The French Revolution 1789–1799

The French Revolution

1789–1799

Peter McPhee

OXFORD
UNIVERSITY PRESS

OXFORD
UNIVERSITY PRESS

Great Clarendon Street, Oxford OX2 6DP

Oxford University Press is a department of the University of Oxford.
It furthers the University's objective of excellence in research, scholarship,
and education by publishing worldwide in

Oxford New York

Athens Auckland Bangkok Bogotá Buenos Aires Cape Town
Chennai Dar es Salaam Delhi Florence Hong Kong Istanbul Karachi
Kolkata Kuala Lumpur Madrid Melbourne Mexico City Mumbai Nairobi
Paris São Paulo Shanghai Singapore Taipei Tokyo Toronto Warsaw

with associated companies in Berlin Ibadan

Oxford is a registered trade mark of Oxford University Press
in the UK and in certain other countries

Published in the United States
by Oxford University Press Inc., New York

© Peter McPhee 2002

The moral rights of the author have been asserted
Database right Oxford University Press (maker)

First published 2002

British Library Cataloguing in Publication Data
Data available

Library of Congress Cataloging in Publication Data
Data available
ISBN 0-19-924414-6

10 9 8 7 6 5 4 3 2 1

Typeset in Stone Serif and Stone Sans
by RefineCatch Limited, Bungay, Suffolk
Printed in Great Britain by
T. J. International Ltd., Padstow, Cornwall

Contents

Introduction

The French Revolution is one of the great turning-points in history. Never before had the people of a large and populous country sought to remake their society on the basis of the principle of popular sovereignty. The drama, success, and tragedy of their project, and of the attempts to arrest or reverse it, has attracted students to it for more than two centuries. Although right-wing journalists at the time of the bicentenary of 1989 rushed to proclaim that 'the French Revolution is finished', its importance and fascination for us are undiminished.[1]

Ever since several thousand armed Parisians seized the Bastille fortress in Paris on 14 July 1789 people have debated the origins and meaning of what had happened. All have agreed on the unprecedented and momentous nature of the storming of the Bastille and associated acts of revolution in the months between May and October 1789. However, such were the consequences of these events that the debate on their origins shows no signs of concluding.

In the years after 1789 successive revolutionary governments sought to remake every aspect of life in accordance with what they understood to be the principles underpinning the Revolution of 1789. However, because there could not be agreement on the practical application of those principles, the question of whose revolution this was quickly became a source of division, driving the Revolution in new directions. At the same time, powerful opponents of change inside and outside France forced governments to take measures to preserve the Revolution itself, culminating in the Terror of 1793–4.

Those in power during these years repeatedly asserted that the Revolution, having achieved its objectives, was over, and that stability was the order of the day. When Louis XVI entered Paris in October 1789; when the National Assembly resolved to disperse by force a crowd of petitioners calling for the king's overthrow in July 1791; when the National Convention introduced the Constitution of the Year III in 1795—each time it was asserted that the time had come to stop the process of revolutionary change. In the end, it was Napoleon Bonaparte's seizure of power in December 1799 which was the most successful of such attempts to impose stability.

The first historians of the Revolution had by then begun to outline not only their narratives of these years but also their judgements about the consequences of revolutionary change. How revolutionary was the French Revolution? Did the protracted political instability of these years disguise a more fundamental social and economic stability? Was the French Revolution a major turning-point in French, even world, history, as its proponents claim, or a protracted period of violent upheaval and warfare which wrecked millions of lives?

This book is a narrative history of the Revolution which also seeks to answer the fundamental questions outlined above. Why was there a Revolution in 1789? Why did it prove so difficult to stabilize the new regime? How might the Terror be explained? What were the consequences of a decade of revolutionary change? The book draws on the great richness of historical writing of the past few decades, some of it part of the renewed debates at the time of the bicentenary of the Revolution in 1789, but much of it influenced by wider changes in approaches to the writing of history.

Four themes stand out among the rich diversity of approaches to the French Revolution in recent years. The first has applied a more imaginative understanding of the world of politics by placing the practice of power within the context of 'political culture' and the 'public sphere'. That is, this approach contends that we can begin to understand the French Revolution only by going beyond the court and parliament to consider a fuller array of ways in which people thought about and acted out politics. Linked to this is a second approach which has examined the masculine domination of institutional politics and the aggressive response to women's challenges to men's power. As a corollary, a third approach has been to reopen debates on the origins of the Terror of 1793–4: are the seeds of the deadly and repressive politics of that year to be found in the earliest moments of the Revolution, in 1789 itself, or was the Terror a direct response to the desperate military crisis of 1793? Finally, and rather differently, a renewed interest in the experience of 'ordinary' people has enabled historians to consider more broadly the rural experience of revolution. One dimension of that experience which will be highlighted here concerns the history of the rural environment.

The decade of the French Revolution was significant, too, for the elaboration of some major statements of political ideas or ideologies, such as the Declaration of the Rights of Man and of the Citizen in 1789 and the Jacobin Constitution of 1793. Contemporary descriptions of some of the most harrowing episodes of the Revolution, such as the 'September Massacres' in 1792, are unusually powerful. For that reason, key sections of a wide array of documents are reproduced here, the better to enable us to listen to the diverse voices of revolutionary France.

My colleague Chips Sowerwine has given the manuscript the benefit of his critical and knowledgeable gaze: I am grateful to him for that, as I am for his friendship and encouragement. The manuscript has also been improved by a critical reading by Charlotte Allen, Judy Anderson, Glenn Matthews, Tim Tackett, and Suzy Schmitz; none of them, of course, is responsible for the book's shortcomings. Further valuable assistance was provided by Juliet Flesch, Marcia Gilchrist, and Kate Mustafa.

Note

1. Steven Laurence Kaplan, *Farewell Revolution: Disputed Legacies, France 1789/1989* (Ithaca, NY, 1995), 470–86.

1

France in the 1780s

The most important feature of eighteenth-century France was that it was essentially a rural society. Ten times as many people inhabited France's villages and farms as do today. Perhaps 28 million people inhabited France in 1780: if we define an urban community as one with more than 2,000 people, then only two persons in ten lived in an urban centre in the eighteenth century. The great majority inhabited 38,000 rural communities or parishes with, on average, about 600 residents. A glimpse of two of them reveals some of the central characteristics of that distant world.

The tiny village of Menucourt was typical of the Vexin region to the north of Paris. It was situated between bends in the Seine and Oise rivers, a few kilometres west of the nearest town, Pontoise, and 35 winding kilometres from Paris. It was a small village: there were just 280 inhabitants in its 70 households (but it had grown from 38 households in 1711). The 'seigneur' or lord of the village was Jean-Marie Chassepot de Beaumont, aged 76 in 1789. In 1785 he had successfully applied to the king for authority to establish a 'livre terrier' in order to systematize the extensive feudal dues his villagers were reluctant to recognize. The seigneur's cereal-growing farm dominated the village economically, just as the chateau dominated the squat houses of the villagers. Cultivated fields covered 58 per cent of the 352 hectares of the surface of the tiny parish; forest covered another 26 per cent. Some inhabitants were involved in winegrowing, or in working wood from the chestnut trees to the south of the village into wine barrels and stakes; others quarried stone for new buildings in Rouen and Paris. This market-oriented activity was supplemented by a subsistence economy on small plots of vegetables and fruit-trees (walnuts, apples, pears, plums, cherries), the gathering in the forest of chestnuts and mushrooms, and the milk and meat of 200 sheep and

50 or 60 cows. As in villages everywhere in France, people plied several trades: for example, Pierre Huard ran the local inn and sold bulk wine, but was also the village stonemason.[1]

Different in almost every way was the village of Gabian, 20 kilometres north of Béziers, near the Mediterranean coastline of Languedoc. Indeed, most people in Gabian could not have communicated with their fellow subjects in Menucourt, for like the mass of the people of Languedoc they spoke Occitan in daily life. Gabian was an important village, with a constant supply of fresh spring water, and since 988 its seigneur had been the bishop of Béziers. Among the dues payable to him were 100 *setiers* (a *setier* was about 85 litres) of barley, 28 *setiers* of wheat, 880 bottles of olive oil, 18 chickens, 4 pounds of bees-wax, 4 partridges, and a rabbit. Reflecting Gabian's ancient role as a market between mountains and coast, it also had to pay 1 pound of pepper, 2 ounces of nutmeg, and 2 ounces of cloves. Two other seigneurs also had minor claims over its produce. Like Menucourt, Gabian was characterized by the diversity of its polycultural economy, its 770 inhabitants producing most of what they needed on the village's 1,540 hectares. Whereas Menucourt was linked to wider markets by the timber and quarrying industries, Gabian's cash economy was based on extensive vineyards and the wool of 1,000 sheep which grazed on the stony hillsides which ringed the village. A score of weavers of the sheep's wool worked for merchants from the textile town of Bédarieux to the north.[2]

The monarchy had long sought to impose linguistic uniformity on villages like Gabian by requiring priests and lawyers to use French. However, most of the king's subjects did not use the French language in daily life; indeed, it could be argued that the language almost all French people heard regularly was Latin, on Sunday mornings. Across most of the country French was the daily language only of those involved in administration, commerce, and the professions. Members of the clergy also used it, although they commonly preached in local dialects or languages. Several million people of Languedoc spoke variants of Occitan; Flemish was spoken in the northeast; German in Lorraine. There were minorities of Basques, Catalans, and Celts. These local 'parlers'—or, more pejoratively, 'patois'—were infinitely varied within regions. Even in the Île-de-France around Paris there were subtle differences in the French spoken from area to area. When the

Abbé Albert, from Embrun in the southern Alps, travelled through the Auvergne, he discovered that

I was never able to make myself understood by the peasants I met on the road. I spoke to them in French, I spoke to them in my native patois, I even tried to speak to them in Latin, but all to no avail. When at last I was tired of talking to them without their understanding a word, they in their turn spoke to me in a language of which I could make no more sense.[3]

The two most important characteristics the inhabitants of eighteenth-century France had in common were that they were the king's subjects, and that 97 per cent of them were Catholic. France in the 1780s was a society in which people's deepest sense of identity attached to their particular province or *pays*. Regional cultures and minority languages and dialects were underpinned by economic strategies which sought to meet the needs of the household within a regional or micro-regional market. The rural economy was essentially a peasant economy: that is, household-based agrarian production which had a primarily subsistence orientation. This complex, polycultural system sought to produce as much as possible of a household's consumption needs, including clothing.

An insight into this world is provided by Nicolas Restif de la Bretonne, born in 1734 in the village of Sacy, on the border of the provinces of Burgundy and Champagne. Restif, who moved to Paris and became notorious for his ribald stories in *Le Paysan perverti* (1775), wrote of his recollections of Sacy in *La Vie de mon père* (1779). He recalled the suitable and happy marriage his relative Marguerite was making to Covin, 'a great joker, well-built, a vain country-bumpkin, the great local story-teller':

Marguerite had about 120 livres worth of arable land, and Covin had 600 livres worth, some in arable land, some under vines, and some fields dispersed in the grasslands; there were six parts of each type, six of wheat, six of oats or barley, and six fallow. . . . as for the woman, she had the profit of her spinning, the wool of seven or eight sheep, the eggs of a dozen hens, and the milk of a cow, with the butter and cheese she could extract from it. . . . Covin was also a weaver, and his wife had some domestic work; her lot in consequence must have been pleasant enough.

Urban people commonly referred to the rural population as 'paysans', that is, as 'people of the land'. However, this simple term—like its English counterpart 'peasant'—disguises the complexities of rural society which were to be revealed in the varied behaviour of rural people during the Revolution. Farm labourers were as much as half the population in areas of large-scale agriculture like the Île-de-France around Paris. In most regions, however, the bulk of the population were either smallholders, tenant-farmers, or sharecroppers, many of whom were also reliant on practising a craft or on wage-work. In all rural communities there was a minority of larger farmers, often dubbed the *coqs du village*, who were large tenant-farmers (*fermiers*) or landowners (*laboureurs*). Larger villages also had a minority of people—priests, lawyers, artisans, textile-workers—who were not peasants at all, but who commonly owned some land, such as the vegetable garden belonging to the priest. The peasantry made up about four-fifths of the 'Third Estate' or 'commoners' but across the country it owned only about 40 per cent of the land outright. This varied from about 17 per cent in the Mauges region of western France to 64 per cent in the Auvergne.

Paradoxical as it may seem, rural France was also the centre of most manufacturing. The textile industry in particular was largely based on women's part-time work in rural areas of Normandy, the Velay, and Picardy. Rural industry of this type was linked to regional specialties centred on provincial towns, such as sheepskin gloves in Millau, ribbons in St-Étienne, lace in Le Puy and silk in Lyons. A recent study of rural industry by Liana Vardi focuses on Montigny, a community of about 600 people in the 1780s located in the northern region of Cambrésis, only part of France since 1677.[4] At the beginning of the eighteenth century, its population of essentially subsistence landowners and tenants had been one-third that size. Across the eighteenth century, large owners and tenants monopolized the land, increasingly specializing in corn; the middling and small peasants instead found spinning and weaving linen the answer to poverty and land-hunger. A flourishing if vulnerable rural industry in Montigny was based on merchants 'putting out' spinning and weaving to rural households. In turn, the textile industry provided the incentive for farmers to increase crop yields substantially to feed an increasing population. A key role was played by middlemen, merchant-weavers from places like Montigny who mortgaged small family holdings to join the rush to be rich. These people remained rural in their links and economic strategies at the same time as they demonstrated a remarkable entre-preneurial ability and enthusiasm.

However, Montigny was an exceptional case. Most of rural France was a place of unremitting manual labour by tillers of the soil. A rural world in which households engaged in a highly complex occu-pational strategy to secure their own subsistence could inevitably expect only low yields for grain crops grown in unsuitable or exhausted soil. The dry and stony soils of a southern village like Gabian were no more suited to growing grain crops than the heavy, damp soils of Normandy: in both places, however, a large proportion of arable land was set aside for grain to meet local needs. Con-sequently most rural communities had restricted 'surpluses' which could be marketed to substantial towns. Far more important to most peasants were nearby small towns or *bourgs*, whose weekly, monthly, or annual market-fairs were as much an occasion for the collective rituals of local cultures as for the exchange of produce.

Rural communities consumed so much of what they produced—and vice versa—that towns and cities faced both chronic problems of food supply and a limited rural demand for their goods and ser-vices. However, although only 20 per cent of French people lived in urban communities, in a European context France was remarkable for the number and size of its cities and towns. There were eight cities with more than 50,000 people (Paris was easily the biggest, with perhaps as many as 700,000 people, then Lyons, Marseilles, Bordeaux, Nantes, Lille, Rouen, and Toulouse), and another seventy with 10,000–40,000. These cities and towns all had examples of large-scale manufacturing involved in an international trading framework, but most were dominated by artisan-type craftwork for the needs of the urban population itself and the immediate hinter-land, and by a range of administrative, judicial, ecclesiastical, and policing functions. They were provincial capitals: only one person in forty lived in Paris, and communication between the capital Ver-sailles and the rest of its territory was usually slow and uncertain. The size and topography of the country was a constant impediment to the rapid movement of instructions, laws, and goods (see Map 1). However, improvements to roads after 1750 meant that no city in France was more than fifteen days from the capital; coaches travel-ling at 90 kilometres a day could in five days bring travellers from

Paris to Lyons, with 145,000 inhabitants France's second largest city.

Like many other cities, Paris was ringed by a wall, largely for the collection of customs duties on goods imported into the city. Within the walls were a number of *faubourgs* or suburbs, each with its distinctive mix of migrant population and trades. Paris was typical of France's major cities in its occupational structure: it was still dominated by skilled, artisanal production despite the emergence of a number of large-scale industries. Some of the most important of the latter were in the *faubourg* St-Antoine, where Réveillon's wallpaper factory employed 350 people and the brewer Santerre had 800 workers. In the western neighbourhoods of the city, the building industry was booming as the well-to-do constructed imposing residences away from the teeming medieval quarters of the central city. However, most Parisians continued to live in congested streets in central neighbourhoods near the river, where the population was vertically segregated in tenement buildings: often, wealthy bourgeois or even nobles would occupy the first and second floors above shops and workplaces, with their domestic servants, artisans, and the poor inhabiting the upper floors and garrets. As in rural communities, the Catholic Church was a constant presence: there were 140 convents and monasteries in Paris (housing 1,000 monks and 2,500 nuns) and 1,200 parish clergy. The Church owned one-quarter of the city's property.[5]

Paris was dominated by small workshops and retail shops: there were thousands of small enterprises employing on average three or four people. In skilled trades, a hierarchy of masters controlled the entry of journeymen, who had qualified by presenting their masterpiece (*chef d'œuvre*) on completion of their *tour de France* through provincial centres specializing in their trade. This was a world in which small employers and wage-earners were bonded by deep knowledge of their trade and of each other, and where skilled workers were identified by their trade as well as by whether they were masters or workers. Contemporaries referred to the working people of Paris as the 'common people' (*menu peuple*): they were not a working class. Nevertheless, frustrations between workers and their masters were evident in trades where entry to a mastership was difficult; in some industries, such as printing, the introduction of new machines was threatening the skills of journeymen and apprentices. In 1776 skilled wage-earners had rejoiced at the prospect of the abolition of guilds and the chance of establishing their own workshops, but the project was suspended; then in 1781 a system of *livrets*, or workers' passbooks, was introduced, strengthening the hand of masters at the expense of fractious employees.

Social relations focused on the neighbourhood and the workplace as much as the family. Large cities like Paris, Lyons, and Marseilles were characterized by tightly packed, medieval centres where most families occupied no more than one or two rooms: most of the routines associated with eating and leisure were public activities. Historians have documented the use made of streets and other public spaces by working women to settle domestic disputes as well as issues to do with rents and food prices. Men in skilled trades found their own solidarities in *compagnonnages*, illegal but tolerated brotherhoods of workers which acted to protect work routines and wages and to provide outlets for leisure and aggression after working days of 14–16 hours. One of these workers, Jacques-Louis Ménétra, recalled later in life his apprenticeship as a glazier before the Revolution, in a rebellious milieu of *compagnons* which relished obscene pranks, casual sex, and ritualized violence with other brotherhoods. However, Ménétra also claimed to have read Rousseau's *Contrat social*, *Émile* and *La Nouvelle Héloïse* and even to have met their author.[6]

Provincial cities were often dominated by specific industries, such as textiles in Rouen and Elbeuf. Smaller, newer urban centres had sprung up around large iron foundries and coal mines, such as at Le Creusot, Niederbronn, and Anzin, where 4,000 workers were employed. However, it was particularly in the Atlantic ports where a booming colonial trade with the Caribbean colonies was developing a capitalist economic sector in shipbuilding and in processing colonial goods, as in Bordeaux, where the population expanded from 67,000 to 110,000 between 1750 and 1790. This was a triangular trade between Europe, North America, and Africa, exporting wines and spirits from ports such as Bordeaux to England and importing colonial produce such as sugar, coffee, and tobacco. One leg of the trade involved scores of purpose-built slave-ships which carried a human cargo from the west coast of Africa to colonies such as St-Domingue. There as many as 465,500 slaves worked in a plantation economy controlled by 31,000 whites according to the rules of the Code Noir of

1685. The code laid down rules for the 'correct' treatment of the slave-owners' property, while denying slaves any legal or family rights: slaves' children were the property of the slave-owner. In 1785 there were 143 ships actively engaged in the slave trade: 48 of them from Nantes, 37 each from La Rochelle and Le Havre, 13 from Bordeaux, and several from Marseilles, St-Malo, and Dunkerque. In Nantes, the slave-trade represented 20–25 per cent of the traffic of the port in the 1780s, in Bordeaux 8–15 per cent and in La Rochelle as much as 58 per cent in 1786. Across the century from 1707, these slave-ships had made more than 3,300 voyages, 42 per cent of them from Nantes: their trade was essential to the great economic boom of the Atlantic ports in the eighteenth century.[7]

However, most middle-class families drew their income and status from more traditional forms of activity, such as the law and other professions, the royal administration, and from investment in property. Perhaps 15 per cent of rural property was owned by such bourgeois. While the nobility dominated the most prestigious positions in the administration, its lower ranks were staffed by the middle classes. The royal administration at Versailles was tiny, with only about 670 employees, but across a network of provincial cities and towns it employed many thousands more in courts, public works, and government. For bourgeois who had substantial means, there were no more attractive and respectable investments than low-return, secure government bonds or land and seigneurialism. The latter, in particular, offered the hope of social status and even marriage into the nobility. By the 1780s as many as one-fifth of the seigneurs in the countryside around Le Mans were of bourgeois background.

Eighteenth-century France was characterized by the multiplicity of links between town and country. In provincial towns, in particular, bourgeois owned extensive rural property from which they drew rent from peasant farmers; in turn, domestic service for bourgeois families was a major source of employment for young rural women. Less fortunate girls worked as prostitutes or in charity workshops. Another important link between town and country involved the practice of working women in cities such as Lyons and Paris sending their babies to rural areas for wet-nursing, often for several years. Babies had a greater chance of survival in the countryside, but one-third would die while in the care of the wet-nurse (conversely, the glazier

Jacques-Louis Ménétra's mother had died while he was in the care of a rural wet-nurse). A human trade of another kind involved scores of thousands of men from highland areas with a long 'dead season' in winter who migrated to towns seasonally or for years at a time to look for work. The men left behind what has been called a 'matricentric' society, where women tended livestock and produced textile fabrics.

However, the most important link between urban and rural France was the supply of foodstuffs, particularly grain. This was a link which was often strained by competing demands of urban and rural consumers. In normal times urban wage-earners spent 40–60 per cent of their income on bread alone. As prices rose during years of shortage, so did the tension between urban populations dependent on cheap and plentiful bread and the poorer sections of the rural community, threatened by local merchants seeking to export grain to lucrative urban markets. Twenty-two of the years between 1765 and 1789 were marked by food riots, either in popular urban neighbourhoods where women in particular sought to impose *taxation populaire* to hold prices at customary levels, or in rural areas where peasants banded together to prevent scarce supplies from being sent away to market. In many areas tension over the food supply aggravated suspicion of large towns as parasitic on rural toil, for elites in the Church and nobility drew their wealth from the countryside and consumed it ostentatiously in towns. In the process, however, they created work for townspeople and the promise of charity for the poor.[8]

Eighteenth-century France was a land of mass poverty in which most people were vulnerable to harvest failure. It is this which explains what historians have called the 'demographic equilibrium', in which very high birth rates (about 4.5 per hundred people) were almost matched by high mortality rates (about 3.5). Men and women married late: usually between 26 and 29 and 24 and 27 years respectively. Especially in devout areas, where couples were less likely to avoid conception by coitus interruptus, women conceived as often as once every twenty months. Across much of the country, however, as many as one-half of all children died of infantile diseases and malnutrition before the age of 5. In Gabian, for example, there were 253 deaths in the 1780s, 134 of them of children younger than 5 years. While old age was not unknown—in 1783 three octogenarians and two nonagenarians were buried—the average life-expectancy of those who survived infancy was just 50 years.

After 1750 a long series of adequate harvests disturbed the demographic equilibrium: the population increased from perhaps 24.5 million to 28 million by the 1780s. However, the vulnerability of this increasing population was not simply a function of the ever-present threat of harvest failure. It was the rural population above all which underwrote the costs of the three pillars of authority and privilege in eighteenth-century France: the Church, nobility, and monarchy. Together, the two privileged orders and the monarchy exacted on average one-quarter to one-third of peasant produce, through taxes, seigneurial dues, and the tithe.

The 169,500 members of the clergy (the First Estate of the realm) made up 0.6 per cent of the population. Their calling divided them between the 81,500 'regular' clergy (26,500 monks and 55,000 nuns) in religious orders and the 59,500 'secular' clergy (39,000 priests or *curés* and 20,500 curates or *vicaires*) who ministered to the spiritual needs of lay society. There were several other types of 'lay' clergy. In social terms the Church was sharply hierarchical. The most lucrative positions as heads of religious orders (often held *in absentia*) and as bishops and archbishops were dominated by the nobility: the archbishop of Strasbourg had a stipend of 450,000 livres per year. Although the minimum annual salaries of priests and curates were raised to 750 and 300 livres respectively in 1786, such stipends made them little more comfortable than most of their parishioners.

The Church drew its wealth largely from a tithe (usually 8–10 per cent) imposed on farm produce at harvest, bringing in an estimated 150 million livres each year, and from extensive landholding by religious orders and cathedrals. From this was paid in many dioceses a *portion congrue* or stipend to parish clergy, which they supplemented by the charges they levied for special services such as marriages and masses said for departed souls. In all, the First Estate owned perhaps 10 per cent of the land of France, reaching up to 40 per cent in the Cambrésis, on which the dues and rents it levied accounted for up to 130 million livres annually. In provincial towns and cities, parish clergy and nuns and monks in 'open' orders were a frequent sight: about 600 of the 12,000 inhabitants of Chartres, for example, were religious personnel. In many provincial cities, the Church was also a major proprietor: in Angers, for example, it owned three-quarters of urban property. Here, as elsewhere, it was a major source of local employment for domestic servants, skilled artisans, and lawyers meeting the needs of the 600 clergy resident in a town of 34,000 people: clerks, carpenters, cooks, and cleaners depended on them, as did the lawyers who ran the Church's fifty-three legal courts for the prosecution of rural defaulters on tithes and rents on its vast estates. The Benedictine abbey of Ronceray owned five manors, twelve barns and winepresses, six mills, forty-six farms, and six houses in the countryside around Angers, bringing in to the town 27,000 livres annually.

Many male religious orders were moribund by the 1780s: Louis XV had closed 458 religious houses (with just 509 religious personnel) before his death in 1774, and the recruitment of monks declined by one-third in the two decades after 1770. Female orders were stronger, such as the Sisters of Charity in Bayeux who provided food and shelter to hundreds of impoverished women through extensive lace-works. Throughout rural France, however, the parish clergy were at the heart of the community: as a source of spiritual comfort and inspiration, as a counsellor in time of need, as a dispenser of charity, as an employer, and as a source of news of the outside world. During the winter months, it was the parish priest who provided the rudiments of an education, although perhaps only one man in ten and one woman in fifty could have read the Bible. In areas of dispersed habitat, such as in parts of the Massif Central or the west, it was at Sunday mass where the inhabitants of outlying farms and hamlets felt a sense of community. In the west parishioners and clergy decided on the full range of local matters after mass in what have been described as tiny theocracies. Even here, however, education was of marginal importance: in the devout western parish of Lucs-Vendée only 21 per cent of bridegrooms could sign the marriage register, and only 1.5 per cent in a way that suggests a degree of literacy. Most Parisians could at least read, but rural France was essentially an oral society.

The Catholic Church enjoyed a monopoly of public worship, even though geographically segregated Jewish communities, in all 40,000 people, preserved a strong sense of identity in Bordeaux, the Comtat-Venaissin and Alsace, as did the approximately 700,000 Protestants in parts of the east and the Massif Central. Memories of the religious wars and intolerance following the revocation of the Edict of Nantes in 1685 remained powerful: the people of Pont-de-Montvert, in the heartland of the Protestant Camisard rising in 1700, had an army garrison and a Catholic seigneur (the Knights of Malta) to remind them daily of their subjection. However, while 97 per cent of French people were nominally Catholic, levels of both religiosity (the external observance of religious practices, such as attendance at Easter mass) and spirituality (the importance that individuals accorded to such practices) varied across the country. The substance of spirituality is, of course, largely beyond the reach of the historian; however, the decline in faith in some areas at least is suggested by increasing numbers of brides who were pregnant (from 6.2 to 10.1 per cent across the century) and a decline in priestly vocations (the number of new recruits declined by 23 per cent across the years 1749–89).

Catholicism was strongest in the west and Brittany, along the Pyrenees, and in the southern Massif Central, regions characterized by a strong clerical recruitment of boys from local families well integrated into their communities and cultures. In the west, too, priestly stipends were far higher than the requisite minimum; moreover, this was one of the few parts of the country where the tithe was paid to the local clergy rather than to the diocese, hence facilitating the capacity of priests to minister to all the needs of the parish. Everywhere, the most devout parishioners were more likely to be older, female, and rural. The theology to which they were exposed was marked by a 'Tridentine' mistrust of worldly pleasures, by emphasis on priestly authority, and by a powerful imagery of the punishments awaiting the lax when they passed beyond the grave. Yves-Michel Marchais, the *curé* of the devout parish of Lachapelle-du-Gênet in the west, preached that 'Everything that might be called an act of impurity or an illicit action of the flesh, when done of one's own free will, is intrinsically evil and almost always a mortal sin, and consequently grounds for exclusion from the Kingdom of God.' Once excluded, sinners were left in no doubt about the punishments which awaited them by preachers such as Father Bridaine, a veteran of 256 missions:

Cruel famine, bloody war, flood, fire . . . raging toothache, the stabbing pain of gout, the convulsions of epilepsy, burning fever, broken bones . . . all the tortures undergone by the martyrs: sharp swords, iron combs, the teeth of lions and tigers, the rack, the wheel, the cross, red-hot grills, burning oil, melted lead . . .[9]

The elite positions in the Catholic Church were dominated by members of the Second Estate or nobility. Historians have never agreed on the numbers of nobles in eighteenth-century France, in part because of the numbers of commoners claiming noble status in an attempt to obtain the positions, privileges, and standing which were beyond the reach of wealth alone. Recent estimates have suggested that there may have been no more than 25,000 noble families or 125,000 individual nobles, perhaps 0.4 per cent of the population.

As an order, the nobility drew on several sources of corporate wealth and power: fiscal and seigneurial privileges, the status which went with insignia of eminence, and exclusive employment in a range of official positions. However, like the First Estate, the nobility was characterized by great internal diversity. The poorest provincial nobles (*hobereaux*) on their country estates had little in common with the several thousand courtiers at Versailles or the magistrates of the high courts (*parlements*) and senior administrators, even though their noble status was usually far more ancient than that of those who had bought a title or been ennobled for their administrative services (*noblesse de robe*). Entry of a son into a military academy and the promise of a career as an officer was one of the favoured ways in which provincial nobles preserved status and economic security. Their standing within the army was buttressed by the 1781 Ségur ordinance requiring four generations of nobility for army officers. Within the elite of the nobility (*les Grands*), boundaries of family and wealth were further fractured by intricate hierarchies of position and prerogative; for example, between those who had been formally presented at court, those permitted to sit on a footstool in the queen's presence, and those allowed to ride in her carriage. What all nobles had in common, however, was a vested interest in a highly complex system of status and hierarchy from which came material privilege and preferment.[10]

Most nobles also drew a significant proportion of their wealth from the land. While the Second Estate owned outright perhaps one-third of the land of France, it exerted seigneurial rights over most of the rest. The most important of these rights was regular payment of a harvest due (*champart*, *censive* or *tasque*) on the major crops produced on all land within the *seigneurie*; this was normally between one-twelfth and one-sixth, but up to one-quarter in parts of Brittany and central France. It was bolstered by other significant rights, such as a monopoly (*banalité*) over the village oven, grape and olive presses, and mill; financial levies on land transfers and even on marriages; and the requirement of unpaid labour by the community on the lord's lands at harvest time. It has been estimated that the value of such dues was as high as 70 per cent of noble income in the Rouergue (where the *champart* took one-quarter of peasant produce) and as low as 8 per cent in the neighbouring region of the Lauragais to the south.

The solution to the paradox of how an essentially peasant society could sustain so many substantial towns and cities lies in the functions of these provincial centres in the eighteenth century. In an important sense, inland towns were dependent on the countryside, for the bulk of the seigneurial dues, rents, tithes, and fees collected by the elite of the first two estates of the realm were spent in urban centres. For example, the cathedral chapter of Cambrai drew its wealth from its properties in villages like Montigny, where it owned 46 per cent of the total area in 1754. It was also the seigneur of the village, though this was a region where the feudal regime weighed relatively lightly.

Rural people were born into a world marked by physical statements of the sources of authority and status. Everywhere the parish church and chateau dominated the built environment and recalled the duties of commoners to labour and defer. While seigneurs were less likely to reside on their estates by the 1780s than earlier in the century, they continued to exercise a maze of prerogatives reinforcing the community's subordinate position, whether by reserving a pew in the parish church, wearing a weapon in public, or naming the village officials. We cannot know the extent to which the deference on which they insisted was a sincere recognition of their eminence; certainly, however, there were repeated instances of peasant animosity which made members of the elite despair. In Provence, for example, local communities were required to respect a death in the seigneur's family by refraining from public festivals for a year. Here a bereaved noble complained that, on the day of the patron saint's festival in the village of Sausses in 1768, 'people had beaten drums, fired muskets and danced the whole day and part of the night, with a remarkable *éclat* and conceit'.[11]

Eighteenth-century France was a society of corporations, in which privilege was integral to social hierarchy, wealth, and individual identity. That is, people were members of social orders born of a medieval conception of a world where people had duties to pray, to fight or to work. This was an essentially fixed or static vision of the social order which did not correspond with other measures of personal worth, such as wealth. The Third Estate, about 99 per cent of the population, included all commoners from beggars to the wealthiest financiers. The first two estates were internally united by privileges belonging to their estate, and by their vision of their social functions and identity, but they, too, were divided internally by differences of status and wealth. In particular, at the summit of every form of privilege—legal, fiscal, occupational, regional—was the noble elite of the first two estates or orders. These ancient and immensely wealthy noble families at the pinnacle of power shared a conception of social and political authority which they expressed through ostentatious display in their dress, dwellings and consumption of luxuries.

The First and Second Estates were privileged corporations: that is, the monarchy had long recognized their privileged status through, for example, separate law codes for their members and by tax exemptions. The Church paid only a voluntary contribution (*don gratuit*) to the state, usually no more than 3 per cent of its income, by decision of its governing synod. Nobles were generally exempt from direct taxation except for the modest *vingtième* surcharge imposed in 1749. However, relations between the privileged orders and the monarch— the third pillar of French society—were based on mutual dependence and negotiation. The king was head of the Gallican Church, which had a certain measure of autonomy from Rome, but in turn was dependent on the goodwill of the personnel of the Church for maintaining the legitimacy of his regime. In return the Catholic Church enjoyed a monopoly of public worship and moral codes. Similarly, in return for the obedience and deference of his fellow nobles, the king accepted that they would be at the pinnacle of every institution, from the Church to the armed forces, from the judiciary to his own administration. Jacques Necker, a Genevan banker who was Finance Minister 1777–81 and Principal Minister from 1788, was Louis XVI's only non-noble member of cabinet.

The king's residence at Versailles was the most imposing physical statement of power in eighteenth-century France. His state bureaucracy was, however, both small in size and limited in function to internal order, foreign policy, and trade. There were only six named ministries, and three were devoted to Foreign Affairs, War, and the Navy; the others were concerned with Finances, Justice, and the Royal Household. Much of the collection of taxes was 'farmed out' to private *fermiers-généraux*. Most important, every aspect of the institutional structures of public life—in administration, customs and measures, the law, taxation, and the Church—bore the imprint of privilege and historical accretion across seven centuries of territorial expansion by the monarchy. The price the monarchy had paid as it expanded its territory since the eleventh century had been to recognize the special 'rights' and 'privileges' of new 'provinces'. Indeed, the kingdom included an extensive enclave—Avignon and the Comtat-Venaissin—which had continued to belong to the papacy since its fourteenth-century exile there.

The constitution by which the king governed France was customary, not written. Essential to it was that Louis was king of France by the grace of God, and that he was responsible to God alone for the well-being of his subjects. The royal line was Catholic and passed only through the oldest sons (the Salic Law). The king was head of the executive: he appointed ministers, diplomats, and senior officials, and had the power to declare war and peace. However, since the high courts or *parlements* had the responsibility of registering the king's decrees, they had increasingly assumed the right to do more than vet them for juridical correctness; rather, the *parlements* insisted that their 'remonstrances' could also defend subjects against violations of their privileges and rights unless the king chose to use a *lit de justice* to impose his will.

The historic compromises which French monarchs had had to make in order to guarantee the acquiescence of newly acquired provinces across several centuries was manifest in the complicated tax arrangements across the country. The major direct tax, the *taille*, varied between provinces and some towns had bought their way out of it entirely. The major indirect tax, the *gabelle* on salt, varied from over 60 livres per 72 litres to just 1 livre 10 sous. Olwen Hufton has described bands of ostensibly pregnant women smuggling salt from

Brittany, the lowest taxed area, eastwards into areas of high taxation in order to profit from clandestine sales of this necessity.[12]

In administration, too, the keywords were exception and exemption. The fifty-eight provinces of eighteenth-century France were grouped for administrative purposes into 33 *généralités* (see Map 2). These units varied enormously in size and rarely coincided with the territory covered by archdioceses. Moreover, the powers the king's chief administrators (*intendants*) could exercise varied considerably. Some of the *généralités*, known as the *pays d'état* (such as Brittany, Languedoc and Burgundy), claimed a measure of autonomy, for example, in the apportionment of taxation, which other areas, the *pays d'élection*, did not. Dioceses ranged in size and wealth from the archdiocese of Paris to the 'évêchés crottés' or 'muddy bishoprics', tiny sees which were the result of political agreements in earlier centuries, particularly in the south during the fourteenth-century exile of the papacy to Avignon.

The map of France's administrative and ecclesiastical boundaries did not coincide with that of the high courts (*parlements* and *conseil souverains*). The *parlement* of Paris exercised power over half the country, whereas the *conseil souverain* of Arras had only a tiny local jurisdiction. Commonly, the centre of administration, the archdiocese, and the judicial capital were located in different cities within the same province. Moreover, cutting across all these boundaries was an ancient division between the written or Roman law of the south and the customary law of the north. On either side of this divide were tens of local law codes; the clergy and nobility, of course, had their own specific codes as well.

Those involved in trade and the professions complained of the difficulties created for their businesses by the multiplicity of legal jurisdictions and codes. Further obstacles were posed by the multiplicity of systems of currency, weights, and measures—there was no commonality in measures of size or volume across the kingdom—and by internal customs houses. Nobles and towns imposed their own tolls (*péages*) as produce moved across rivers and canals. In 1664 much of northern France had formed a customs union; but there were customs houses between it and the rest of the country, though not always between border provinces and the rest of Europe. It was easier for eastern provinces to trade with Prussia than with Paris.

Every aspect of public life in eighteenth-century France was marked by regional diversity and exceptionalism, and the continuing strength of local cultures. The institutional structures of the monarchy and the corporate powers of the Church and nobility were everywhere complicated by local practices, exemptions and loyalties. The Corbières region of Languedoc provides an example of this institutional complexity and of the limitations on the control of the monarchy over daily life. Here was a geographically well-defined area whose 129 parishes all spoke Occitan with the exception of three Catalan villages on its southern border. Yet the region was divided for administrative, ecclesiastical, judicial, and taxing purposes between offices in Carcassonne, Narbonne, Limoux, and Perpignan. The boundaries of these institutions were not consistent: for example, neighbouring villages administered from Perpignan were in different dioceses. Across the Corbières, there were ten different volumes for which the term *setier* was used (normally about 85 litres), and no fewer than fifty different measures of area: the *sétérée* ranged from just 0.16 hectares on the lowlands to 0.51 in highland areas.

Voltaire and other reformers campaigned against what they saw as the intolerance and cruelty of the judicial system, most famously in the case of the torturing and execution in 1762 of the Toulouse Protestant Jean Calas, condemned for allegedly killing his son to prevent him from converting to Catholicism. The system of punishments which Voltaire and others castigated was a manifestation of the regime's need to instil control of its large, diverse kingdom through intimidation and awe. Physical punishments were severe and often spectacular. In 1783, a defrocked Capucin monk accused of sexually assaulting a boy and stabbing his victim seventeen times was broken on the wheel and burned alive in Paris; two beggars from the Auvergne were broken on the wheel in 1778 for threatening a victim with a sword and rifle. In all, 19 per cent of the cases before the Prevotal Court in Toulouse in 1773–90 resulted in public execution (reaching 30.7 per cent in 1783) and as many again to life imprisonment in naval prisons.

However, to most contemporaries the monarchy of Louis XVI appeared the most stable and powerful of regimes. While protest was endemic—whether in the form of food-rioting or of complaints about the presumptions of the privileged—this was almost always within the system: that is, against threats to idealized ways in which the system was believed to have once worked. Indeed, during the most extensive popular unrest in the years prior to 1789—the 'Flour War' in northern France in 1775—rioters shouted that they were lowering the price of bread to its customary price of 2 sous per pound 'in the name of the king', tacit recognition of the king's responsibility to God for his people's well-being. By the 1780s, however, a series of long-term changes in French society was undermining some of the fundamental bases of authority and challenging a social order based on privilege and corporations. Deep-seated financial difficulties would further test the capacity for elites to respond to the imperatives of change. An abrupt political crisis would then bring these tensions and problems to the surface.

Notes

1. Denise, Maurice, and Robert Bréant, *Menucourt: un village du Vexin français pendant la Révolution 1789–1799* (Menucourt, 1989).

2. Peter McPhee, *Une communauté languedocienne dans l'histoire: Gabian 1760–1960* (Nîmes, 2001), ch. 1.

3. Fernand Braudel, *The Identity of France*, trans. S. Reynolds, vol. 1 (London, 1988), 91–7; Daniel Roche, *France in the Enlightenment*, trans. Arthur Goldhammer (Cambridge, Mass., 1998), chs. 1–2, 6, pp. 488–91.

4. Liana Vardi, *The Land and the Loom: Peasants and Profit in Northern France 1680–1800* (Durham, NC, 1993). On rural France in general, see Roche, *France in the Enlightenment*, ch. 4, P. M. Jones, *The Peasantry in the French Revolution* (Cambridge, 1988), ch. 1.

5. Daniel Roche, *The People of Paris: An Essay on Popular Culture in the Eighteenth Century*, trans. Marie Evans (Berkeley, Calif., 1987). Among the many other studies of Paris, see David Garrioch, *Neighbourhood and Community in Paris, 1740–1790* (Cambridge, 1986); Arlette Farge, *Fragile Lives: Violence, Power, and Solidarity in Eighteenth-Century Paris*, trans. Carol Shelton (Cambridge, Mass., 1993).

6. Jacques-Louis Ménétra, *Journal of My Life*, trans. Arthur Goldhammer (New York, 1986); Roche, *France in the Enlightenment*, 342–6, ch. 20.

7. Jean-Michel Deveau, *La Traite rochelaise* (Paris, 1990); Roche, *France in the Enlightenment*, ch. 5.

8. Among the important studies of the grain trade are Steven Kaplan, *Provisioning Paris: Merchants and Millers in the Grain and Flour Trade during the Eighteenth Century* (Ithaca, NY, 1984); Cynthia Bouton, *The Flour War: Gender, Class, and*

Community in late Ancien Regime French Society (University Park, Pa., 1993); Judith Miller, *Mastering the Market: the State and the Grain Trade in Northern France, 1700–1860* (Cambridge, 1998).

9. Ralph Gibson, *A Social History of French Catholicism 1789–1914* (London, 1989), 24, 27. For the Church in the eighteenth century see, too, Roche, *France in the Enlightenment*, ch. 11; and the outstanding survey by John McManners, *Church and Society in Eighteenth-Century France*, 2 vols. (Oxford, 1998). Ch. 46 of the latter analyses the position of Protestants and Jews.

10. See Roche, *France in the Enlightenment*, ch. 12. One of many excellent local studies is Robert Forster, *The House of Saulx-Tavanes: Versailles and Burgundy 1700–1830* (Baltimore, 1977).

11. Alain Collomp, *La Maison du père: famille et village en Haute-Provence aux XVIIe et XVIIIe siècles* (Paris, 1983), 286.

12. Olwen Hufton, 'Women and the Family Economy in Eighteenth-Century France', *French Historical Studies*, 9 (1975), 1–22; Hufton, *The Prospect before Her: A History of Women in Western Europe, 1500–1800* (New York, 1996), esp. ch. 4; Roche, *France in the Enlightenment*, ch. 7, 287–99.

2

The Crisis of the Old Regime

Historians have long debated whether the eighteenth-century bourgeoisie was 'class conscious': that is, whether the French Revolution was the work of a bourgeoisie determined to overthrow the privileged orders and which therefore accelerated the transition from feudalism to capitalism in line with the Marxist model of historical development. The terms of this debate have often been cast in simplified terms, about whether the wealthiest members of the bourgeoisie were integrated into the ruling elites. If they were, could it not be argued that there was no deep-seated, long-term crisis within this society, that the Revolution had only short-term and therefore relatively unimportant causes? There is certainly evidence for this argument.[1] Individual nobles played active roles in agricultural change and mining, in contrast to their reputation then and now, and kings ennobled individuals among the most successful financiers and manufacturers, such as the Bavarian migrant Christophe-Philippe Oberkampf who had established a printed-fabrics factory at Jouy, near Versailles. Among the choicest objects of bourgeois acquisition were about 70,000 venal offices, upwards of 3,700 of which conferred nobility on their owners. Some of those ambitious young bourgeois who were to be most distinguished in the forefront of militant anti-noble initiative after 1789 found it desirable at times to add a noble prefix or suffix to their plebeian names: de Robespierre, Brissot de Warville, and d'Anton. It is also the case that the various occupational groups who made up the bourgeoisie did not define themselves as members of a 'class' united across the country by similar socio-economic roles and interests.

However, it might be more fruitful to understand the elite of the bourgeoisie as seeking entry into the aristocratic world while at the same time inadvertently subverting that world. The wealthiest bourgeois sought to buy noble office and title, for they brought with them wealth as well as status in their society. This is hardly surprising, for they were trying to get ahead in a world which they never imagined would end. For example, Claude Périer, a wealthy textile-factory owner from Grenoble, who also had a sugar plantation in St-Domingue, paid one million livres for several seigneuries and the huge château of Vizille in 1780, where he constructed a new textile factory. The return of his seigneuries—37,000 livres annually—was about the same as he could have expected from alternative invest-ment possibilities. However, even where the well-to-do among the bourgeoisie pinned their hopes and fortunes on entry into the nobil-ity they were necessarily still 'outsiders': not only were their claims to eminence based on different grounds of achievement, but their very success was subversive of the *raison d'être* of noble status. In turn, nobles who emulated the bourgeoisie by seeking to appear 'progres-sive', for example, by joining a Freemasons' lodge, were undermining the exclusivity of their order.

Other historians have shunned questions about the social and eco-nomic origins of the Revolution as 'fruitless' and 'defunct' and have decided that the origins and nature of the Revolution are best observed through an analysis of 'political culture', in Lynn Hunt's words, the role of 'symbols, language, and ritual in inventing and transmitting a tradition of revolutionary action'.[2] Indeed, some his-torians have contested the applicability of terms such as 'class' and 'class consciousness' in eighteenth-century France. David Garrioch begins his study of 'the formation of the Parisian bourgeoisie' by stat-ing that 'there was no Parisian bourgeoisie in the eighteenth century', that is, that individual bourgeois did not define themselves as part of a 'class' with similar interests and outlook. Dictionaries of the time defined bourgeois by what they were not—neither nobles nor manual workers—or by using 'bourgeois' as a disparaging term.

However, as Sarah Maza has shown, this is not to say that there was no critique of the nobility: on the contrary, the *causes célèbres* she has studied through published trial briefs with print runs of up to 20,000 in the 1780s demonstrate a powerful and more frequent repudiation of a traditional aristocratic world depicted as violent, feudal and immoral and as opposed to values of citizenship, rationality and utility.[3] In the increasingly commercial world of the late eighteenth century, nobles and others debated whether abolishing laws of *dérogeance* to permit nobles to engage in trade would resuscitate the 'utility' of the nobility in the eyes of commoners. What all this suggests is that, while there was no self-conscious class of bourgeois with a political programme, there was certainly a vigorous critique of the privileged orders and of the allegedly outmoded claims to social order and function on which they rested.

If changes were evident in the way public debate was expressed in the years before 1789, might not this have something significant to tell us about wider changes in French society? Most recently historians have returned to study what they call the 'material culture' of eighteenth-century France, that is the material objects and practices of economic life. They have not done this to repeat older Marxist understandings of intellectual and cultural life as 'reflections' of economic structure; rather, they wish to comprehend the meanings people at the time gave to their world through behaviour as well as words. From this it seems clear that a series of interrelated changes—economic, social, and cultural—was undermining the bases of social and political authority in the second half of the eighteenth century. The limited but highly visible expansion of capitalist enterprise in industry, agriculture in the Paris hinterland, and above all commerce, linked to the colonial trade, generated forms of wealth and values discordant with the institutional bases of absolutism, an ordered society of corporate privilege and the claims to authority of aristocracy and Church. Colin Jones has estimated that the number of bourgeois increased from about 700,000 in 1700 to perhaps 2.3 million in 1780; even among petits-bourgeois a distinctive 'consumer culture' was thriving, apparent in the taste for writing tables, mirrors, clocks, and umbrellas. The decades after 1750 were a time of a 'clothing revolution', in Daniel Roche's words, in which values of respectability, decency, and solid wealth were expressed by clothing across all social groups, but among the 'middling' classes in particular. Bourgeois also marked themselves off from noble and artisan by their *cuisine bourgeoise*, featuring smaller, more regular meals, and by the private virtues of simplicity in housing and manners.

Jones has studied several expressions of these changing values in magazines of the time. In the 1780s the *Journal de santé* and other periodicals devoted to hygiene and health were launched, calling for schemes to wash the streets and to circulate air: the heavy mix of sweat and perfume of bewigged courtiers was as intolerable as the 'stench' of the urban poor and peasantry, with their belief in the medical value of dirt and urine. The content of the advertising and news-sheets known as *Affiches* which were produced in forty-four towns and read by up to 200,000 people became perceptibly more 'patriotic'. This ranged from the increasing use of terms such as 'public opinion', citizen', and 'nation' in political commentary to an advertisement in the *Affiches de Toulouse* in December 1788 for 'véritables pastilles à la Neckre (sic)': patriotic cough-drops 'for the public good'.[4]

Coinciding with the articulation of such values and with gradual, long-term, and uneven economic change was a series of intellectual challenges to established forms of politics and religion which historians have called the 'Enlightenment'. The relationship between economic change and intellectual life is at the heart of the social history of ideas, and social theorists and historians have remained divided over the nature of such a relationship. Historians, particularly Marxist historians for whom the origins of the Revolution are inextricably linked with fundamental economic change, have long understood the Enlightenment as a symptom of a society in crisis, as expressive of the values and frustrations of the middle classes. Hence, for Albert Soboul, writing in 1962, the Enlightenment was effectively the ideology of the bourgeoisie:

The economic base of society was changing, and with it ideologies were being modified. The intellectual origins of the Revolution are to be found in the philosophical ideals which the middle classes had been propounding since the seventeenth century . . . their class-consciousness had been fortified by the exclusive attitude of the nobility and by the contrast between their advancement in economic and intellectual matters and their decline in the field of civic responsibility.[5]

Such a view of the Enlightenment has been contested by other historians who have pointed to the interest many nobles took in the new philosophy. Moreover, whereas an older generation of intellectual historians tended to look backwards from the Revolution to the ideas which seemed to inspire it, such as Rousseau's *Contrat social*, others have since noted that pre-revolutionary interest instead focused on his romantic novel, *La Nouvelle Héloïse*.

Just as the Enlightenment was not a unified intellectual crusade which alone undermined the fundamental assumptions of the Old Regime, so the Catholic Church was not a monolith which always shored up the power of the monarchy. Some of the most prominent *philosophes* were themselves clerics: Mably, Condillac, Raynal, and Turgot, for example. In addition, Dale Van Kley has insisted on the importance of the long-term religious legacy of Protestant and Jansenist notions of political liberty and challenges to ecclesiastical hierarchy. If, towards 1730, police estimated support for the Jansenist critics of church hierarchies at three-quarters in the popular neighbourhoods of Paris, what might the long-term consequences have been? Despite the suppression of Jansenism across the century, its values survived among the 'Richerists', followers of a seventeenth-century canon lawyer who had argued that Christ had commissioned not only the twelve apostles as 'bishops', but also the seventy-two disciples or 'priests' mentioned in Luke.[6]

Nevertheless, there was an essential connection between the major themes of the new philosophy and the society it was challenging. The vibrant intellectual life of the second half of the century was a product of that society. It is no coincidence that the chief and linked targets of critical writing were royal absolutism and theocracy. In the words of Diderot in 1771:

Every century has its own characteristic spirit. The spirit of ours seems to be liberty. The first attack against superstition was violent, unchecked. Once people dared in whatever manner to attack the barrier of religion, this barrier which is the most formidable as well as the most respected, it was impossible to stop. From the time when they turned threatening looks against the heavenly majesty, they did not fail the next moment to direct them against the earthly power. The rope which holds and represses humanity is composed of two strands: one of them cannot give way without the other breaking.[7]

For most *philosophes*, such a critique was limited by an acceptance of the social value of parish priests as guardians of public order and morality. Resigned to what they saw as the ignorance and superstition of the masses, intellectuals similarly turned to enlightened monarchs as the best way of ensuring liberalization of public life.

Such a liberation would necessarily also encourage the unleashing of creativity in economic life: for 'physiocrats' such as Turgot and Quesnay, worldly progress lay in freeing initiative and commerce (*laissez-faire, laissez-passer*). By removing obstacles to economic freedom—guilds and controls on the grain trade—and by encouraging agricultural 'improvement' and enclosures, the economic wealth would be created which would underpin the 'progress' of civil liberties. Such liberties were to be for Europeans alone: with few exceptions, *philosophes* from Voltaire to Helvétius rationalized plantation slavery as the natural lot of inferior peoples. In 1716–89 the volume of trade through the great ports grew fourfold, by some 2 or 3 per cent annually, in part because of the slave trade. Marseilles, with 120,000 inhabitants in 1789, was economically dominated by 300 great trading families. They were the force behind the Enlightenment as well as economic growth, said one of them in 1775:

The trader of whom I am speaking, whose status is not incompatible with the most ancient nobility or the most noble sentiments, is the one who, superior by virtue of his views, his genius, and his enterprise, adds his fortune to the wealth of the state . . .[8]

In these terms the Enlightenment does appear as a class-based ideology. But what was the social incidence of its readership? It is in this area, of the social history of the Enlightenment, that historians have moved closest to assessing the cultural changes of the 1770s and 1780s. Starting from the premiss that publishing is a multi-layered business activity, Robert Darnton has sought, by analysing the clandestine Swiss book trade, to discover what the reading public wanted. In a regime of tight censorship, the cheap pirate editions of the *Encyclopédie* smuggled in from Switzerland sold an estimated 25,000 sets in 1776–89. While the state authorities tolerated the trade in cheap editions of works from the *Encyclopédie* to the Bible, it was the underground trade in banned books which is most revealing, for a whole network of people from printers, booksellers, peddlers, and mule-drivers risked imprisonment to profit from public demand. The Swiss catalogues offered readers at every level of urban society a socially explosive mixture of philosophy and obscenity: the finest works of Rousseau, Helvétius, and d'Holbach jostled with titles such as *Vénus dans le cloître, ou la religieuse en chemise*, and *La Fille de joie. L'Amour de*

Charlot et Toinette began with a description of the queen masturbating and of her affairs with her brother-in-law, and ridiculed the king:

> It is very well known that poor Sire
> Three or four times condemned . . .
> For complete impotence
> Cannot satisfy Antoinette.
> Of this misfortune we are sure
> Given that his 'match'
> Is not fatter than a straw
> Always soft and always curved . . .

The subversive tone of these books and pamphlets was paralleled in popular songs. A clerk in the department which was responsible for regulating the book trade called on his superior to impose more severe censorship: 'One observes that the songs sold in the street for the amusement of the populace instruct them in the system of liberty. Rabble of the most vile sort, mistaking themselves for the Third Estate, no longer respect the high nobility.'[9]

The ribald yet moralistic tone of these publications and songs mocked the Church, nobility, and the royal family itself for its decadence and impotence, undermining at the same time the mystique of those born to rule as well as their capacity to do so. Nor did it matter that Louis's daughter was born in 1778, and sons in 1781 and 1785. Even in provincial towns dominated by the privileged orders, such as Toulouse, Besançon, and Troyes, the *Encyclopédie* and the ribaldry of the literary underground found a ready market. After 1750, argues Arlette Farge, the working people of Paris also became more involved in public debate, not because the writings of the Enlightenment intellectuals filtered down to them but in response to what they felt to be the arbitrary rule of the monarchy.

The Enlightenment was not simply a self-conscious cultural movement: it was lived out subconsciously, in shifting values. In 1700 estate inventories in Paris showed that books were owned by 13 per cent of wage-earners, 32 per cent of magistrates and 26 per cent of nobles of the sword: by the second half of the century the figures were 35, 58 and 53 per cent. The historian of the *faubourg* St-Marcel, David Garrioch, has contrasted the wills of two wealthy tanners. Nicolas Bouillerot left 73 books, all of them about religion, when he died in

1734. Jean Auffray, who died in 1792, was less wealthy but left 500 books, including works of history and Latin classics, and a number of maps and pamphlets. Of course, this may be no more than the literary tastes of two individuals, but Garrioch sees it as typifying changing values and interests among bourgeois for whom the Enlightenment was 'a way of life'.[10]

Yet another approach to the Enlightenment has drawn heavily on the work of the German sociologist Jürgen Habermas, writing in the 1960s in the context of his nation's recent history and emerging knowledge of Stalin's Russia. For Habermas, the Enlightenment was best understood as the intellectual expression of democratic political culture. Recent historians have expanded on Habermas's notions of political culture and public space by going beyond elite intellectual history to the 'spaces' in which ideas were articulated and contested. For example, at variance with the corporate, privileged world of the aristocratic academies were the more open, freethinking Masonic lodges, a form of bourgeois and male sociability which proliferated remarkably after 1760: despite injunctions from several popes (which did not prevent 400 priests from joining), there were some 210,000 members in 600 lodges in the 1780s. This expansion of Freemasonry was in part of the expression of a distinctive bourgeois culture outside the norms of the aristocratic elite. Businessmen, excluded from noble academies, comprised 35–50 per cent of the lodges, which also attracted soldiers, public officials and professional men. In Paris, 74 per cent of Freemasons were from the Third Estate. Dena Goodman, however, has argued that Freemasonry was a masculine space in contrast to the world of Paris salons in which women played a central role in the creation of spaces which were both feminized and 'freethinking'.[11]

The real significance of the Enlightenment, then, is as a symptom of a crisis of authority and as part of a wider political discourse. Well before 1789, the language of 'citizen', 'nation', 'social contract', and 'general will' was articulated across French society, clashing with an older discourse of 'orders', 'estates', and 'corporations'. Daniel Roche has underscored the importance of 'cultural crisis' evident in a new 'public sphere of critical reason' in Parisian salons, learned societies, and Masonic lodges: 'The rupture with the past had in some respects already taken place: censorship was accomplishing nothing, and a realm of freedom was being established through increasingly intense, rapid, and eloquent consumption of commodities.'[12] The same complex relationship between reading public and writer existed in the art world, exemplified in the public reception of David's 'Oath of the Horatii' in 1785, with its celebration of civic behaviour perceived as virtuous. Its subject-matter resonated among middle-class audiences schooled in the classics. The author of *Sur la peinture* (1782) attacked conventional painting and the decadence of the social elite, exhorting art critics to engage 'considerations which are moral and political in character'.

The lively world of literature in the 1780s was essentially an urban phenomenon: in Paris, for example, there was a primary school for every 1,200 people and most men and women could read. In rural areas, the major sources of the printed words which the few literate people occasionally read aloud to evening gatherings (*veillées*) were the Bible, popular almanacs of festivals and seasons, and the *Bibliothèque bleue*.[13] The latter, cheap, and mass-produced paperbacks, offered the rural poor an escape from the misery of daily life into a medieval wonderland of the supernatural, lives of saints, and magic. While there seems to have been a secularization of the type of information contained in the almanacs, there is no evidence at all that the reading matter peddled through the countryside by *colporteurs* was imbued with 'enlightened' precepts.

Nevertheless, rural France was in crisis in the 1780s. In Montigny (see Chapter 1), the free trade treaty with England in 1786 was a body blow to the textile industry; rural producers, too, were battered by a trebling of rents on church lands in the 1780s and by harvest failure in 1788. At least in Burgundy, the discourse through which villages contested seigneurial rights was increasingly marked by appeals to social utility, reason and even notions of citizenship. There is abundant evidence of nobles employing lawyers (*feudistes*) to check or tighten the exaction of dues as a way of increasing income in a time of inflation, what came later to be called the 'feudal reaction'. For example, in 1786, the family of Saulx-Tavanes in Burgundy used their elevation to a dukedom to double all dues for a year, resurrecting a practice not used since the thirteenth century. Their investment in farm improvements, never more than 5 per cent of their receipts, shrank to nothing in the late 1780s while rents were doubled as the nobles attempted to pay off their debts. A tax official travelling through the southwest of France was astonished to find nobles enforcing 'rights and dues unknown or forgotten', such as an extraordinary *taille* a noble magistrate in the Toulouse Parlement exacted every time he bought land. This reaction occurred in the context of long-term inflation, whereby grain prices had outstripped labourers' wages, and short-term harvest failures in 1785 and 1788 which doubled grain prices. Taken together, they explain the escalation of conflict in the countryside: some three-quarters of 4,400 recorded collective protests in the years 1720–88 occurred after 1765, mostly in the form of food riots and anti-seigneurialism.[14]

This conforms with Tocqueville's thesis of an increasingly intrusive and powerful State effectively rendering the nobility 'dysfunctional' by undermining the theoretical justification of its privileges. Seigneurial dues could no longer be legitimized as the price the non-privileged paid for poor relief, protection, and assistance from seigneurs who were rarely present in the community. Increasingly, the seigneurial system appeared as little more than a cash-racket. It was precisely the response of seigneurs to this challenge to their authority and wealth—from above and below—which made them seem particularly aggressive. Whilst some historians have argued that feudalism had effectively ceased to exist by the late eighteenth century, they have a point only in so far as the concept of *noblesse oblige* seemed to have lost all pertinence to absentee seigneurs who extracted surplus from a grudging peasantry. If the seigneurial regime was relatively light and non-intrusive in the Roussillon and Brittany, at opposite ends of the country, this was not at all the case in areas of central France or of Languedoc. It was this resentment of seigneurialism above all which bonded rural communities together against their lords.[15]

Peasants did not acquiesce unquestioningly in the power of those to whom they had been taught to defer. On the lowlands of Languedoc in particular there is evidence of the *mentalité* Olwen Hufton and Georges Fournier have described, of young men in particular more commonly contesting the authority of seigneur, *curé*, and local officials, and exhibiting a contrariness denounced as a 'republican spirit' by the authorities. Consider some examples from the Corbières region of Languedoc, southeast of Carcassonne. A day-labourer from Albas commented to others as the seigneur passed: 'If you would do as I do we'd soon put to rights this young —— of a seigneur.' Later he had continued to a blacksmith, 'If you would all do as I do, not only would you not raise your hats when you pass in front of them, but you wouldn't even recognize them as seigneurs, because as for me I've never and will never in my life raise my hat, they're a huge load of scum, thieves, young ——'. At nearby Termes a man took his brother-in-law to court in the years before the Revolution for having said 'that he carried on like a seigneur, with his arrogant tone'. Those described by priests, nobles, and the local well-to-do as 'libertins' and 'séditieux' were overwhelmingly young peasant men, and three-quarters of the incidents in which they were involved concerned their refusal to make 'signs of submission'. In 1780 the young men of Tuchan mocked a local seigneur, with a provocative song in Occitan, accusing him of being a 'skirt-chaser' and referring to one of his conquests:

Regardas lo al front	Look at her, she has the cheek
Sen ba trouba aquel homme	To go and seek this man
Jusquos dins souns saloun.	In his very parlour.
Bous daisi a pensa	I leave you to imagine
Se que naribara	What will happen there.[16]

Georges Fournier has discerned clear signs of developing friction in Languedoc within such rural communities and between them and their seigneurs in the second half of the eighteenth century. Long-standing resentments at the seigneurial system were aggravated by, for example, the consistency with which the rigidly aristocratic Parlement of Toulouse upheld the rights of seigneurs against their communities over access to the rough hillsides (*garrigues*) used for grazing sheep. Members of the elite at the time were also sure that social relations were changing. In 1776, towards the end of his long and active term as bishop of Carcassonne, Armand Bazin de Bezons warned his superiors at Versailles that

for some time the spirit of revolt and the lack of respect for one's elders has become intolerable . . . no remedies avail since people believe themselves to be free; this word 'liberty' known even in the most isolated mountains has become an unchecked license . . . I hope that this impunity does not lead to and produce in the end some very bitter fruits for the government.

Certainly, it is commonplace for a man in such a position to regret the collapse of idealized patterns of behaviour, but there is evidence which suggests that he was not mistaken about the erosion of deference. Bazin de Bezons's warning was delivered in the same year in which Britain's North American colonies declared their independence, triggering French involvement on their side and a financial crisis. The successful war of independence waged by the United States may have assuaged somewhat the humiliations France had suffered from England in India, Canada and the Caribbean; however, the war had cost over one billion livres, more than twice the usual annual revenue of the state. As the royal state lurched into financial crisis after 1783, the changing economic and cultural structures of French society conditioned conflicting responses to Louis XVI's pleas for assistance. Increasing costs of war, maintaining an expanding court and bureaucracy, and servicing a massive debt impelled the monarchy to seek ways of eroding noble taxation immunity and the capacity of *parlements* to resist royal decrees. The entrenched hostility of most nobles towards fiscal and social reform was generated by two long-term factors: first, the long-term pressures of royal state-making which reduced the nobility's autonomy; and, secondly, by the challenge from a wealthier, larger and more critical bourgeoisie and an openly disaffected peasantry towards aristocratic conceptions of property, hierarchy and social order.

Successive attempts by royal ministers to convince meetings of Notables to agree to lift the fiscal privileges of the Second Estate foundered on their insistence that only a gathering of representatives of the three orders as an Estates-General could agree to such innovation. Initially, Calonne sought to convince an assembly of 144 'Notables', only ten of whom were non-noble, in February 1787, by offering concessions such as the establishment of assemblies in all provinces in return for the introduction of a universal land-tax, the reduction of the *taille* and *gabelle*, and the abolition of internal customs barriers. His proposals foundered in particular on the principle of the land-tax. Following Calonne's dismissal in April, his successor, Loménie de Brienne, archbishop of Toulouse, failed to convince the Notables of similar proposals, and they were dismissed at the end of May.

Brienne pursued his wide-ranging programme of reforms; this time, in July, it was the Paris *parlement* which refused to register the uniform land-tax. Tension between crown and aristocracy came to a head in August, with the exile of the *parlement* to Troyes; such was the popular and elite support for the *parlement*, however, that the king was forced to recall it. On 28 September it re-entered Paris amid popular celebrations. The principle of universal taxation was set aside.

At the same time as the crisis between crown and *parlements* was reaching a head in September 1787, news arrived that on the 13th Prussian troops had crossed the border to support the Hohenzollern princess of Orange against the 'patriot' party in the Dutch Republic. Assumptions that French intervention to support the patriots was imminent were dashed when the government announced that the military were unprepared.

The resistance of the *parlements* was increasingly expressed through calls for an Estates-General, an advisory body composed of representatives of the three estates which had last been consulted in 1614. In November 1787 Lamoignon, the *garde des sceaux* or Minister of Justice, made a speech to a royal sitting of the *parlement* of Paris. Lamoignon, a former president of the *parlement*, reminded his peers of Louis XVI's pre-eminence by dismissing their call for a meeting of the Estates-General:

> These principles, universally accepted by the nation, testify that *sovereign power in his kingdom belongs to the king alone;*
> *That he is accountable only to God for the exercise of supreme power;*
> *That the link that unites the king and the nation is by nature indissoluble;*
> *That the reciprocal interests and duties of the king and his subjects ensure the perpetuity of this union;*
> *That the nation has a vested interest that the rights of its ruler remain unchanged;*
> *That the king is the sovereign ruler of the nation, and is one with it;*
> *Finally that legislative power resides in the person of the sovereign, depending upon and sharing with no-one.*
> These, sirs, are the invariable principles of the French monarchy.

'When our kings established the *parlements*', he reminded them, 'they wished to appoint officers whose duty it was to administer justice and to maintain the edicts of the kingdom, and not to build up in their bodies a power to rival royal authority.'[17] Lamoignan's resounding statement of the principles of the French monarchy did not, however, intimidate the king's most eminent subjects into submission.

The following May Lamoignon issued six edicts aimed at undermining the judicial and political power of the *parlements*, provoking rioting in Paris and provincial centres. Even entrenched noble interests were couched in the language of the *philosophes*: the *parlement* of Toulouse asserted that 'the natural rights of municipalities, common to all men, are inalienable, imprescriptible, as eternal as nature which forms their basis'. This language of opposition to the royal state, appeals to provincial autonomy in provincial centres such as Bordeaux, Rennes, Toulouse, and Grenoble, and the vertical bonds of economic dependency generated an alliance between urban working people and local *parlements* in 1788. When the *parlement* of Grenoble was exiled in June 1788 for its defiance towards the ministry's strike at noble judicial power, royal troops were driven from the city by popular rebellion on the 'Day of the tiles'. The self-interest behind noble appeals to 'natural law', 'inalienable rights', and the 'nation' ensured that such an alliance could not last. From a meeting of local notables in July 1788 at Claude Périer's recently acquired chateau at Vizille came another call for the Estates-General, but this time for the Third Estate to have double the representation of the other orders in recognition of its importance in the life of the nation. The same month, Louis decided that he would after all convoke an Estates-General in May 1789, and Lamoignon and Brienne resigned.

In September 1788, the English agronomist Arthur Young found himself in the Atlantic port of Nantes just six weeks after Louis XVI had announced the convocation of the Estates-General. A keen observer and recorder, Young noted in his journal that

Nantes is as *enflammée* in the cause of liberty, as any town in France can be; the conversations I witnessed here prove how great a change is effected in the minds of the French, nor do I believe it will be possible for the present government to last half a century longer, unless the clearest and most decided talents be at the helm.[18]

Nantes was a bustling port of 90,000 people which had boomed with the rapid growth of the colonial trade with the Caribbean throughout the eighteenth century. The merchants with whom Young conversed had convinced him of the rights of the 'talented' to participate more fully in public life. Moreover, their enthusiasm for reform reveals how much further the crisis of absolutist France went beyond friction between nobles and monarch. Nor was this political awareness limited to elites. The Parisian cobbler Joseph Charon recalled in his memoirs that before the disturbances of August–September 1788 political ferment had descended 'from men of the world of the highest rank to the very lowest ranks through various channels . . . people acquired and dispensed enlightenment that one would have searched for in vain a dozen years earlier . . . and they have acquired notions about public constitutions in the past two or three years'.[19]

The calling of the Estates-General facilitated the expression of tensions at every level of French society, and revealed social divisions which challenged the idea of a society of 'orders'. The remarkable vibrancy of debate in the months before May 1789 was in part a function of the suspension of press censorship. It has been calculated that 1,519 pamphlets on political issues were published between May and December 1788; in the first four months of 1789 they were followed by a flood of 2,639 titles. This war of words was fuelled by Louis's indecision about the procedures to be followed at Versailles. Torn between a loyalty to the established corporate order of rank and privilege and the exigencies of fiscal crisis, the king vacillated on the crucial political question of whether the three orders would meet separately, as in 1614, or in a common chamber. In September the *parlement* of Paris had decreed that tradition would be followed in this matter; then Louis's decision on 5 December to double the size of the Third Estate representation served only to highlight the crucial issue of political power, because he remained silent on how voting would occur. By January 1789, a Swiss journalist, Mallet du Pan, had commented: 'the public debate has totally changed in its emphasis; now the King, despotism, and the Constitution are only very secondary questions; and it has become a war between the Third Estate and the other two orders.'[20]

Louis's younger brother, Provence, was prepared to countenance increased representation for the Third Estate, but his youngest brother, Artois, and the 'princes of the blood' made their recalcitrance and fear known in a 'memoir' to Louis in December:

Who can say where the recklessness of opinions will stop? The rights of the throne have been called into question; the rights of the two orders of the State divide opinions; soon property rights will be attacked; the inequality of fortunes will be presented as an object for reform; the suppression of feudal rights has already been proposed, as has the abolition of a system of oppression, the remains of barbarism . . .

May the Third Estate therefore cease to attack the rights of the first two orders; rights which, no less ancient than the monarchy, must be as unchanging as its constitution; that it limit itself to seeking the reduction in taxes with which it might be burdened; then the first two orders, recognizing in the third citizens who are dear to them, will, by the generosity of their sentiments, be able to renounce those prerogatives which have a financial interest, and consent to bear public charges in the most perfect equality.[21]

At the same time, a 40-year-old priest of bourgeois background, Emmanuel Sieyès, contributed the most remarkable of his several pamphlets, titled *What is the Third Estate?*[22] Castigating the nobility's obsession with its 'odious privileges', Sieyès issued a ringing declaration of commoner capacity. Certainly, Sieyès was no democrat—he noted that women and the poor could not be entrusted with political responsibilities—but his challenge articulated a radical intransigence:

We have three questions to ask ourselves.
1. What is the Third Estate?—everything.
2. What has it been until now in the political order?—nothing.
3. What is it asking?—to be something . . .

Who thus would dare to say that the Third Estate does not contain everything that is needed to make up a complete nation? It is a strong and robust man who still has one arm in chains. If the privileged orders were removed, the nation would not be worse off for it, but better. So, what is the Third? Everything, but a fettered and oppressed everything. What would it be without the privileged order? Everything, but a free and flourishing everything . . . the fear of seeing abuses reformed inspires more fear in the aristocrats than the desire they feel for liberty. Between it and a few odious privileges, they have chosen the latter. . . . Today, they dread the Estates General that they once called upon with such fervour.

Sieyès's pamphlet resonated with the language of patriotism: that the nobility were too selfish to be committed to a process of national 'regeneration' and could therefore be excluded from the body politic. Significantly, too, Sieyès wrote here of just one privileged order, evidently assuming that the clergy, too, were irrevocably divided between noble elite and commoner parish priests.

The savage winter of 1788–9, with devastating hailstorms in July which flattened crops in the Paris basin, did nothing for the peasants' capacity to pay taxes. The winter was correspondingly one of sharp misery in cities as well: contemporaries spoke of 80,000 unemployed in Paris and half or more of the looms idle in textile towns such as Amiens, Lyons, Carcassonne, Lille, Troyes, and Rouen. The response to crisis in the supply of food took 'traditional' forms, of collective action by consumers to forcibly lower the price of bread. However, in many northern regions there were also reports of opposition to the seigneurial system, particular its game laws and hunting restrictions. On the estates of the Prince de Conti near Pontoise, not far from Menucourt (see Chapter 1), peasants and farm-labourers trapped rabbits in defiance of seigneurial privilege. In Artois, peasants from a dozen villages banded together to seize the Count d'Oisy's game.

In the spring of 1789, people all over France were required to formulate proposals for the reform of public life and to elect deputies to the Estates-General. In particular, parish and guild assemblies, and meetings of clergy and nobles were engaged in compiling their 'lists of grievances' to guide their deputies in the advice they would offer the king. The drawing up of these *cahiers de doléances* in the context of subsistence crisis, political uncertainty, and fiscal chaos was the decisive moment in the mass politicization of social friction. At least on the surface, the *cahiers* of all three orders show a remarkable level of agreement, particularly at the level of the district (*sénéchaussée* or *bailliage*). First, whatever the undoubtedly sincere expressions of gratitude and loyalty towards the king, the *cahiers* of all three orders assumed that the absolute monarchy was moribund, that the meeting of the Estates-General in May would be but the first of a regular cycle. If there is no reason to doubt the sincerity of the repeated expressions of gratitude and devotion towards the king, his ministers were nonetheless castigated for their fiscal inefficiency and arbitrary powers. The king was urged to make a full disclosure of the level of state debt and to concede to the Estates-General (often called the 'nation assemblée') control over expenditures and taxes.

Secondly, there was consensus that the Church was in urgent need of reform to check abuses within its hierarchy and to improve the lot of its parish clergy. Thirdly, it would seem that, across the mass of nobles, priests, and bourgeois, there was already general acceptance of the basic principles of fiscal equality, that the nobles and clergy would renounce their tax immunity, at least in part. The *cahiers* of all three estates exhibited similar agreement on the need for judicial reform: that the laws should be made uniform across society and between regions, that the administration of justice should be more expeditious and less costly, and that laws be more humane. Finally, the advantages of internal free trade and of facilitating transport and commerce were widely accepted.

On several fundamental matters of social order and political power, however, entrenched divisions were to undermine the possibilities of consensual reform. The sharpest contrasts in the *cahiers* lay in the polarized world-views of the peasantry, bourgeoisie and provincial nobles. Even small-town bourgeois spoke openly of a new society characterized by 'careers open to talent', encouragement of enterprise, equality of taxation, liberal freedoms, and the ending of privilege. The nobility responded with a utopian vision of a reinforced hierarchy of social orders and obligations, protection of noble exemptions and renewed political autonomy. To provincial nobles, seigneurial rights and noble privileges were too important to be negotiable, and from this came the intransigence of most of the 270 noble deputies elected to Versailles. To self-respecting officials, professional men and property owners, such pretensions were offensive and demeaning, reflected in the repeated insistence in *cahiers* at the *bailliage* level that Third Estate deputies should refuse to meet separately. To the insistence of villagers that seigneurial dues be abolished or at the very least made redeemable, the nobility reasserted its belief in an idealized social order of hierarchy and mutual dependence, recognizing the sacrifices noble warriors had made for France. In general, the nobility sought a wider political role for itself within a limited constitutional monarchy, with a system of representation which would guarantee the stability of the social order by ensuring only a restricted role for the elite of the Third Estate.

A typical rhetorical device of nobles across France was to make ringing statements of preparedness to join with the Third Estate in the programme of reform and common acceptance of duties coupled with subtle qualifying clauses which effectively negated the initial generosity. Hence, for example, the Second Estate of the province of Berry meeting in Bourges expressed its delight that 'the spirit of unity and agreement, which had always reigned between the three orders, is equally manifest in their *cahiers*. The question of voting by head in the assembly of the Estates-General was the only one to divide the Third Estate from the other two orders, whose constant wish has been to deliberate there by order.' In fact, however, there were a series of matters on which there was no agreement. For example, in the parish of Levet, 18 kilometres south of Bourges, where no fewer than seventeen ecclesiastics and nine lay persons had seigneurial rights, a meeting of four farmers and thirty labourers insisted:

Article 1. That the Third Estate vote by head at the assembly of the Estates-General . . .
Article 4. That all types of exemptions be abolished, such as those concerning the *taille*, *capitation*, lodging of soldiers, etc., entirely borne by the most unfortunate class of the Third Estate . . .
Article 9. That seigneurial justice be abolished and those called to justice instead plead before the closest royal judge.[23]

As members of a corporate, privileged body, parish priests similarly envisaged a rejuvenated social order under the auspices of a Catholic monopoly of worship and morality. However, as commoners by birth, they were also ominously sympathetic to the needs of the poor, the opening of positions—including the church hierarchy—to 'men of talent', and to calls for universal taxation. Unlike the Third Estate, however, the clergy were consistently hostile to surrendering their monopoly of religious worship or public morality. The First Estate of Bourges called on 'His Majesty' 'to order that all those who, through their writings, seek to spread the poison of incredulity, attack religion and its mysteries, discipline and dogmas, be seen as enemies of the Church and the State and severely punished; that printers be once again forbidden to print books contrary to religion'. It asserted that 'The apostolic and Roman Catholic religion is the only true religion.' Whereas the noble *cahiers* were agreed upon by consensus, those of the clergy reveal a genuine tension between the parish clergy and the cathedral chapters and monasteries of the towns. The clergy of Troyes insisted on the traditional distinction of the three orders meeting separately, but made a crucial exception on the matter of taxation; on this issue they urged a common assembly to adopt a tax 'proportionately borne by all individuals of the three orders'.[24]

The *cahiers* of urban *menu peuple* were variously expressed through meetings of master craftsmen, parish assemblies and, very occasionally, groups of tradeswomen. Most urban working people were too poor to meet the minimal property requirements necessary to participate: in Paris only one in five men over 25 years were eligible. Artisans' *cahiers*, like those of the peasantry, revealed an overlapping of interests with those of the bourgeoisie on fiscal, judicial, and political questions, but a clear divergence on economic regulation, calling for protection against mechanization and competition, and for controls on the grain trade. 'Let us not call the rich capitalists egoists: they are our brothers', conceded the hatters and furriers of Rouen, before calling for the 'suppression of machinery' so 'there will be no competition and no problems about markets'. The *cahier* of the Norman village of Vatimesnil, too, called on 'His Majesty for the good of the people to abolish spinning machines because they do great wrong to all poor people'. A similar point was made eloquently in one of the rare women's *cahiers*, that of the Parisian flower-sellers, complaining about the effects of deregulation of their trade:

The multitude of sellers is far from producing the salutary effect that we apparently should expect from competition. As the number of consumers does not increase proportionately to the number of producers, they necessarily do each other damage . . . Today when everyone can sell flowers and make bouquets, their modest profits are divided up to the point of no longer giving them means to subsist . . . since their profession cannot feed them, they seek the resources they lack in licentiousness and the most shameful debauchery.[25]

The veracity of the 40,000 rural *cahiers de doléances* as statements of popular attitudes is often questioned: not only did the number of those participating in their drafting vary widely, in many cases model *cahiers* were circulated through the countryside from towns, even if frequently added to or adapted at a local level. Despite this, they are an unparalleled resource for the historian. A sample of 1,112 of the *cahiers*, 748 of them from village communities, has been the subject of quantitative analysis by John Markoff and Gilbert Shapiro. Their analysis demonstrates that peasants were far more concerned in 1789 with material rather than symbolic burdens, that they largely ignored the trappings of seigneurial status which weighed little in material terms, such as the public display of arms and reserved pews in churches. Hostility to seigneurial exactions tended to go together with criticism of the tithes, fees, and practices of the Church; that is, they were seen as interdependent within the seigneurial regime.

Peasant *cahiers* ranged in length from many pages of detailed criticisms and suggestions to the three sentences written in a mixture of French and Catalan from the tiny village of Serrabone in the stony foothills of the Pyrenees. In the districts of Troyes, Auxerre, and Sens, an analysis of 389 parish *cahiers* by Peter Jones shows that seigneurial dues and *banalités* were explicitly criticized in 40 per cent, 36 per cent, and 27 per cent respectively, leaving aside other common complaints about hunting rights and seigneurial courts. Inevitably, the composite *cahiers* drawn up by urban bourgeois at the district (*bailliage*) level excised many rural grievances deemed too parochial; nevertheless, 64 per cent of the 666 *cahiers* at this level across France called for the abolition of seigneurial dues. In stark contrast, 84 per cent of noble *cahiers* were simply silent on the whole matter.[26]

At the heart of tensions in the countryside were long-standing frictions over the control of resources. As Andrée Corvol has shown, well before 1789 the administration and conservation of forests was under great strain because of increased pressure from rising population and wood prices and more commercial attitudes from owners of forest resources.[27] The *cahiers* of parish assemblies were concerned to preserve resources, especially wood, and targeted as enemies of the local environment the excessive demands of local industry and seigneurs. In eastern France, in particular, the proliferation of wood-fuelled extractive industries was the focus of peasant ire such as that demonstrated in the widely repeated article of parish *cahiers* around Amont in eastern France that 'all forges, furnaces and factories established in the province of Franche-Comté within the past thirty years be destroyed as well as older ones whose proprietors do not personally possess a forest large enough to power them for six months per year'. Others were angered by effluent from mines, 'whose cesspit and drain empty into the rivers which water the fields or in which the stock drink,' causing sickness in stock and killing fish. From Brittany, the parish of Plozévet expressed a very common point of view:

The poor vassal who has the misfortune to cut a foot off a tree of little value, but of which he has great need for a house or a cart or a plough, is plagued and crushed by his seigneur for the value of a whole tree. If everybody had the right to plant and to cut for oneself, without being able to sell, there would not be so much loss of wood.

Many rural *cahiers* also targeted the monarchy's attempt to encourage land clearances. Royal decrees of 1764, 1766, and 1770 had offered tax concessions on all state taxes and tithes for fifteen years for land cleared and duly reported to the authorities. Although the decree stipulated that Colbert's forest code of 1669 remained in force, outlawing the clearing of wooded terrain, river banks, and hillsides, parishes complained bitterly of the erosion caused by land clearances. They targeted for criticism not only their fellow peasants, but seigneurs who were too mean or neglectful to replant areas they had cleared. For example, from Quincé and other parishes near Angers came the demand that large proprietors and seigneurs be required to replant sections of *landes* with trees; from nearby St-Barthélemy the *cahier* insisted that all who cut trees be required to replace them 'following the prudent example of the English'.

As Markoff has properly insisted, the *cahiers* are an imperfect guide to what was to happen in the countryside thereafter, not only because of the circumstances in which they were drafted, but because of the changing context of local and national politics once the Estates-General assembled. In any case, people were being consulted about reform proposals, not about whether they wanted a revolution. Peasant demands about how the world might be—which had previously been in the realm of the imagination—were only later to become the focus of concerted action. In rural communities, the economically dependent were also acutely aware of the potential costs of being outspoken about noble privilege. Nevertheless, some parish assemblies were so bold as to criticize the tithe and the seigneurial system directly. In the southern corner of the kingdom, the few lines submitted from the tiny community of Périllos were unreservedly hostile to the seigneurial system under which they claimed the seigneur treated them 'like slaves'.[28]

Most obviously of all, nobles and commoners could not agree on arrangements for voting at the Estates-General. Louis's decision on

5 December to double the size of the Third Estate representation, while remaining silent on how voting would occur at Versailles, served only to highlight the crucial issue of political power. There was a shared commitment in all three orders to the need for change, and general agreement on a plethora of specific abuses within the church and state apparatus; however, the divisions over fundamental issues of political power, seigneurialism, and claims to corporate privilege were already irreconcilable by the time the deputies arrived in Versailles.

Historians have long debated whether there were deep-seated, long-term causes of the political friction which erupted in 1788, and whether there were clear lines of social antagonism. Some have insisted that political conflict was short-term and avoidable, and have pointed to the coexistence of nobles and wealthy bourgeois in an elite of notables, united as property-owners, office-holders, investors, and even by involvement in profit-oriented industry and agriculture. However, within this bourgeois and noble elite was a ruling class of nobles with inherited titles who dominated the highest echelons of privilege, office, wealth, and status. While ennoblement was the ambition of the wealthiest bourgeois, the Second Estate's *recherches de noblesse*, set up to investigate claims to noble status, guarded the boundaries closely. And within the Second Estate was, in a contemporary's words, a 'cascade of contempt' for those in descending positions of status.[29]

While the upper echelons of bourgeoisie and nobility were coalescing into an elite of notables, the bulk of the Second Estate was unwilling to give up its privileges for a new social order of equal rights and obligations. The attempts at institutional reform after 1774 would always founder on the rocks of this intransigence and the inability of the king to direct basic changes to a system in which he was at the pinnacle. Social changes since 1750 had aggravated tensions between this elite and the less eminent majority of the privileged orders while nourishing rival conceptions of the bases of social and political authority among commoners. Fraudulent names such as de Robespierre, Brissot de Warville, and d'Anton fooled nobody. The lionizing in Paris and even at Versailles of Benjamin Franklin, Thomas Jefferson, and John Adams—representatives of a popularly elected republican government—suggests how deep was the crisis of confidence in the juridical structures of the Old Regime. The debate over the specific provisions for the convening of the Estates-General had served to focus noble, bourgeois, and peasant images of a regenerated France with dramatic clarity.

Notes

1. The classic Marxist formulation of the origins of the crisis of 1789 is in Georges Lefebvre, *The Coming of the French Revolution*, trans. R. R. Palmer (Princeton, 1947); and Soboul, *The French Revolution*, 25–113. Their argument is contested by William Doyle, *Origins of the French Revolution*, 2nd edn. (Oxford, 1980); and T. C. W. Blanning, *The French Revolution: Aristocrats versus Bourgeois?* (London, 1987). The argument that wealthy nobles and bourgeois formed an élite of notables is put by William Doyle, *The Oxford History of the French Revolution* (Oxford, 1989), ch. 1.

2. Lynn Hunt, 'Foreword' to Mona Ozouf, *Festivals and the French Revolution*, trans. Alan Sheridan (Cambridge, Mass. 1988), ix–x; Sarah Maza, 'Luxury, Morality, and Social Change: Why there was no Middle-Class Consciousness in Prerevolutionary France', *Journal of Modern History*, 69 (1997), 199–229.

3. David Garrioch, *The Formation of the Parisian Bourgeoisie 1690–1830* (Cambridge, Mass., 1996), 1; Sarah Maza, *Private Lives and Public Affairs: The Causes Célèbres of Prerevolutionary France* (Berkeley, Calif., 1993); and 'Luxury, Morality, and Social Change'.

4. Colin Jones, 'Bourgeois Revolution Revivified: 1789 and Social Change', in Colin Lucas (ed.), *Rewriting the French Revolution* (Oxford, 1991); and 'The Great Chain of Buying: Medical Advertisement, the Bourgeois Public Sphere, and the Origins of the French Revolution', *American Historical Review*, 101 (1996), 13–40; Georges Vigarello, *Concepts of Cleanliness: Changing Attitudes in France since the Middle Ages*, trans. J. Birrell (Cambridge, 1988), chs. 9–11. This theme of the development of a commercial, consumer culture is addressed in engaging fashion by Roche, *France in the Enlightenment*, chs. 5, 17, 19, and *The Culture of Clothing: Dress and Fashion in the 'Ancien Régime'*, trans. Jean Birrell (Cambridge, 1994).

5. Albert Soboul, *The French Revolution 1787–1799: From the Storming of the Bastille to Napoleon*, trans. Alan Forrest and Colin Jones (London, 1989), 67, 74. A lucid discussion is Dorinda Outram, *The Enlightenment* (Cambridge, 1995).

6. Roche, *France in the Enlightenment*, ch. 11; Dale Van Kley, *The Religious Origins of the French Revolution: From Calvin to the Civil Constitution, 1560–1791* (New Haven, 1996).

7. John Lough, *An Introduction to Eighteenth-Century France* (London, 1960), 317; Roche, *France in the Enlightenment*, ch. 18, 20.

8. Roche, *France in the Enlightenment*, 159, 167.

9. Robert Darnton, *The Literary Underground of the Old Regime* (Cambridge, Mass., 1982), 200; Roche, *France in the Enlightenment*, 671. The cultural origins of the French Revolution are successfully explored in the 1989 film version of Choderlos de Laclos's 1782 novel *Dangerous Liaisons*, and in the 1997 film *Ridicule*.

10. Garrioch, *Formation of the Parisian Bourgeoisie*, 278; Roche, *France in the Enlightenment*, 199; Arlette Farge, *Subversive Words: Public Opinion in Eighteenth-Century France*, trans. Rosemary Morris (Oxford, 1994).

11. On the 'spaces' of public life, see Thomas E. Crow, *Painters and Public Life in Eighteenth-Century Paris* (New Haven, 1985); Joan B. Landes, *Women and the Public Sphere in the Age of the French Revolution* (Ithaca, NY, 1988), ch. 1; Jack Censer and Jeremy Popkin (eds.), *Press and Politics in Pre-Revolutionary France* (Berkeley, Calif., 1987); Dena Goodman, *The Republic of Letters: A Cultural History of the French Enlightenment* (Ithaca, NY, 1994); Margaret C. Jacob, *Living the Enlightenment: Freemasonry and Politics in Eighteenth-Century Europe* (Oxford, 1991); and Roche, *France in the Enlightenment*, ch. 13. A lucid statement of the use historians have made of Habermas is in Maza, *Private Lives and Public Affairs*, Introduction.

12. Roche, *France in the Enlightenment*, 669.

13. Emmet Kennedy, *A Cultural History of the French Revolution* (New Haven, 1989), 38–47. Roger Chartier doubts the practice of reading aloud in *Cultural History: Between Practices and Representations*, trans. Lydia Cochrane (Cambridge, 1988), ch. 7.

14. Hilton L. Root, *Peasant and King in Burgundy: Agrarian Foundations of French Absolutism* (Berkeley, Calif., 1987); Forster, *The House of Saulx-Tavanes*, ch. 2; Jones, *Peasantry*, 53–8.

15. The argument that 'feudalism' was dead is put most famously by Alfred Cobban, *The Social Interpretation of the French Revolution* (Cambridge, 1964; a second edition, with an introduction by Gwynne Lewis, was published in 1999); and Emmanuel Le Roy Ladurie, in Georges Duby and Armand Wallon (eds.), *Histoire de la France rurale* (Paris, 1975), vol. 2, esp. 554–72.

16. Peter McPhee, *Revolution and Environment in Southern France: Peasants, Nobles and Murder in the Corbières, 1780–1830* (Oxford, 1999), 36–9; Olwen Hufton, 'Attitudes towards Authority in Eighteenth-Century Languedoc', *Social History*, 3 (1978), 281–302; Georges Fournier, *Démocratie et vie municipale en Languedoc du milieu du XVIIIe au début du XIXe siècle*, 2 vols. (Toulouse, 1994).

17. *Archives parlementaires*, 19 November 1787, Series 1, vol. 1, pp. 265–9.

18. Arthur Young, *Travels in France during the years 1787–1788–1789* (New York, 1969), 96–7. The Museum of the French Revolution is today housed in Périer's former château at Vizille.

19. Roche, *France in the Enlightenment*, 669–72.

20. Soboul, *French Revolution*, 120; Jeremy Popkin, *Revolutionary News: The Press in France* (London, 1990), 25–6. For sharply contrasting political histories of 1788–92 see, too, Doyle, *Oxford History of the French Revolution*; Simon Schama, *Citizens: A*

Chronicle of the French Revolution (New York, 1989). Neither account is able to evoke the social dynamics underpinning politics as effectively as Soboul.

21. *Archives parlementaires*, 12 December 1788, Series 1, vol. 1, 487–9.

22. Emmanuel Sieyès, *What is the Third Estate?*, trans M. Blondel (London, 1963). See, too, Jay M. Smith, 'Social Categories, the Language of Patriotism, and the Origins of the French Revolution: The Debate over *noblesse commerçante'*, *Journal of Modern History*, 72 (2000), 339–74; William Sewell, *A Rhetoric of Bourgeois Revolution: The Abbé Sieyès and 'What is the Third Estate?'* (Durham, NC, 1994).

23. *Cahiers de doléances du bailliage de Bourges et des bailliages secondaires de Vierzon et d'Henrichement pour les États-Généraux de 1789* (Bourges, 1910); *Archives parlementaires, États Généraux 1789. Cahiers, Province du Berry*.

24. Paul Beik (ed.), *The French Revolution* (London, 1971), 56–63.

25. Jeffry Kaplow (ed.), *France on the Eve of Revolution* (New York, 1971), 161–7; Richard Cobb and Colin Jones (eds.), *Voices of the French Revolution* (Topsfield, Mass., 1988), 42; 'Doléances particulières des marchandes bouquetières fleuristes chapelières en fleurs de la Ville et faubourgs de Paris', in Charles-Louis Chassin, *Les Élections et les cahiers de Paris en 1789*, 4 vols. (Paris, 1888–9), vol. 2, 534–7.

26. On the limitations to the usefulness of the *cahiers*, see Jones, *Peasantry*, 58–67; John Markoff, *The Abolition of Feudalism: Peasants, Lords, and Legislators in the French Revolution* (Philadelphia, 1996), 25–9.

27. Peter McPhee, ' "The misguided greed of peasants"? Popular Attitudes to the Environment in the Revolution of 1789', *French Historical Studies*, 24 (2001), 247–69.

28. McPhee, *Revolution and Environment*, 49. The *cahier* is reproduced in Cobb and Jones (eds.), *Voices of the French Revolution*, 40. For a detailed analysis of the rural *cahiers*, see Markoff, *Abolition of Feudalism*, ch. 6; Gilbert Shapiro and John Markoff, *Revolutionary Demands: A Content Analysis of the Cahiers de Doléances of 1789* (Stanford, Calif., 1998).

29. Roche, *France in the Enlightenment*, 407.

3

The Revolution of 1789

More than 1,200 deputies from the three estates gathered in Versailles late in April 1789. The expectations of their constituents were boundless, exemplified in the publication by a self-styled 'roturier' (commoner) from Anjou in western France of a seven-page *Ave et le crédo du tiers-état*, which concluded with an adaptation of the Apostles' Creed:

> I believe in the equality that Almighty God, maker of heaven and earth, has established among men: I believe in the liberty which was conceived by courage and born of magnanimity; which suffered under Brienne and Lamoignon, was crucified, died, and was buried, and descended into hell; which will soon be resurrected, will appear in the midst of the French, will be seated at the right hand of the Nation, from where she will judge the Third Estate and the Nobility.
>
> I believe in the King, in the legislative power of the People, in the Assembly of the Estates-General, in the more equal distribution of taxes, in the resurrection of our rights and in eternal life. Amen.[1]

It is, of course, difficult to be certain whether the author was being deliberately satirical and sacrilegious or genuinely believed that enlightened reform was God's gospel. Whatever the case, however, the 'Ave' shows how indebted to the language of the Church would be attempts to articulate a new symbolic order.

The formulation of the *cahiers de doléances* in March had been complemented by the election of deputies of the three estates for the Estates-General due to convene at Versailles on 4 May 1789. Priests rushed to make the most of Louis's decision to favour the parish clergy in the election of First Estate delegates: they were to vote individually in the assemblies to elect deputies, while monasteries would have only one representative and cathedral chapters one for every ten canons. This was done as a way of further pressuring the nobility, and as a mark of Louis's own religious convictions. 'As *curés* we have rights', exclaimed a parish priest from Lorraine, Henri Grégoire, son of a tailor: 'such a favourable opportunity to enforce them has not occurred, perhaps, for twelve centuries ... Let us take it.' His plea was heard: when the clergy gathered to elect its deputies early in 1789, 208 of the 303 chosen were lower clergy; only 51 of the 176 bishops were delegates. Most of the 282 noble deputies were from the highest ramks of the aristocracy, but less reformist than those like Lafayette, Condorcet, Mirabeau, Talleyrand, and others active in the reformist Society of Thirty in Paris who were wealthy and worldly enough to accept the importance of surrendering at least fiscal privileges.

In small rural parishes Third Estate meetings of male taxpayers over 25 years of age were to elect two delegates for the first 100 households and one more per extra hundred; the delegates in turn were to elect deputies for each of the 234 constituencies. Participation was significant everywhere, but varied sharply, ranging in Upper Normandy from 10 to 88 per cent between parishes, around Béziers from 4.8 to 82.5 per cent, in Artois from 13.6 to 97.2 per cent. In what was to become a common feature of the revolutionary period, it was often in smaller communities with a stronger sense of solidarity that participation levels were highest. An indirect system of elections operated for the Third Estate, whereby parishes and guilds elected delegates who in turn voted for the district's deputies. This ensured that virtually all of the 646 deputies of the Third were lawyers, officials, and men of property, men of substance and repute in their region. Only 100 of these bourgeois deputies were from trade and industry. A rare exception in the ranks of middle-class men was Michel Gérard, a peasant from near Rennes who appeared at Versailles in his working clothes.

Once at Versailles the First and Second Estates were to wear the costume appropriate to their particular rank within their order, whereas the Third Estate were to dress uniformly in suits, stockings and cloaks of black cloth: in the words of an English doctor then in Paris, 'even worse than that of the inferior sort of gownsmen at the English universities'. 'A ridiculous and bizarre law has been imposed upon our arrival', commented one deputy, 'by the grand-master of court puerilities'.[2] Reminded of their inferior status in the hierarchy of this corporate society from the very opening of the Estates-General, these men, mostly provincial and wealthy, soon discovered a common outlook. It was a solidarity which, within six weeks, was to encourage them to mount a revolutionary challenge to absolutism and privilege. The immediate issue was that of voting procedures: while the Third Estate deputies refused to vote separately, the nobility was in favour (by 188 votes to 46) as, very narrowly, were the clergy (134 votes to 114). Ultimately, Louis's acquiescence in the nobility's demand for voting to be in three separate chambers galvanized the outrage of the bourgeois deputies. In this they were encouraged by defections from the privileged orders. On 13 June three *curés* from Poitou joined the Third Estate, followed by six others, including Grégoire, the next day.

On the 17th the deputies of the Third Estate went further, and claimed that 'the interpretation and presentation of the general will belong to it . . . The name National Assembly is the only one which is suitable . . .'. Three days later, finding themselves locked out of their meeting hall, the deputies moved to an indoor royal tennis court and, under the presidency of the astronomer Jean-Sylvain Bailly, insisted by oath on their 'unshakeable resolution' to continue their proceedings wherever necessary:

> The National Assembly, whereas it is called on to lay down the constitution of the kingdom, implement the regeneration of public order, and maintain the true principles of the monarchy, nothing can stop it from continuing its deliberations in whatever place it may be obliged to establish itself, and that finally, anywhere its members are gathered together, that is the National Assembly.
>
> It is decided that all the members of this Assembly will now swear a solemn oath never to separate, and to gather together anywhere that circumstances demand, until the constitution of the kingdom is established and consolidated on solid foundations, and that the said oath being sworn, each and every one of the members will confirm this unshakeable resolution with their signature.[3]

There was only one dissenting voice, that of Martin Dauch, elected from Castelnaudary in the south.

The Third Estate deputies' resolve was sustained by the steady trickle to their ranks of liberal nobles and of many among the more reformist parish priests who numerically dominated the First Estate representation. The vote to join the Third Estate taken by 149 clerical deputies, against 137, on 19 June was a decisive turning-point in the political stand-off. A key reason for their decision was anger at the gulf between them and their episcopal fellows. The Abbé Barbotin wrote home to a fellow priest:

Upon arriving here I was still inclined to believe that bishops were also pastors, but everything I see obliges me to think that they are nothing but mercenaries, almost Machiavellian politicians, who mind only their own interests and are ready to fleece—perhaps even devour—their own flocks rather than to pasture them.[4]

On the 23rd, Louis attempted to meet this challenge by proposing modest tax reform while maintaining a system of separate orders and leaving seigneurialism untouched. The Third Estate was unmoved, however, and its resolve was strengthened by the arrival two days later of forty-seven liberal nobles at the Assembly, led by Louis's own cousin, the Duke d'Orléans. By 27 June Louis had seemed to capitulate and ordered the remaining deputies to join their fellows in the Assembly. However, despite their apparent victory, the bourgeois deputies and their allies were soon confronted by a counter-attack from the court. Paris, 18 kilometres from Versailles and a crucible of revolutionary enthusiasm, was invested with 20,000 mercenaries and, in symbolic defiance, Louis dismissed Jacques Necker, his one non-noble minister, on 11 July.

The men of the Assembly were saved from summary dismissal by a collective action by Parisian working people. Though largely barred by gender or poverty from participation in the formulation of *cahiers* or the election of deputies, from April the *menu peuple* had demonstrated their conviction that the bourgeois deputies' revolt was in the people's name. Indeed, an offhand remark about wages by the wealthy manufacturer Réveillon at a Third Estate meeting on 23 April had triggered a riot in the *faubourg* St-Antoine during which, in imitation of Sieyès, shouts of 'Long live the Third Estate! Liberty! We will not give way!' were heard (see Map 4). The riot was put down by troops at the cost of perhaps several hundred lives. Pamphlets expressed the anger of the *menu peuple* at their exclusion from the political process. Sustaining this anger was an escalation in the price of a four-pound loaf of bread from 8 to 14 sous, an increase widely assumed to be the result of deliberate withholding of supplies by noble landowners. The Paris bookseller Sébastien Hardy, whose diaries are an unparalleled source for the early months of the Revolution, noted that people were saying 'that the princes were hoarding grains deliberately in order to more effectively trip up M. Necker, whom they are so keen to overthrow'.[5]

The signal for popular action was the dismissal of Necker, replaced by the Queen's favourite, the Baron de Breteuil. Among the orators to whom Parisians flocked for news and inspiration was Camille Desmouslins, friend of the Third Estate deputy from Arras, Maximilien Robespierre, whom he had met while they were scholarship boys at the Collège Louis-le-Grand in the 1770s. During the four days after 12 July forty of the fifty-four customs houses ringing Paris were destroyed. The abbey of Saint-Lazare was searched for arms; popular suspicions that the nobility were trying to starve the people into submission were confirmed when stocks of grain were also discovered there. Arms and ammunition were also seized from gunsmiths and the Invalides military hospital, and royal troops were confronted. The ultimate target was the Bastille fortress in the *faubourg* St-Antoine, both for its supplies of arms and gunpowder and because this powerful fortress dominated the popular neighbourhoods of eastern Paris. It was also an awesome symbol of the arbitrary authority of the monarchy. On the 14th, up to 8,000 armed Parisians laid siege to the fortress; the governor, the Marquis de Launay, refused to surrender and, as crowds forced their way into the courtyard, ordered his 100 soldiers to fire upon the crowd, killing perhaps 98 and wounding 73. Only when two detachments of Gardes Françaises sided with the crowd and trained their cannon on the main gate, did he surrender.

Who were the people who took the Bastille? Several official lists were made of the *vainqueurs de la Bastille*, as they came to be known, including one by their secretary Stanislas Maillard. Of the 662 survivors he listed, there were perhaps a score of bourgeois, including manufacturers, merchants, and the brewer Santerre, and 76 soldiers. The rest were typical of the *menu peuple*: tradesmen, artisans, and wage-earners from about thirty different trades. Among them were 49 joiners, 48 cabinetmakers, 41 locksmiths, 28 cobblers, 10 hairdressers and wig-makers, 11 wine-merchants, 9 tailors, 7 stonemasons, and 6 gardeners.[6]

The triumphant seizure of the Bastille on the 14th had several important revolutionary consequences. In political terms, it saved the

National Assembly and legitimized a sharp shift in power. The control of Paris by bourgeois members of the Third Estate was institutionalized by a new city government under Bailly and a bourgeois civil militia commanded by the French hero of the American War of Independence, Lafayette. Early on the morning of 17 July, Louis's youngest brother, the Count d'Artois, left France in disgust at the collapse of respect evident in the Third Estate. A steady trickle of disgruntled courtiers would join him in his *émigré* court in Turin. On the same day, however, Louis formally accepted what had occurred by entering Paris to announce the withdrawal of troops and the recalling of Necker. Later in the month Lafayette would join the white of the Bourbon flag to the red and blue colours of the city of Paris: the revolutionary tricolour cockade was born.

However, the storming of the Bastille also confronted revolutionaries with a dilemma they found distressing and intractable. The collective action of the people of Paris had been decisive in the triumph of the Third Estate and the National Assembly; however, the subsequent response of some in the exultant crowd which took the Bastille had been to exercise violent retribution by killing the governor of the fortress, de Launay and six of his troops. Was this an understandable—indeed justifiable—act of popular vengeance on a man whose decision to defend the prison at all costs had resulted in the deaths of one hundred of the assailants? Was it, alternatively, a thoroughly regrettable and retrograde moment of madness, the actions of a crowd too used to the spectacular punishments meted out by the monarchy in the violent society which the Revolution would reform? Or, finally, was this a totally inexcusable act of barbarity, the antithesis of all for which the Revolution should stand? In the first issue of one of the new newspapers which rushed to report on the unprecedented events, *Les Révolutions de Paris*, Elysée Loustallot seemed to find de Launay's killing disgusting but legitimate:

For the first time, august and sacred liberty finally entered this abode of horrors [the Bastille], this dreadful asylum for despotism, monsters and crimes . . . people who were so impatient to avenge themselves allowed neither de Launai, nor the other officers to go into the city court; they tore them from the hands of their conquerors and trampled them underfoot one after the other; de Launai was pierced by countless blows, his head was cut off and carried at the end of a spear, and his blood ran everywhere. . . . This glorious day must surprise our enemies, and portends finally the triumph of justice and freedom.

Loustallot, a young lawyer from Bordeaux, may have hoped that the incident would be unique, but worse was to come. On the 22nd, the royal governor of Paris since 1776, Louis Bertier de Sauvigny, was caught as he tried to flee Paris. He and his father-in-law Joseph Foulon, who had replaced Necker in the ministry, were battered to death and decapitated, their heads paraded through Paris, apparently in retribution for allegedly conspiring to worsen the long period of hunger through which Parisians had lived in 1788–9. Foulon had allegedly stated that if the poor were hungry they should eat straw. Loustallot's report of the 'frightening and terrible' day was now marked by anxiety and despair. After Foulon was decapitated,

A handful of hay was in his mouth, a striking allusion to the inhuman sentiments of this barbarous man . . . the revenge of a justifiably furious people! . . . A man . . . O God! The barbarian! pulls [Berthier's] heart from its palpitating entrails. . . . What a horrible sight! Tyrants, look at this terrible and revolting spectacle! Shudder and see how you are treated . . . I sense, my fellow citizens, how these revolting scenes afflict your soul; like you, I am struck by it; but think how ignominious it is to live as a slave. . . . Never forget, however, that these punishments outrage humanity, and make Nature shudder.

Simon Schama has argued that such punitive violence was at the heart of the Revolution from the very first, and that the middle-class leadership was complicit in its barbarity. According to Schama, Loustallot, who was to become the most important and admired of revolutionary journalists, had used mock horror at the violence to condone and encourage it: 'while he pretended to be shocked by much of the violence he described, his prose wallowed in it'. Loustallot's distressed reportage makes such a claim difficult to sustain.[7]

The taking of the Bastille was only the most spectacular instance of popular conquest of local power. All over France, from Paris to the smallest hamlet, the summer and spring of 1789 was the occasion of a total and unprecedented collapse of centuries of royal state-making. In provincial centres 'municipal revolutions' occurred, as nobles retired or were forcibly removed from office, as in Troyes, or accommodated an influx of new men, as in Reims. The vacuum of authority caused by the collapse of the Bourbon state was temporarily filled in villages and small towns by popular militias and councils. This seizure of power was accompanied everywhere by generalized refusal of the claims of the state, seigneurs, and Church to the payment of taxes, dues and tithes; moreover, as royal troops openly fraternized with civilians, the judiciary was powerless to enforce the law.

The municipal revolution was paralleled by an even greater consequence of the taking of the Bastille. News of this unprecedented challenge to the might of the state and nobility reached a countryside in an explosive atmosphere of conflict, hope, and fear. Since December 1788, peasants had refused to pay taxes or seigneurial dues, or had seized food supplies, in Provence, the Franche-Comté, the Cambrésis and Hainaut in the northeast, and the Paris basin. The desperate hope invested in the National Assembly was caught by Arthur Young, on his third tour of France, while talking with a peasant woman in Lorraine on 12 July:

Walking up a long hill, to ease my mare, I was joined by a poor woman, who complained of the times, and that it was a sad country; demanding her reasons, she said her husband had but a morsel of land, one cow, and a poor little horse, yet they had a *franchar* (42 pounds) of wheat, and three chickens, to pay as a quit-rent to one Seigneur; and four *franchar* of oats, one chicken and one livre to pay to another, besides very heavy tailles and other taxes . . . It was said, at present, *that something was to be done by some great folks for such poor ones, but she did not know who nor how,* but God send us better, *car les tailles & les droits nous écrasent.* This woman, at no great distance, might have been taken for sixty or seventy, her figure was so bent, and her face so furrowed and hardened by labour,—but she said she was only twenty-eight.[8]

Fear of aristocratic revenge replaced such hope as news of the Bastille arrived: were bands of beggars roaming through ripening corn the agents of vengeful seigneurs? Hope, fear, and hunger made the countryside a tinder-box ignited by imagined sightings of 'brigands'. Panics spread from five separate sparks as bushfires of angry rumours, spreading from village to village at several kilometres an hour, engulfed every region but Brittany and the east. When noble revenge failed to materialize, village militias instead turned their weapons on the seigneurial system itself, compelling seigneurs or their agents to hand over feudal registers to be burned on the village square. This extraordinary revolt came to be known as the 'Great Fear'. Other objects of hatred were also singled out: in Alsace, this extended to violence against Jews. On the northern outskirts of Paris, at St-Denis, an official who had mocked a crowd complaining about food prices was dragged from his hiding-place in the steeple of a church, stabbed to death and decapitated; however, this was a rare case of personal violence in these days. Like the *menu peuple* of Paris, peasants adopted the language of bourgeois revolt to their own ends; on 2 August the steward of the Duke of Montmorency wrote to his master at Versailles that:

The populace, attributing to the Lords of the kingdom the high price of grain, is fiercely against all that belongs to them. All reasoning fails: this unrestrained populace listens only to its own fury . . .

Just as I was going to finish my letter, I learned that approximately three hundred brigands from all the lands associated with the vassals of Mme the marquise of Longaunay have stolen the titles of rents and allowances of the seigniory, and demolished her dovecotes: they then gave her a notice of the theft signed *The Nation*.[9]

On the night of 4 August, in an extraordinary atmosphere of panic, self-sacrifice and exhilaration, a series of nobles mounted the rostrum of the Assembly to respond to the Great Fear by renouncing their privileges and abolishing feudal dues. In the succeeding week, however, they made a distinction between instances of 'personal servitude', which were abolished outright, and 'property rights' (seigneurial dues payable on harvests) for which peasants had to pay compensation before ceasing payment:

Article 1. The National Assembly completely destroys the feudal regime. It decrees that, in rights and duties, both feudal and *censuel*, deriving from real or personal mortmain, and personal servitude, and those who represent them, are abolished without compensation; all the others are declared redeemable, and the price and the manner of the redemption will be set by the National Assembly. Those of the said rights that are not abolished by this decree will continue nonetheless to be collected until settlement.

Accordingly, the Assembly abolished outright serfdom, dovecotes, seigneurial and royal hunting privileges, and unpaid labour. Seigneur-ial courts were also abolished: in future justice was to be provided free of charge according to a uniform set of laws. Tithes, like existing state taxes, were to be replaced by more equitable ways of funding Church and state; in the meantime, however, they were to be continued to be paid.

Later, on the 27th of August, the Assembly voted a carefully debated Declaration of the Rights of Man and of the Citizen. Fundamental to the Declaration was the insistence that 'ignorance, forgetfulness, or contempt of the rights of man are the sole causes of public misfortune'; the Assembly repudiated the suggestion from nobles that a declaration of duties be joined to those of rights lest the common people abuse their liberties. Instead, it asserted the essence of liberalism, that 'liberty consists of the power to do whatever is not injurious to others'. Accordingly, the Declaration guaranteed rights of free speech and association, of religion and opinion, limited only—and rather ambiguously—by 'the law'. This was to be a land in which all were to be equal in legal status, and subject to the same public responsibilities: it was an invitation to become citizens of a nation instead of subjects of a king.

The August Decrees and the Declaration of the Rights of Man represented the end of the absolutist, seigneurial, and corporate structure of eighteenth-century France. They were also a revolutionary proclamation of the principles of a new golden age. The Declaration in particular was an extraordinary document, one of the most powerful statements of liberalism and representative government. While universal in its language, and resounding in its optimism, it was nonetheless ambiguous in its wording and silences. That is, while proclaiming the universality of rights and the civic equality of all citizens, the Declaration was ambiguous on whether the propertyless, slaves and women would have political as well as legal equality, and silent on how the means to exercise one's talents could be secured by those without education or property. As a women's *cahier* from the Pays de Caux region north of Paris had posed the question in the spring of 1789:

Whether from reason or necessity men permit women to share their work, to till the soil, to plough, to run the postal service; others undertake long and difficult travel for commercial reasons . . .

We are told there is talk of freeing the Negroes; the people, almost as enslaved as them, is recovering its rights . . .

Will men persist in wanting to make us victims of their pride or injustice?[10]

The August Decrees were of great importance for another reason, for they were based on the assumption that henceforth all individuals in France were to enjoy the same rights and be subject to the same laws: the age of privilege and exception was over:

Article X ... all special privileges of the provinces, principalities, counties, cantons, towns and communities of inhabitants, be they financial or of any other nature, are abolished without compensation, and will be absorbed into the common rights of all French people.[11]

The Declaration, like the August Decrees, explicitly asserted that all careers and positions would be open to talent, and that henceforth 'social distinctions may be based only on general usefulness'. It was therefore felt politic to exclude clauses from an earlier draft which sought to explain the limits to equality rather more directly:

II. To ensure his own preservation and find well being, each man receives faculties from nature. *Liberty* consists in the full and entire usage of these faculties.
V. But nature has not given each man the same means to exercise his rights. Inequality between men is born of this. Thus inequality is in nature itself.
VI. Society is formed by the need to maintain equality in rights, in the midst of inequality in means.[12]

As a profoundly revolutionary set of founding principles of a new order, both the August Decrees and the Declaration met with refusal from Louis. The Estates-General had been summoned to offer him advice on the state of his kingdom: did his acceptance of the existence of a 'National Assembly' require him to accept its decisions? Moreover, as the food crisis worsened and evidence multiplied of open contempt for the Revolution on the part of army officers, the victory of the summer of 1789 seemed again in question. For the second time, the *menu peuple* of Paris intervened to safeguard a revolution they assumed to be theirs. This time, however, it was particularly the women of the markets: in the words of the observant bookseller Hardy, 'these women said loudly that the men didn't know what it was all about and that they wanted to have a hand in things'.[13] On 5 October, up to 7,000 women marched to Versailles; among their spontaneous leaders were Maillard, a hero of 14 July, and a woman from Luxembourg, Anne-Josephe Terwagne, who became known as Théroigne de Méricourt. They were belatedly followed by the

National Guard, who compelled their reluctant commander Lafayette to 'lead' them. At Versailles the women invaded the Assembly. A deputation was then presented to the king, who promptly agreed to sanction the decrees. It soon became apparent, however, that the women would be satisfied only if the royal family returned to Paris; on the 6th it did so, and the Assembly followed in its wake.

This was a decisive moment in the Revolution of 1789. The National Assembly owed its existence and success once again to the armed intervention of the people of Paris. Convinced now that the Revolution was complete and secure, and determined that never again would the common people of Paris exercise such power, the Assembly ordered an inquiry into the 'crimes' of 5–6 October. Among the hundreds of participants and observers interviewed was Madelaine Glain, a 42-year-old cleaner, who made a link between the imperatives of securing cheap and plentiful bread and the fate of the key revolutionary decrees:

she went with the other women to the hall of the National Assembly, where they entered in great numbers; that some of these women having demanded 4 pound bread for 8 sols, and meat for the same price, the witness . . . came back with Mr Maillard and two other women to the Paris town hall, bringing the decrees that were given to them in the National Assembly.

The mayor, Bailly, recalled that, when the women returned to Paris on the 6th, they were singing 'vulgar ditties which apparently showed little respect for the queen'. Others claimed to have brought with them the royal family as 'the baker and his wife, and the baker's apprentice'.[14] The women were here making explicit the ancient assumption of royal responsibility to God for the provision of food. The key decrees sanctioned, and the court party in disarray, the Revolution's triumph seemed assured; to signify the magnitude of what they had achieved, people now began to refer to the *ancien régime*.

Elsewhere in Europe, people were similarly struck by the dramatic events of the summer. Few failed to be enthused by them: among the crowned heads of Europe, only the kings of Sweden and Spain and Catherine of Russia were resolutely hostile from the outset. Others may have felt a certain pleasure at seeing one of Europe's great powers incommoded by its own people. Among the general European populace, however, support for the Revolution was far more common, and there were few obvious 'counter-revolutionaries' such as Edmund Burke. While many in England started to become disturbed at reports of punitive bloodshed or when the National Assembly quickly ruled out the possibility of emulating Britain's bicameral system, with its House of Lords, most were openly enthusiastic. Poets such as Wordsworth, Burns, Coleridge, Southey, and Blake joined with their creative peers in Germany and Italy (such as Beethoven, Fichte, Hegel, Kant, and Herder) in celebrating what was seen as an exemplary moment of liberation in the history of the European spirit. Lafayette had sent a set of the keys of the Bastille to George Washington as 'a tribute which I owe as a son to my adoptive father, as an aide-de-camp to my general, and as a missionary of liberty to its patriarch'. In turn, Washington, elected six months earlier as first president of the United States, wrote to his envoy in France, Gouverneur Morris, on 13 October: 'The revolution which has been effected in France is of so wonderful a nature, that the mind can hardly recognise the fact. If it ends as . . . [I] predict, that nation will be the most powerful and happy in Europe.'

Jostling with the potent sense of euphoria and unity in the autumn of 1789 was the realization of how revolution had been achieved and the magnitude of what remained to be done. The Revolution of the bourgeois deputies had only been secured by the active intervention of the working people of Paris; the deputies' misgivings were expressed in the temporary proclamation of martial law on 21 October. On the other hand, Louis's reluctant consent to change was only thinly disguised by the fiction that his obstinacy was solely due to the malign influence of his court. Most important of all, the revolutionaries' declaration of the principles of the new regime presupposed that every aspect of public life would be reshaped. To that task they now turned.

Notes

1. *Ave et le crédo du tiers-état* (n.p., 1789).

2. J. M. Thompson (ed.), *English Witnesses of the French Revolution* (Oxford, 1938), 58; Aileen Ribeiro, *Fashion in the French Revolution* (London, 1988), 46. On the elections of 1789, see Malcolm Crook, *Elections in the French Revolution: An Apprenticeship in Democracy, 1789–1799* (Cambridge, 1996), ch. 1.

3. *Gazette nationale ou le Moniteur universel*, no. 10, 20–4 June 1789, vol. 1, 89. Charles Panckoucke, publisher of the *Encyclopédie*, was the proprietor of this paper, which linked the pre-revolutionary *Gazette* to the 'patriotic' *Moniteur*. With its reprint in the 1840s, it is an invaluable source for parliamentary debates.

4. Dale Van Kley, *The Religious Origins of the French Revolution* (New Haven, 1996), 349.

5. George Rudé, *The Crowd in the French Revolution* (Oxford, 1959), 46.

6. On the storming of the Bastille, see ibid., ch. 4; and Jacques Godechot, *The Taking of the Bastille: July 14th, 1789*, trans. Jean Stewart (London, 1970).

7. Schama, *Citizens*, 446; *Les Révolutions de Paris*, no. 1, 12–18 July 1789, 17–19, no. 2, 18–25 July 1789, 18–25. An excellent collection of newspaper articles is J. Gilchrist and W. J. Murray (eds.), *The Press in the French Revolution* (Melbourne, 1971).

8. Arthur Young, *Travels in France during the Years 1789–1788–1789* (New York, 1969).

9. *Annales historiques de la Révolution française* (1955), 161–2. The rural revolt is the subject of the classic 1932 study by Georges Lefebvre, *The Great Fear of 1789: Rural Panic in Revolutionary France*, trans. Joan White (New York, 1973); a recent study is Clay Ramsay, *The Ideology of the Great Fear: The Soissonnais in 1789* (Baltimore, 1992).

10. 'Cahier des doléances et réclamations des femmes par Mme. B. . . B. . .', 1789', in *Cahiers des doléances des femmes et autres textes* (Paris, 1981), 47–59.

11. *Moniteur universel*, no. 40, 11–14 August 1789, vol. 1, 332–3.

12. *Moniteur universel*, no. 44, 20 August 1789, vol. 2, 362–3; *Archives parlementaires*, 2 September 1791, 151–2. There is a detailed discussion of the Declaration in Dale Van Kley (ed.), *The French Idea of Freedom: The Old Regime and the Declaration of Rights of 1789* (Stanford, Calif., 1994).

13. Rudé, *Crowd in the French Revolution*, 69 and ch. 5.

14. *Réimpression de l'Ancien Moniteur, seule histoire authentique et inaltérée de la Révolution française, depuis la réunion des États-Généraux jusqu'au Consulat*, 32 vols. (Paris, 1847), vol. 2, 1789, 544; Cobb and Jones (eds.), *Voices of the French Revolution*, 88.

4

The Reconstruction of France, 1789–1791

The Constituent or National Assembly of 1789–91 was the largest parliament in French history, with more than 1,200 members of the clergy, nobility and commons who had previously convened for the Estates-General in May 1789. Over the next two years, the deputies threw themselves with extraordinary energy into the task of reworking every dimension of public life. The work of its thirty-one committees was facilitated by the preparedness to co-operate of a large number of nobles, styled 'patriots', by abundant harvests in 1789 and 1790, and above all by the deep reservoir of popular goodwill. However, the rostrum and committees of the Assembly were dominated by about one-tenth of the deputies, and it could be suggested that the seeds of later southern misgivings about the Revolution were sown in the domination of the Assembly from the outset by men from the north.

The remaking of France was based on a belief in the common identity of French citizens whatever their social or geographic origin. This was a fundamental change in the relationship between the state, its provinces, and the citizenry. In every aspect of public life— administration, the judiciary, the armed forces, the Church, policing—traditions of corporate rights, appointment, and hierarchy gave way to civil equality, accountability, and elections within national structures. The institutional structure of the *ancien régime* had been characterized by recognition of extraordinary provincial diversity controlled by a network of royal appointees. Now this was reversed: at every level officials were to be elected, and the institutions in which they worked were everywhere to be the same.

The 41,000 new 'communes', mostly based on the parishes of the *ancien régime,* were to be the base of an administrative hierarchy of cantons, districts and departments. The 83 departments announced in February 1790 were designed to facilitate the accessibility of administration, for each capital was to be no more than a day's ride from any commune (see Map 3). The creation of this new map of France was the work of urban elites with a distinctive vision of spatial organization and institutional hierarchy. It was designed to give reality to two of their keywords: to 'regenerate' the nation while cementing its 'unity'. There was usually a valid geographic rationale to each department; but they also represented an important victory of the new state over the resurgent provincial identities expressed since 1787. Their very names, drawn from rivers, mountains, and other natural features, undercut claims to other provincial and ethnic loyalties: the Basque country would be the 'Basses-Pyrénées', not the 'Pays Basque', nor would there be any institutional recognition whatsoever of regions such as Brittany or Languedoc.

The Assembly was also concerned to accelerate 'from above' the coincidence of the new nation of French citizens with use of the French language. The Abbé Grégoire's inquiry of 1790 was sobering for legislators who wrongly assumed that a facility in French was indispensable to be a patriot. Only fifteen departments, with three million people, were identified as purely French speaking. In the Gascon-speaking Lot-et-Garonne in the southwest, priests complained of peasants falling asleep during the reading of decrees from the Assembly, 'because they do not understand a word, even though the decrees are read in a loud and clear voice and are explained'. In consequence, successive assemblies encouraged the translation of decrees into local languages and over much of France the new elements of political life were assimilated through the medium of translation.[1]

The Declaration of the Rights of Man had already held out the promise that henceforth all citizens would share equal rights to freedom of conscience and the external practice of their faith. By the end of 1789 full citizenship had been granted to Protestants and, the following January, to the Sephardic Jews of Bordeaux and Avignon (by only 374 votes to 280). The Assembly hesitated, however, in the face of the anti-Semitism of deputies from Alsace, such as Jean-François Reubell from Colmar, who opposed citizenship for eastern (but not southern) Jews as vigorously as he campaigned for the rights of 'people of colour'. This prompted a spirited reminder from eastern, Ashkenazim Jews in January 1790:

France must, for justice and interest, grant them the rights of citizenship, in that their home is in this empire, that they live there as subjects, that they serve their fatherland through all the means that are in their power, that they contribute to the maintenance of the public force like all the other citizens of the kingdom, independently of the onerous, degrading, arbitrary taxes that ancient injustices, ancient prejudices, supported by the old regime, accumulated on their head: they say, there can only be two classes of men in a State; citizens and foreigners; to prove that we are not foreigners is to prove that we are citizens.[2]

Only during the final sessions of the National Assembly in September 1791 were the eastern Jews granted full equality and able to stand for election.

The complex set of royal, aristocratic, and clerical courts and their regional variations was replaced by a national system deliberately made more accessible, humane, and egalitarian. In particular, the introduction of elected justices of the peace in every canton was immensely popular for its provision of cheap and accessible justice. For example, the range of capital offences was sharply reduced, and those who committed them would henceforth be punished by the painless machine promoted by the chairman of the Assembly's health committee, Dr Joseph Guillotin. The assumption of individual liberty also extended to prostitution: in July 1791, new municipal regulations removed all reference to prostitution and its policing. While many women were thereby freed from the repressive constraints of religious reformatories to which they were sent under the *ancien régime*, it was simultaneously assumed that prostitution and its side-effects were an individual choice and responsibility. The 'liberty' achieved in 1789 was thus a two-edged sword in its practical applications.

National Guard units of 'active' citizens in every commune chose their leaders. However, while officer positions in the armed forces were opened to non-nobles, the Assembly stalled at applying popular sovereignty to their election. The army and navy were wracked by internal conflict between noble officers and soldiers over control of regimental funds and the role of the army in repressing civilian protests. There were serious rebellions in the fleets at Toulon in December 1789 and Brest in September 1790. A rebellion in the garrison at Nancy in August 1790 was bloodily repressed by the commander Bouillé, cousin of the commander-in-chief of the army, Lafayette. The Assembly endorsed Bouillé's actions. For Elysée Loustallot of *Les Révolutions de Paris*, already despondent over the violence which had continued since July 1789, the news of the massacre was intolerable:

How can I narrate with a leaden heart? How can I reflect when my feelings are torn with despair? I see them there, these corpses strewn about the streets of Nancy . . . Await rascals, the press that uncovers all crimes and dispels all errors will deprive you of your joy and your strength: how sweet it would be to be your last victim!

Loustallot died shortly thereafter, at just 29 years; his funeral oration was delivered by another prominent journalist and revolutionary, Camille Desmoulins.[3]

The National Assembly had to address the urgent necessity of fundamental reform in three major areas: fiscal reform to implement the Assembly's commitment to the principle of uniform, proportional taxation; administrative reform to establish the practice of popular sovereignty within reformed institutional structures; and measures to resolve the ambiguities concerning feudalism within the August legislation.

The Assembly had inherited the monarchy's bankruptcy, further aggravated by popular refusal to pay taxes, and took several measures to meet this crisis. Across the country people responded to calls for 'patriotic contributions' or donations. In November 1789, church lands were nationalized and, from November 1790, sold at auction. These lands were also used to back the issue of *assignats*, paper currency which soon began to decline in real purchasing power. The need for a radically new and universal taxation system took far longer to meet. On 25 September 1789 the Assembly decreed that the nobility, clergy, and others who so far had had fiscal immunity would now have to pay a proportionate share of direct taxes, backdated to cover the second half of 1789. The difficulties of completing new tax registers and assessments for every community was time-consuming, however, and resulted in the Assembly having to continue the *ancien régime* tax system for 1790. The Assembly's announcement, on 14 April 1790, that the tithe was to be abolished from 1 January of the following year as part of a general reform of taxation, meant that it would be payable to the state in 1790.

However, the decree was interpreted by communities across France as meaning that there seemed little reason to pay it in the meantime. Communes objected to paying the tithe at all, and brought in crops without waiting for the tithe-collector. Finally a new system of taxation, based on the estimated value of and income from property, was introduced from the beginning of 1791. The new taxes were considerably higher than under the *ancien régime* and, for tenant-farmers, were often added to rents. In Brittany, where the feudal regime and taxes had been relatively light and tenants had had long-term leases (known as the *domaine congéable*), the Revolution substantially increased the burden of taxation without meeting tenant-farmers' demands for security of tenure. For most peasants, however, the 15–20 per cent increase in state taxes was more than offset by the ending of tithes and, ultimately, of seigneurial dues.

The second broad area for immediate attention concerned the exercise of popular sovereignty and power. While an English bicameral system was repudiated because of deep mistrust of the nobility, Louis was left with extensive executive powers, for example, to appoint his ministers and diplomats. He was also to possess a veto enabling him to suspend unacceptable legislation for several years (though not on matters pertaining to finance or the constitution). The ambiguity about the meaning of citizenship in the Declaration of the Rights of Man was resolved by excluding women and 'passive' male citizens, those—perhaps 40 per cent of adult men—paying less than three days' labour in taxes, and by imposing sharp property qualifications on those eligible to be electors and deputies. While there were at least four million active citizens, only about 50,000 of them paid enough in taxes to be electors; the 745 deputies in the Legislative Assembly in turn had to pay the 'silver mark', equivalent to fifty-four days' labour in taxes. In his newspaper *Les Révolutions de France et de Brabant*, Camille Desmoulins denounced the new 'aristocratic system': 'But what is this much repeated word *active citizen* supposed to mean? The active citizens are the ones who took the Bastille.'[4]

The National Assembly passed its municipal law on 14 December 1789. This drew in large measure on Calonne's attempt in 1787 to reform and make uniform local government across the country, but was far more democratic. The mayor, municipal officers, and notables were to be elected on the basis of a property franchise. The local government law represented a significant change in the autonomy and electorate of village councils. Now municipalities were liberated from the control of seigneurs. The new law placed a huge burden of responsibility on villagers; they were now responsible for apportioning and collecting direct taxes, carrying out public works, overseeing the material needs of church and school and maintaining law and order. In very small communities these were awesome, even impossible, responsibilities. In the west, moreover, the local government law created a puzzling separation of municipality and vestry and excluded many men and all women used to discussing parish matters after mass.

The third area of urgent need concerned seigneurialism. Rural communities all over France were waiting to transcribe one particular decree. From the outset of the Revolution, the National Assembly had been caught between the radical demands of the peasant revolution and its commitment to principles of private property and to preserving the support of liberal nobles. Moreover, the king, whom peasant communities had assumed to be their protector at the time they drew up their *cahiers* had initially refused his assent to even the compromise legislation on feudalism. Not until 20 October, after the women's march to Versailles, did the feudal legislation of 4–11 August finally become law. Even then, it was fraught with ambiguities concerning the extent to which seigneurialism had been abolished.

But peasants only accepted without question the opening phrase of the August decree, that 'the National Assembly completely destroys the feudal regime'. In the four months after December 1789, peasants from 330 parishes in the southwest invaded over 100 chateaux to protest against the requisite payment of harvest dues. Similar protests, whether by violent action or non-compliance, occurred in the departments of the Yonne, Loiret, Aisne, and Oise, and in regions such as the Massif Central, Brittany, the Dauphiné, and Lorraine. Many of these rebellions were accompanied by what Mona Ozouf has called 'wild festivals' whereby villagers began to invent new forms of spontaneous celebrations around improvised 'liberty trees'. In Picardy,

demands for a more radical revolution focused on taxes and seigneurialism. For example, in the village of Hallivillers (department of the
Somme), most of the inhabitants decided that they intended to 'put
an end to the payment of the *champart* and force the other landholders to unite with them to refuse the tax'. Widespread protest of this
type created the context for the activism of the young, self-educated
François-Noël Babeuf (born 1760). Babeuf had himself worked for the
seigneurial system before 1789 as a 'feudiste': it was there, he later
claimed, that he learned the darkest secrets of the system. Now he
called for land distribution to the poor (the 'agrarian law'), the complete abolition of seigneurialism, and for a tax on incomes rather than
property. In 1790 he began calling himself Camille, after Camillus, the
fourth-century BC campaigner for equal pay in the Roman army.[5]

On 15 March 1790 debates began within the Committee on Feudalism of the National Assembly concerning a proposed comprehensive
law on the implementation of the August 1789 decisions. Not only
were communes warned that the payment of such rights could not be
suspended while they were being legally contested, but the nature of
the acceptable proof seemed heavily weighted towards former seigneurs, requiring only the evidence drawn from 'the statutes, customs
and rules observed up until the present'. In other words, the burden of
proof rested with those who paid. The Assembly also voted to abolish
banalités without compensation only if there was no proof of the con-
tractual acceptance of their existence: this could take the form of an
original document or subsequent ones assuming such a contract.
Finally, on 3 May a decree set out the value of the redemption of
seigneurial rights. For *corvées, banalités,* and those dues paid in
money, the rate of redemption was set at twenty times the annual
value and, for those paid in kind, at twenty-five times.

It rapidly became apparent, through agitated reports pouring in
from the new departments and from personal correspondence
received by deputies, that across most of the country the compromise
legislation of March and May 1790 had encountered stubborn and at
times violent resistance. This action took two forms. First, since the
1789–90 legislation treated seigneurial exactions as a legal form of
rent which peasants could only terminate by compensating the
seigneur, many communities decided to take legal action to force seigneurs to submit their feudal titles for judicial verification. Such

action was quite legal, but reflects the extent to which small rural communities were prepared to contest the legality of the seigneurial system under which they had lived, for they had to pay the legal costs of verification. This legal challenge was often connected with an illegal, second type of action, the refusal to pay feudal dues in the meantime. In the Corbières region of Languedoc, at least 86 of the 129 communes were involved in legal action against seigneurs or in open refusal to pay dues in 1789–92. Moreover, the nation had placed itself in an awkward position by its simultaneous partial dismantling of the seigneurial regime and nationalization of church property, for it now found itself the proprietor of all those non-suppressed seigneurial dues belonging to former ecclesiastical seigneurs.

The Revolution was, and long remained, overwhelmingly popular: the extent of change in public life cannot be understood except in a context of mass optimism and support. Michael Fitzsimmons, for example, has stressed the nationwide goodwill for the prospects of social harmony and 'regeneration' (a keyword throughout the Revolution) as the National Assembly went about its awesome work after 1789. Those who moved to fill the power vacuum left by the collapse of the *ancien régime* and those who were among the major initial beneficiaries of the Revolution were bourgeois. The dramatic reorganization of institutional structures had meant that many thousands of middle-class officials and lawyers lost their positions, venal or not. However, not only did they succeed in being elected to positions in the new structures, but they were also compensated for their lost offices. Indeed, the final cost of paying compensation to owners of venal offices was more than 800 million livres, necessitating massive issues of *assignats* and precipitating inflation. This compensation came at an ideal time for investment in the vast amounts of church property thrown onto the market from November 1790. Sold at auction and in large lots, this fine property was mainly purchased by urban bourgeois and wealthy peasants, and by a surprising number of nobles. In the district of Grasse, in southeastern France, for example, where only about 6.8 per cent of land changed hands, it was local bourgeois who dominated the auctions. Three-quarters of the property sold was bought by one-quarter of the buyers; 28 of the 39 largest purchasers were merchants from Grasse.[6]

However, particular groups within the bourgeoisie were among those who regretted the collapse of the *ancien régime* because it threatened their livelihoods. For example, those whose wealth was drawn from the slave system as slave-traders or colonial planters were anxious lest the principles underpinning the Declaration of the Rights of Man were extended to the Caribbean colonies. A bitter debate pitted the colonial lobby (the Club Massiac) against the Société des Amis des Noirs, which included Brissot, Robespierre, and Grégoire.

No French city was more vulnerable to the vicissitudes of international relations—or more dependent on the slave trade and its privileged trading relationship with St-Domingue (the *exclusif*)—than La Rochelle. Here the Revolution was enthusiastically welcomed, especially by Protestants, who were only about 7 per cent of the city's 18,000 people, but who dominated every aspect of the economy and society, except for political power. In 1789 they made that their own, too. Nine of the twelve men on the first municipal council of La Rochelle were merchants, and five of them were Protestants. The merchants constructed a Protestant church with remarkable speed, and placed their considerable resources behind the new nation. Daniel Garesché, owner of six slave-ships (*négriers*), and mayor in 1791–2, gave 17,000 livres, then 50,000 more, as a 'contribution patriotique'.

The merchants' enthusiasm for the Revolution was as pragmatic as it was enthusiastic. Rochelais had always been able to reconcile their principles with their self-interest. The *cahier* of the Third Estate of La Rochelle was a long, eloquent plea for liberty and humanity: the use of the whip on slaves was condemned as contrary to humanity, as 'irreconcilable with the enlightenment and humanity which distinguish the French nation'. However, the slave trade itself was not mentioned. The merchants knew that Africans were human beings wishing to live freely: slaves were automatically freed once ashore in France, and there were 44 free blacks in the city in 1777 (there were also as many as 750 in Paris). One of La Rochelle's observers at the Estates-General, Pierre-Samuel Demissy, made the mistake of joining the Amis des Noirs and calling for abolition of slavery in 1789. By the following year he had seen the error of his ways. He came to agree with his fellow observer Jean-Baptiste Nairac, who always hoped that 'the political aspects which are so important will triumph over moral considerations'. When the Assembly finally changed nothing in its decree of 8 March 1790, Nairac was exultant: 'Without giving things their real names, it maintains the slave-trade, slavery, the exclusive regime.' Only five deputies had voted against the decree.[7] The Assembly's next response, in May 1791, granted 'active' citizen status to free blacks with free parents and the necessary property, but avoided the issue of slavery:

The National Assembly decrees that it will never deliberate on the station of people of colour who are not born of free father and mother, without the prior, free and spontaneous wish of the colonies; that the colonial assemblies currently in existence will stay on; but that people of colour born of free father and mother, will be admitted to all future parish and colonial assemblies, if they moreover have the required qualities. (The hall echoes with applause.)[8]

The example of La Rochelle points to the continuing importance of foreign affairs. Historians have agreed that, before 1789 and after 1791, issues of foreign policy and military strategy dominated the domestic reform agenda; they generally assume, too, that the two intervening years of sweeping revolutionary change, 1789–91, were a time when radical internal reform preoccupied the Assembly. On the contrary, as Jeremy Whiteman has argued, a major impulse for this revolutionary reform was in fact the desire to 'regenerate' as well France's capacity to act as the key military and commercial player in Europe and the Caribbean. Central to the reforming zeal of the National Assembly was the belief that the new nation would thereby be 'regenerated' and return to the international status it had enjoyed before the successive foreign affairs humiliations since 1763. As before 1789, three of the six ministries were War, Navy, and Foreign Affairs.[9]

Despite anxiety over its future prosperity, La Rochelle was staunchly in support of the Revolution. Elsewhere, resentment towards the Revolution stemmed from various disappointments, such as the loss of status following administrative reorganization, as in Vence (department of the Var), where a vigorous campaign failed to protect its bishopric, relocated in nearby St-Paul. As Ted Margadant has shown, the location of departmental, district and cantonal *chefs-lieux* swamped legislators with a flood of complaints and rivalries which could call into question support for the Revolution in towns formerly sustained by the presence of the maze of courts and offices of the Bourbon regime.

Where denominational loyalties coincided with class tensions, the Revolution triggered open hostilities. In parts of the south, where a Protestant bourgeoisie had won religious freedom and civil equality, opening the way to political power, the Assembly's refusal to proclaim Catholicism the state religion in April 1790 provided the pretext for large-scale violence in Montauban and Nîmes. Here, as in the Protestant communities of the southern Massif Central, memories of the *ancien régime* underscored Protestant support for a Revolution which had brought them civil equality. In Nîmes, popular Catholic hostility to the political and economic role of wealthy Protestants was bloodily crushed when bands of Protestant peasants from the nearby regions of the Cévennes and Vaunage marched on the city. The violence in Nîmes was to become known as the brawl or *bagarre de Nîmes*, a misnomer for four days of fighting which left 300 Catholics dead, but few Protestants. News of the killings fuelled suspicions that Protestants were manipulating the Revolution: had not a Protestant pastor, Rabaut de Saint-Étienne, been elected president of the Assembly? The seriousness of such religious divisions was made alarmingly clear in the first instance of mass popular disaffection with the Revolution, when in mid-1790 20,000–40,000 Catholic peasants from 180 parishes established the short-lived 'Camp de Jalès' in the Ardèche.

Nevertheless, the popular alliance of the Third Estate and its allies among the clergy and 'patriotic' nobility continued to draw on a powerful sense of national unity and regeneration well into 1790. This unity was enacted in Paris by the great 'Fête de la Fédération', on the first anniversary of the storming of the Bastille. On the Champ de Mars, which had been levelled by voluntary labour, Louis, Talleyrand (former bishop of Autun), and Lafayette proclaimed the new order in front of 300,000 Parisians. This ceremony occurred in different forms all over France, an example of the use of festivals as an element of revolutionary political culture. In a society rich in religious rituals and displays of royal splendour, ceremonies celebrating revolutionary unity drew on the old for style if not for substance or imagery. The colliers of Montminot adapted a traditional festival by swearing on 'the axe always raised in order to defend, at the risk of their lives, the finest edifice that ever was, the French Constitution'. At Beaufort-en-Vallée, in the Loire valley in western France, eighty-three women slipped away during the festivities and returned costumed as the new departments. For fashion-conscious, well-to-do women, the Parisian *Journal de la mode et du goût* was full of recommended dresses for the new age, self-consciously simpler and with patriotic motifs such as patterns of tiny liberty caps.[10]

The Festival of Federation celebrated the unity of Church, monarchy and Revolution. Two days earlier, the Assembly had voted a reform which was to shatter all three. The widespread agreement in the *cahiers* on the need for reform guaranteed that the Assembly had been able to push through the nationalization of church lands, the closing of contemplative orders and the granting of religious liberty to Protestants, in 1789, and Jews, in 1790–1. Mounting clerical opposition to these changes ultimately focused on the Civil Constitution of the Clergy voted on 12 July 1790. There was no question of separating Church and state: the public functions of the Church were assumed to be integral to daily life, and the Assembly accepted that public revenues would financially support the Church after the abolition of the tithe. It was therefore argued that, like the monarchy before it, the government had the right to reform the Church's temporal organization.

Many priests were materially advantaged by the new salary scale, and only the upper clergy would have regretted that bishops' stipends were dramatically reduced. However, the Assembly reallocated diocesan and parish boundaries, eliciting a chorus of complaints from small communities and urban parishes now required to worship in a neighbouring church. Most contentious, however, was the issue of how the clergy were to be appointed in future. To the trenchant objections from clerical deputies in the Assembly that the hierarchy of the Church was based on the principle of divine authority and inspired appointment by superiors, deputies such as Treilhard retorted that this had resulted in nepotism. Only the people could choose their priests and bishops:

Far from undermining religion, in ensuring that the faithful have the most honest and virtuous ministers, you are paying it the most worthy homage. He who believes that this would be to wound religion, is forming a truly false idea of religion.[11]

However, in applying popular sovereignty to the choice of priests and bishops, the Assembly crossed the narrow line separating temporal and spiritual life.

Many historians have seen the Civil Constitution of the Clergy as the moment which fatally fractured the Revolution, and have wondered why the Assembly seemed unwilling to negotiate or compromise. In the end, however, it proved impossible to reconcile a Church based on divinely ordained hierarchy and dogma and a certainty of one true faith with a Revolution based on popular sovereignty, tolerance and the certainty of earthly fulfilment through the application of secular reason. Above all, by applying the practice of 'active' citizenship to the choice of clergy, the Assembly excluded women and the poor from the community of the faithful, and theoretically included Protestants, Jews and non-believers who were wealthy enough to vote. Nor could a compromise be reached, for, with the abolition of corporations in 1789, the majority of the Assembly insisted that it alone could make laws about public life: a church synod could not be consulted about whether it agreed with reforms voted by the people's representatives.

In the face of the opposition of most clerical deputies, but impelled by increasing impatience with the intransigence of most bishops, the Assembly sought to force the issue by requiring elections to be held on New Year's Day 1791, with those elected to swear an oath of loyalty to the law, the nation and the king. Everywhere the oath faced parish priests with an agonizing choice of conscience. The Constitution had been sanctioned by the king, but did that remove their anxiety that the oath contradicted loyalty to the pope and long-established practice? Many priests sought to resolve the dilemma by taking a qualified oath, such as the priest of Quesques and Lottinghem in the north of the department of Pas-de-Calais:

I declare that my religion does not allow me to take an oath such as the National Assembly requires; I am happy and I even promise to watch over as well as we possibly can the faithful of this parish who are entrusted to me, to be true to the nation and the king and to observe the constitution decreed by the National Assembly and sanctioned by the king in all that is within the competence of his power, in all that belongs to it in the order of purely civil and political matters, but where the government and the laws of the Church are concerned, I recognise no superior and other legislators other than the Pope and the bishops . . .[12]

Ultimately, only a handful of bishops and perhaps half the parish clergy took this oath. A large number of the latter subsequently retracted when, in April 1791, the pope, also antagonized by the absorption of his lands in and around Avignon into the new nation, condemned the Civil Constitution and the Declaration of the Rights of Man as inimical to a Christian life. He counselled the clergy of France to regard the constitutional clergy as heretics:

Take special care lest you proffer ears to the insidious voices of this secular sect, which voices furnish death, and avoid in this way all usurpers whether they are called archbishops, bishops or parish priests, so that there is nothing in common between you and them, especially in divine matters . . . for no one can be in the Church of Christ, unless he is unified with the visible head of the Church itself . . .[13]

By mid-1791 two Frances had emerged, contrasting the pro-reform areas of the southeast, the Paris basin, Champagne and the centre with the 'refractory' west and southwest, the east, and the southern Massif Central. The strength of refractory clergy in border areas fed Parisian suspicions that peasants who could not understand French were prey to the 'superstitions' of their 'fanatical' priests.

The sharp regional contrasts in preparedness to take the oath suggests that it was not only a matter of individual choice, but also of local ecclesiastical culture. In broad regional terms, the refractory clergy saw themselves as servants of God, while the constitutional clergy saw themselves as servants of the people. To the former, sustained by a strong clerical presence, the Civil Constitution was anathema to the corporate, hierarchical structure of the Church and the leadership of the pope; to the latter, in areas where the Church had accommodated itself to a weaker temporal role in daily life, it was the will of God's people and reinforced Gallicanism at the expense of the church hierarchy.

Clerical responses must also be seen as a reflection of the attitudes of the wider community, for only a minority of priests felt sufficiently independent from their communities to flout public opinion. In large cities like Paris, priests who opposed the Civil Constitution risked ridicule. The incisive observer and revolutionary Louis-Sébastien Mercier described how the *curé* of the parish of St-Sulpice tried to preach against the Assembly's reforms:

A universal cry of indignation reverberated through the arches of the church. . . . Suddenly, the majestic organ filled the church with its harmonious music and echoed through every heart the famous tune: *Ah! ça ira! ça ira!* . . . the counterrevolutionary instigator was invited to sing *ça ira*. He climbed down from his chair, covered with laughter, shame, and sweat.[14]

In rural France, the oath became a test of popular acceptance of the Revolution as a whole. In the southeast and the Paris basin, where public life had long been relatively 'secularized' and priests were seen as providing only a spiritual service, there was massive acceptance of the Civil Constitution as of the Revolution in general. In regions with prominent Protestant minorities, such as the Cévennes, the oath-taking instead aroused wider fears about attacks on a way of life to which Catholic ritual and charity was pivotal. In the small southern town of Sommières, milling crowds of poor women and children aimed their anger not only at local Protestants but also at pro-revolutionary Catholic administrators deemed to be destroying established forms of religious life.

The retraction of the oath by a popular priest was harrowing for a community. In the foothills of the Pyrenees, at Missègre, municipal officers reported with palpable regret in April 1792 that their priest had retracted:

M. Lacaze, our priest, did not retract in any way his oath concerning the temporal. Quite the contrary: he exhorts us to stay obedient and faithful to the law, the nation and the king and he desires nothing more than the good, the peace and the happiness of the people. And he exhorts us very strongly as well to follow the Christian religion, which causes us a profound sorrow when we think of the fine and beautiful qualities of this person we know. He renounces the tithe and says that he wants the nobles to pay taxes like any commoner, these were the very words he used on the eleventh of March last, when he retracted everything that his conscience dictated on the spiritual level. Moreover he declared that he is ready to swear to maintain the *patrie* with all his might and that he has no other desire than to stay among us for the rest of his days to continue to give us his good example and good instruction every Sunday and on feast-days . . .[15]

By August, thousands of communes had found themselves without a priest and the regular routines of parish life.

The radical decentralization of power created a situation where revolutionary legislation from Paris was interpreted and adapted to local needs. Everywhere, the birth of new systems of administration within a context of popular sovereignty and hectic legislative activity was part of the creation of a revolutionary political culture. In this process, the half-million or more men who were elected to local government, the judiciary and administrative positions played the key role in the void that existed between the Assembly's national programme and the exigencies of the local situation. The volume of legislation arriving from Paris, as well as the expectation that communes would participate in its execution, was in sharp contrast to the situation under the *ancien régime*. Executing laws which to most people often seemed foreign in content as well as language, and often lacking in resources, these 'active' citizens—professional men, wealthy peasants, businessmen and landowners—made an enormous commitment of time and energy. Where particular legislation was unpopular, especially that concerning the redemption of seigneurial dues or religious reform, this was a commitment which could also earn them isolation and contempt.

The work of the Assembly was vast in scope and energy. The foundations of a new social order were laid, underpinned by an assumption of the national unity of a fraternity of citizens. At the same time, the Assembly was walking a tightrope: whose revolution was this? On one side lay a growing hostility from nobles and the elite of the Church angered by the loss of status, wealth, and privilege, and bolstered by a disillusioned parish clergy and their parishioners. On the other, the Assembly was alienating itself from the popular base of the Revolution by its compromise on feudal dues, its antipathy to non-juring clergy, its exclusion of the 'passive' from the political process, and its implementation of economic liberalism.

The Declaration of the Rights of Man had been silent on economic matters, but in 1789–91 the Assembly passed a series of measures revealing its commitment to economic liberalism. It removed internal customs and controls on the grain-trade, in the interests of encouraging a national market and encouraging initiative. From such an outlook, all the corporate structures of the *ancien régime*—from the privileged orders themselves to theatres and guilds—were seen as contrary to individual freedom. Impediments to freedom of occupation were removed with the abolition of guilds (the d'Allarde law, April 1790) and, most importantly, a free market in labour was imposed by the Le Chapelier law of 14 June 1791 outlawing associations of employers and employees:

Article 1. The destruction of all types of corporations of citizens of the same trade and profession being one of the fundamental bases of the French constitution, it is forbidden to reestablish them in fact, under any pretext and in any form whatsoever.

II. Citizens of the same trade or profession, entrepreneurs, those who have an open boutique, workers and craftsmen of whatever art, may not, when they find themselves together, name a president, secretary, or syndic, keep registers, give decrees or make decisions, form regulations on their supposed common interests.[16]

Le Chapelier, an ennobled lawyer, had presided over the session of 4 August 1789 in the National Assembly, and was one of the radical Breton deputies who had founded the Jacobin Club. While his law, with d'Allarde's, were decisive in the creation of a *laissez-faire* economy, they were also aimed at the 'counter-revolutionary' practices and privileges of the *ancien régime*. No longer were there specific orders of clergy or nobility, or guilds, provinces, and towns which could claim particular monopolies, privileges, and rights. The old world of corporations was dead.

In the countryside, frustration at the level of the new taxes coincided in mid-1791 with renewed anger at the unresolved question of seigneurial dues. While simple refusals to pay continued through 1791, the new year was distinguished by a mass of litigation, in which communes, despite their poverty, raised local taxes to launch legal action requiring former seigneurs to make their title-deeds available for adjudication and verification. In addition, the flash-points of rural revolution in the south in particular concerned not only seigneurial rights, but access to land. For many centuries the marginal 'wastelands' (*vacants*) had been used for pastures by local communities in return for payment of a fee to the seigneur. Seigneurs had also allowed a limited amount of clearing of uncultivated land, though this clearing had been limited by the need for sheep pastures and the knowledge that cultivated land would immediately become liable for the payment of seigneurial dues.

Underpinning the Assembly's measures to reassure former seigneurs and to put a brake on popular initiative in the countryside was concern about direct action on land belonging to the state and to seigneurs. In October and November 1789, news of widespread forest invasions prompted royal proclamations warning that all such infractions would be punished. On 11 December, the Assembly had passed a further decree warning that forests were now under the control of the nation, and reiterated the king's warning. Concerned by the massive 'dévastation' of woods of all types, the Assembly also warned communities that they could not simply assume control of woods or wastelands instead of 'taking action, by legal means, against usurpations about which they feel justified in complaining'.

It was readily apparent that such warnings were having negligible effect. In January 1791 Raymond Bastoulh, the *procureur-général-syndic* or chief administrator of the department of the Aude, expressed his anxieties to his departmental administration that

people are complaining on all sides about the misguided greed of peasants who are spending every day clearing the woods and the uncultivated land on mountain-sides, without realising that this soil will only be productive for a year or two. . . . This pernicious clearing has accelerated since the destruction of the feudal régime because the people of the countryside imagine that the communes have become the owners of the *vacants* [wastelands], that the former seigneurs were stripped of them at the same time as they were of judicial power . . .[17]

It was already obvious, he noted, that gravel and stones were being washed down into streams, congesting their beds and causing them to spill over onto the best land. Local authorities and successive revolutionary assemblies were, however, unsuccessful in their attempts to halt extensive felling in forests and occupation of the 'wastelands'. Despite regular missives from Paris reminding municipalities of laws protecting forests dating from 1669 and 1754 and reinforced in 1791, illegal woodcutting went on unchecked.

In response to a plethora of similar reports from many regions of France, the National Assembly sought, in its decree of 22 February 1791, to resolve the issue of ownership of the 'wastelands'. Here the Assembly had difficulty in resolving the contradiction between its policy of dealing with the land according to principles of private ownership and ancient popular assumptions of collective rights of usage. The legislation was clear that former seigneurs no longer had the right to appropriate the *vacants*: they were henceforth to be common land unless the seigneur could demonstrate acquisition before

1789, either by having put them to productive use at least forty years beforehand or 'by virtue of the laws, customs, statutes, or local usages then existing'. Even where former seigneurs could justify this ownership, however, communal rights of usage—for grazing and wood in particular—were to be respected. The legislation inevitably generated further confusion and contestation over what constituted adequate proof of prior ownership. This marginal, uncultivated land—which sustained a rich fauna and flora—was seized and cleared by the rural poor, desperate for an arable plot. Such was the extent of post-1789 land clearances that a durable myth quickly took hold that the Revolution had unleashed the essentially rapacious attitudes of peasants towards their environment, that the Revolution was an ecological disaster. The reality was more complex.

The legislators in the National Assembly were caught between their commitment to the sanctity of private property, their uneasy awareness of the strength of peasant attachment to collective practices, and their horror at environmental damage in many parts of France. This confusion was evident in two key pieces of legislation passed in late September 1791. First, on 28 September, the Assembly voted the Rural Code. In this decree 'on rural property and practices, and their policing', the revolutionary deputies, in one of the final acts of the National Assembly, made their great statement of agrarian individualism. It decreed that collective practices of *droit de parcours* (allowing livestock access to forests across private land) and *vaine pâture* (sending livestock onto private fallow land) could not oblige owners of sheep to leave them as part of a communal flock, nor could individuals be prevented from enclosing their land for their private use. Yet it also acknowledged the continued existence of collective practices. Next day, the Assembly passed its long-awaited Forest Code. This amounted essentially to a restatement of the major provisions of Colbert's 1669 code, with an administrative reorganization to match the new departments. True to the principles enunciated since 1789, however, the Assembly insisted that privately owned forests were fully at the owners' disposition, 'to do with as he wishes'.

The Assembly's vision of a new society was sweeping and ambitious, and its commitment to political freedom facilitated a dramatic revelation of new assumptions about citizenship and rights. Already apparent in some urban and rural areas well before 1789, new assumptions about the legitimate bases of local power were the most corrosive—and contested—cultural change of the revolutionary period. For example, in the tiny community of Fraïsse, southwest of Narbonne, the mayor had once described the terror of his fellow villagers at the behaviour of the seigneur, the Baron de Bouisse, and his nephews, 'possessors of imposing physique and walking about with four-pound sticks'. By 1790, the 86-year-old baron was in turn horrified by the behaviour of formerly 'peaceful' peasants at Fraïsse: people had refused outright to pay seigneurial dues or the tithe. The baron despaired:

I have cherished and I still cherish the people of Fraïsse as I have cherished my own children; they were so sweet and so honest in their way, but what a sudden change has taken place among them. All I hear now is 'corvée, lanternes, démocrates, aristocrates', words which for me are barbaric and which I can't use. . . . the former vassals believe themselves to be more powerful than Kings.[18]

Electoral participation was only one part of this new political culture. The voter turnout at local elections was rarely high in small communities and neighbourhoods where it was well known who would win because choices had already been expressed in public, on the market-place, in taverns, or after church. Nationally, electoral participation was also generally low, perhaps 40 per cent for the Estates-General (though reaching 85 per cent in the villages of upper Normandy). Such figures do not imply apathy: the proportion of voters who exercised their rights was generally low because of a cumbersome system of indirect voting, whereby the electorate voted for electors who then chose between candidates. Moreover, voting was only one of the ways by which French people exercised sovereignty. Another was the extraordinary volume of unofficial correspondence which criss-crossed the country. This travelled both vertically, to and from constituents and their deputies in Paris, and horizontally, in particular between the Jacobin Clubs (or Societies of Friends of the Constitution). The Paris Jacobin Club had been founded by some radical deputies as the Society of the Friends of the Constitution in January 1790, and was soon known by the name of its premises in a former convent. One of the common activities in thousands of Jacobin clubs and other popular societies was the exchange of letters with similar gatherings across the country. With the repeated experience of men gathering to cast votes in elections, the contours of a new type of public space became established.[19]

Whereas Jacobin clubs were normally limited to 'active' citizens, in Paris and elsewhere alternative forums of revolutionary sociability developed for the 'passive'. In Paris, the Cordelier Club, led by Danton and Marat, welcomed all-comers. From the insistence that all citizens constituted the sovereign people developed an understanding of 'democracy' as an entire political system rather than, as in England and the United States, only one arm of government balanced by the upper house and executive power. 'Patriots' increasingly referred to themselves as 'democrats'.

Women, too, were welcome at some clubs. In Paris, the Fraternal Society of Citizens of Both Sexes, gathering up to 800 men and women at its sessions, deliberately sought to integrate women into institutional politics. The rights of women were also advocated by individual activists such as Olympe de Gouges, the Marquis de Condorcet, Etta Palm, and Théroigne de Méricourt, and the Cercle Social urged the vote for women, the availability of divorce, and the abolition of inheritance laws which favoured the first-born son. The last of these demands, at least, was quickly recognized, although more with a view to breaking the power of great noble patriarchs than to strengthening the economic position of women. On 15 March 1790, the Assembly decreed:

Article 11. All privileges, all feudalism and noble property being destroyed, birthright and rights of masculinity with regard to noble fiefs, domains and ancestors, and unequal distribution by reason of someone's quality are abolished.

Consequently, the Assembly orders that all inheritances, whether direct or collateral, personal or real estate, to which it would fall to count from the day of publication of the present decree, will be, without regard for the ancient noble quality of possessions and persons, shared between heirs according to the laws, statutes and customs that regulate distributions between all citizens.[20]

The legislation was to have a dramatic impact in those regions (for example, most of the south and Normandy) where testamentary freedom had favoured first-born sons; in western regions such as Maine and Anjou, on the other hand, partible inheritance was already the norm.

The contradiction between the inclusive, universalist promises of the Declaration of the Rights of Man and the Citizen and the exclusions enshrined in subsequent legislation was not lost on women activists. In 1791 de Gouges published a draft social contract for marriage arrangements concerning children and property and a Declaration of the Rights of Woman and of the Citizeness:

First Article: Woman is born free and remains equal to man in rights. Social distinctions can only be founded on common utility . . .
VI: The law must be the expression of the general will; all female and male Citizens must assist personally, or through their representatives, in its formation; it must be the same for all: all female and all male Citizens, being equal in its eyes, must also be eligible for all public dignities, positions and employments according to their abilities, and without any distinction other than that of their virtues and their talents.[21]

Such participation by men and women in 'associational' life in clubs and elections was only one of the means through which the struggle over the nature of the Revolution was expressed. In early 1789, there were perhaps eighty newspapers in the whole country; over the next few years about 2,000 others were launched, though four-fifths produced fewer than twelve issues. The newspaper-reading public perhaps trebled within three years. The counter-revolutionary press thrived on the same freedoms as its enemies. The ultra-royalist *Ami du Roi* summarized the division over the clerical oath in emotive terms:

The right wing of the National Assembly, or The élite of the defenders Of religion and of the Throne.	The left wing, and the monstrous assembly of the principal enemies of the Church and of the Monarchy, Jews, Protestants, Deists.
All worthy and virtuous citizens	All the libertines, cheats, Jews and Protestants.

The newspaper here mentioned in passing one of the most durable innovations of the Revolution's political language: the use of 'left' and 'right', referring to the clusters of like-minded deputies on the benches of the National Assembly.[22]

The production of books declined: 216 novels were printed in 1788, but only 103 in 1791. On the other hand, in the same period the number of new political songs increased from 116 to 308, including the 'Ça ira', apparently first sung as the Champ de Mars was prepared for the Festival of the Federation in 1790. For this was a society in which the most vibrant expressions of opinion were conveyed through the spoken and sung word, or through the thousands of cheap engraved images which circulated throughout the country popularizing images of what the Revolution had achieved. At about the same time as the Festival of the Federation in July 1790, for example, 'funeral rites for the aristocracy' were held as a comic farce on the Champ de Mars:

A log had been bizarrely dressed as a priest: band, calotte, short coat, everything was there. A long line of mourners followed this black cortège, from time to time raising their hands to heaven and repeating in hoarse, yapping voices, sobbing *Mori!* . . . *Mori!*[23]

Through such vehicles of expression, millions of people learned the language and practice of popular sovereignty and, in a protracted period of state weakness, came to question the most deeply ingrained assumptions about the sanctity and benevolence of monarchy and about their own place in the social hierarchy. By mid-1791 the Constitution was nearing completion. This was a delicate balancing act between the king (with the power to name ministers and diplomats, to temporarily block legislation, and to declare peace and war) and the legislature (with a single chamber, with powers over finance and initiating legislation). The dilemma for Louis was how to interpret the contrasting voices of a sovereign people, hitherto his subjects, who were increasingly divided about the changes the Revolution had wrought and the future direction it should take.

Notes

1. Jones, *Peasantry*, 209. Grégoire's inquiry is discussed in Martyn Lyons, 'Politics and Patois: The Linguistic Policy of the French Revolution', *Australian Journal of French Studies*, 18 (1981), 264–81.

2. *Moniteur universel*, no. 46, 15 February 1790, vol. 2, 368–9; Gary Kates, 'Jews into Frenchmen: Nationality and Representation in Revolutionary France', in Ferenc Fehér (ed.), *The French Revolution and the Birth of Modernity* (Berkeley, Calif., 1990), 103–16.

3. J. Gilchrist and W. J. Murray (eds.), *The Press in the French Revolution* (Melbourne, 1971), 15. On the impact of the Revolution on the armed forces, see Jean-Paul Bertaud, *The Army of the French Revolution: From Citizen-Soldiers to Instrument of Power*, trans. R. R. Palmer (Princeton, 1988), ch. 1; Alan Forrest, *Soldiers of the French Revolution* (Durham, NC, 1990), ch. 2; William S. Cormack, *Revolution and Political Conflict in the French Navy, 1789–1794* (Cambridge, 1995).

4. Doyle, *Oxford History of the French Revolution*, 124.

5. Bryant T. Ragan, 'Rural Political Equality and Fiscal Activism in the Revolutionary Somme', in Ragan and Elizabeth A. Williams (eds.), *Re-creating Authority in Revolutionary France* (New Brunswick, NJ, 1992), 46; Ozouf, *Festivals and the French Revolution*, 37–9; R. B. Rose, *Gracchus Babeuf 1760–1797, the First Revolutionary Communist* (Stanford, Calif., 1978), chs. 5–7. The continuing revolution in the countryside is studied by Jones, *Peasantry*, 67–85; Markoff, *Abolition of Feudalism*, chs. 5–7; and Anatoli Ado, *Paysans en Révolution: terre, pouvoir et jacquerie 1789–1794*, trans. Serge Aberdam et al. (Paris, 1996), chs. 4–6.

6. Aimé Coiffard, *La Vente des biens nationaux dans le district de Grasse (1790–1815)* (Paris, 1973), 94–103; William Doyle, *Venality: The Sale of Offices in Eighteenth-Century France* (Oxford, 1996). On the provincial support for the regeneration of France: Michael P. Fitzsimmons, *The Remaking of France: The National Assembly with the Constitution of 1791* (Cambridge, 1994).

7. The Revolution in La Rochelle has been little studied by other than local historians. See Claude Laveau, *Le Monde rochelais des Bourbons à Bonaparte* (La Rochelle, 1988); J. -M. Deveau, *La Traite rochelaise* (Paris, 1990); and *Le Commerce rochelais face à la Révolution: correspondance de Jean-Baptiste Nairac (1789–1790)* (La Rochelle, 1989).

8. *Moniteur universel*, no. 136, 16 May 1791, vol. 8, 404; Robert Forster, 'Who is a Citizen? The Boundaries of "La Patrie": The French Revolution and the People of Color, 1789–91', *French Politics & Society*, 7 (1989), 50–64.

9. Jeremy Whiteman, 'Trade and the Regeneration of France 1789–91: Liberalism, Protectionism, and the Commercial Policy of the National Constituent Assembly', *European History Quarterly*, 31 (2001), 171–204; Orville T. Murphy, *The Diplomatic Retreat of France and Public Opinion on the Eve of the French Revolution, 1783–1789* (Washington, DC, 1998).

10. Ozouf, *Festivals and the French Revolution*, 51; Aileen Ribeiro, *Fashion in the French Revolution* (London, 1988).

11. *Moniteur universel*, no. 150, 30 May 1790; no. 151, 30 May 1790, 498–9. On the Civil Constitution of the Clergy, see Timothy Tackett, *Religion, Revolution, and Regional Culture in Eighteenth-Century France* (Princeton, 1986); Jones, *Peasantry*,

191–204; Dale Van Kley, *The Religious Origins of the French Revolution* (New Haven, 1996), 349–67.

12. Marcel Coquerel, 'Le Journal d'un curé du Boulonnais', *Annales historiques de la Révolution française*, 46 (1974), 289. On priests' reactions in general, see Tackett, *Religion, Revolution, and Regional Culture*, chs. 3–4.

13. Augustin Theiner, *Documents inédits rélatifs aux affaires religieuses de la France* (Paris, 1857), 88.

14. Laura Mason, *Singing the French Revolution: Popular Culture and Politics, 1787–1799* (Ithaca, NY, 1996), 50.

15. McPhee, *Revolution and Environment*, 77–8.

16. *Moniteur universel*, no. 166, 15 June 1791, 662.

17. Peter McPhee, ' "The misguided greed of peasants"? Popular Attitudes to the Environment in the Revolution of 1789', *French Historical Studies*, 24 (2001), 247.

18. McPhee, *Revolution and Environment*, 60.

19. Crook, *Elections in the French Revolution*; Timothy Tackett, *Becoming a Revolutionary: The Deputies of the French National Assembly and the Emergence of a Revolutionary Culture (1789–1790)* (Princeton, 1996). This 'political culture', one of the most fertile current areas of research in social history, is explored in the four volumes of *The French Revolution and the Creation of Modern Political Culture* (Oxford, 1987–94); Michael Kennedy, *The Jacobin Clubs in the French Revolution: The First Years* (Princeton, 1982); Ozouf, *Festivals and the French Revolution*.

20. *Archives parlementaires*, 15 March 1790, 173.

21. Olympe de Gouges, *Les Droits de la femme* (Paris, 1791). Among the expanding literature on the women's rights movement, see Landes, *Women and the Public Sphere*, 93–129.

22. Cobb and Jones (eds.), *Voices of the French Revolution*, 110.

23. Rolf Reichardt, 'The Politicization of Popular Prints in the French Revolution', in Ian Germani and Robin Swales (eds.), *Symbols, Myths and Images: Essays in Honour of James A. Leith* (Regina, Saskatchewan, 1998), 17. The development of the popular movement is outlined in R. B. Rose, *The Making of the 'sans-culottes': Democratic Ideas and Institutions in Paris, 1789–92* (Manchester, 1983).

5

A Second Revolution, 1792

Ever since July 1789 the Assembly had had to face a double challenge—how to preserve the Revolution from its opponents? Whose Revolution was it to be? These questions came to a head in mid-1791. Outraged by the changes to the Church and the limitations to his own power, Louis fled Paris on 21 June, publicly repudiating the direction the Revolution had taken: 'the only recompense for so many sacrifices is to witness the destruction of the kingdom, to see all powers ignored, personal property violated, people's safety everywhere in danger'. Louis made an appeal to his subjects to return to the certainties they had once known:

People of France, and especially you Parisians, inhabitants of a city that the ancestors of His Majesty delighted in calling 'the good city of Paris', be wary of the suggestions and lies of your false friends; come back to your king; he will always be your father, your best friend.[1]

As news of the king's flight swept the city, however, the mood was one of shock rather than repentance.

The royal family's desperate flight to safety towards Montmédy, near the border, was a series of blunders from the outset. On the evening of the 21st, Louis was recognized by Drouet, the postmaster at Ste-Menehould, who dashed to the next town, Varennes, to arrest him. The Assembly was stunned: Louis was suspended from his position as king, but it was determined to quell any unrest during his return to the capital. 'Whoever applauds the king will be batonned,' it warned, 'whoever insults him will be hanged.' Louis's return was humiliating, the roads lined with his resentful subjects, reportedly refusing to remove their hats in his presence. During his suspension by the Assembly, Jacobins such as the Abbé Grégoire argued that he should be forced to abdicate:

The premier public servant abandons his post; he arms himself with a false passport; after having said, in writing to the foreign powers, that his most dangerous enemies are those who pretend to spread doubts about the monarch's intentions, he breaks his word, he leaves the French a declaration which, if not criminal, is at the least—however it is envisaged—contrary to the principles of our liberty. He could not be unaware that his flight exposed the nation to the dangers of civil war; and finally, in the hypothesis that he wished only to go to Montmédy, I say: either he wanted to content himself with making peaceful observations to the National Assembly regarding its decrees, and in that case it was useless to flee; or he wanted to support his claims with arms, and in that case it was a conspiracy against liberty.

Nevertheless, despite his humiliating capture and return, the Assembly on 15 July decreed that he had in fact been mentally 'kidnapped' and that the monarchist provisions of the Constitution of 1791 would stand. For most of the deputies, the issue was clear; in the words of Barnave:

any change today would be fatal: any prolonging of the Revolution today would be disastrous . . . Are we going to end the Revolution, or are we going to start it all over again? . . . if the Revolution takes one more step, it can only be a dangerous one: if it is in line with liberty its first act could be the destruction of royalty, if it is in line with equality its first act could be an attack on property . . . It is time to bring the Revolution to an end . . . is there still to be destroyed an aristocracy other than that of property?[2]

Barnave was here referring to a wave of strikes and demonstrations by wage-earners and the unemployed in the capital, and continuing unrest in the countryside. Louis had therefore become a symbol of stability against the increasingly radical demands of 'passive' citizens and their supporters.

On the 17th, an unarmed demonstration was organized on the Champ de Mars by the Cordeliers Club to demand Louis's abdication, at the same 'altar of the homeland' on which the Fête de la Fédération had been celebrated a year earlier. The original petition was destroyed in the destruction by fire of the Hôtel de Ville in Paris in 1871; from the *Révolutions de Paris*, however, we know that its substance was

to take into consideration the fact that Louis XVI's crime is proven, that the king has abdicated; to receive his abdication, and to call a new constituent body so as to proceed in a truly national fashion with the judgement of the guilty party, and especially with the replacement and organization of a new executive power.[3]

Lafayette, the commander of the National Guard, was ordered to disperse the petitioners. At the Champ de Mars, he ordered the red flag raised as a signal that troops would fire if the crowd did not disperse, then the solid citizens of his National Guard opened fire on the petitioners, killing perhaps fifty of them.

Of course, this was not the first large-scale bloodshed of the Revolution; however, for the first time, it was the result of open political conflict within the Parisian Third Estate which had acted so decisively in 1789. The king's flight and the Assembly's response had divided the country. Several days after the killings on the Champ de Mars, a delegation from Chartres representing the governing body of the department of Eure-et-Loir was warmly received into the Assembly. The delegates expressed their delight that the Assembly had decided that Louis would retain his throne and that the Constitution would be presented to him:

We have come to assure you, with the most exact truthfulness, that this decree that decides the empire's destiny was received with joy and gratitude by all the citizens of the department; that it has only added to the confidence, the admiration that is due to you on so many grounds. Finally, we have come to repeat at your hands the solemn oath to shed the last drop of our blood for the fulfillment of the law and the upholding of the Constitution. (There is applause.)[4]

On 14 September Louis promulgated the Constitution which embodied the Assembly's work since 1789. France was to be a constitutional monarchy in which power was shared between the king, as head of the executive, and a legislative assembly elected by a restrictive property franchise. However, the issues of his loyalty and whether the Revolution was over were far from resolved. Democrats within the Jacobin Club drew closer to the radical trend of the popular movement, notably the Cordelier Club. Outside France, monarchs expressed concern at Louis's safety, and fears that the Revolution might spread, in threatening declarations from Padua (5 July) and Pillnitz (27 August). On the second anniversary of the taking of the Bastille, on 14 July 1791, 'Church and King' rioters wrecked the Birmingham home of the chemical scientist Joseph Priestley, a strong defender of the Revolution against Edmund Burke. Inside France, de Rozoi's royalist *Gazette de Paris* called for 'hostages to the king' to offer themselves in return for Louis's 'freedom'. Thousands of letters were received, including over 1,400 from Paris and large numbers from Normandy, the northeast, Alsace, and Guyenne. In towns throughout the west the Marquis de La Rouërie established secret royalist committees. From the predominantly Protestant Provençal village of Lourmarin, on the other hand, the council petitioned the Assembly to hasten to 'banish the monster of feudalism' so that 'the countryside, so desolated today, will become the strongest bulwark' of what they already called 'the Republic'.[5]

It was in this highly-charged context that the new Legislative Assembly was elected and convened in Paris in October 1791. It was composed of 'new men' following the self-denying ordinance, proposed by Robespierre to the National Assembly, which disqualified the framers of the Constitution from being those who implemented it. At the outset most of its members sought to consolidate the state of the Revolution as expressed in the Constitution, and deserted the Jacobin Club for the Feuillants, similarly named after its meeting-place in a former convent. However, the mounting hostility of opponents of the Revolution inside and outside France focused the deputies' concern on the counter-revolution centred on Coblenz, where the Count d'Artois joined his brother the Count de Provence, who had emigrated in July. The officer corps of the royal army began to disintegrate, with over 2,100 noble officers emigrating between 15 September and 1 December 1791 and 6,000 in all during the year. In this context the increasingly anxious deputies of the Legislative Assembly, who had originally been committed to the Feuillant project of stabilizing the Revolution under the king and Constitution, found compelling the agitated rhetoric of a group of Jacobins led by Jacques-Pierre Brissot who blamed the Revolution's difficulties on internal conspiracies linked to external enemies.

As Timothy Tackett has demonstrated by analysing speeches and letters by the deputies, there was a dramatic increase in fears of 'conspiracies' in the months after the king's flight. Their rhetoric also resonated outside the Assembly. On 16 October 1791 supporters of the annexation of the papal territories around Avignon massacred sixty opponents imprisoned in the former palace of the popes. The rebellion of hundreds of thousands of mulattos and slaves in St-Domingue, beginning in August 1791, pressured the Legislative Assembly in April 1792 into extending civil equality to all 'free persons of colour'. The importance of the Caribbean colonies for the French economy further convinced the deputies of the insidious intentions of its rivals, England and Spain.

The followers of Brissot agitated the Assembly. In a debate on the *émigrés*, Vergniaud declared that 'a wall of conspiracy' had been formed around France; Isnard expressed his fear that 'a volcano of conspiracy is about to explode and that we are being lulled to sleep with a false sense of security'. On 9 November, the Assembly passed a sweeping law, effectively declaring the *émigrés* outlaws should they not return by the start of the new year:

Those Frenchmen gathered beyond the kingdom's borders are, from this moment, declared to be suspected of conspiracy against the fatherland. . . . If, on January 1, 1792, they are still gathered in the same way, they will be declared guilty of conspiracy; as such they will be prosecuted, and punished with death.[6]

Three days later, the king used his suspensive veto to block the legislation.

The 'Brissotins' argued that the Revolution would not be safe until this foreign threat was destroyed. A military strike at Austria and Prussia, which would be brief because of the welcome the commoners in those countries would give their liberated brothers, would expose internal counter-revolutionaries in the cauldron of armed conflict between old and new Europe. In its decree of 22 May 1790 placing the power to declare war and make peace in the hands of the Assembly rather than the king, the Assembly had declared that 'the French nation renounces the undertaking of any war with a view to making conquests, and that it will never use its forces against the freedom of any people'. By early in 1792, such was the combination of anxiety, exhilaration and fear pervading the Assembly that most deputies convinced themselves that the rulers of Austria and Prussia in particular were engaged in naked aggression towards the Revolution. They were encouraged in their optimism by the urgings of political refugees in Paris who had formed themselves into a force of fifty-four companies of volunteers ready to depart to liberate their homelands. On 20 April 1792 the Assembly declared that

> the French nation, true to the principles established in the Constitution, *not to undertake war with a view to making conquests, and never to use its forces against the freedom of a people*, only takes up arms in order to maintain its liberty and its independence; that the war that it is obliged to support is in no way a nation to nation war, but the rightful defence of a free people against the unjust aggression of a king.[7]

The war may have exposed internal opposition, as the Brissotins hoped, but it was neither limited nor brief. With the Civil Constitution of the Clergy, it marks one of the major turning-points of the revolutionary period, influencing the internal history of France for twenty-three years. Within a few months of its outbreak, it had a series of major consequences. First, it immediately raised the hopes and stakes of the counter-revolution, by adding a military function to the small, embittered *émigré* communities in exile in Europe, particularly at Coblenz. Not only were there members of the old élite inside France, particularly the court, who looked to defeat as a way of crushing the Revolution, but the initial defeats the disorganized revolutionary armies suffered were welcomed by *émigré* nobles and army officers bent on restoring a rejuvenated *ancien régime*.

Secondly, while the counter-revolution could now also aim to be fighting a holy crusade to restore religion, inside France the war made the position of non-juring clergy intolerable. On 27 May they were ordered to leave the country if denounced by twenty citizens, a law vetoed by the king. For all those seeking a ready target to blame for the difficulties the Revolution now faced, the clergy were the most obvious. Was not the pope himself blessing the foreign troops killing Frenchmen? A former priest who had been saying mass for the school-teaching order of Ursuline nuns in Lille on 29 April was murdered in angry revenge as revolutionary troops retreated in disarray after their first battle with the Austrians. Within months the Ursulines had been expelled and their order closed; while most slipped across the border into Austrian Flanders, thirteen of them whose sense of duty impelled them to stay were later to be guillotined for counter-revolutionary activity in support of the enemy.[8]

A third consequence was that the war revitalized the popular revolution; after the call citizens to volunteer to fight at a time of worsening inflation, the political and social demands of working people became more insistent and harder to deny. Among them were women insistent on participating actively in the war effort. A petition from the Société Fraternelle des Minimes with 300 signatures (including that of the activist Pauline Léon) was read to the Legislative Assembly:

Our fathers, husbands and sons may perhaps be the victims of our enemies' fury. Could we be forbidden the sweetness of avenging them or of dying at their sides? . . . We wish only to be allowed to defend ourselves. You cannot refuse us, and society cannot deny us this right, which is given us by nature, unless it is claimed that the Declaration of Rights does not apply to women.[9]

The Assembly did not act on the petition.

The initial months of the war were disastrous for revolutionary armies in a state of disarray consequent to the mass defection of most of the officer corps. Louis's dismissal of his Brissotin or 'patriot' ministers on 13 June provoked an angry demonstration a week later. Among the placards paraded past the king were some carrying slogans such as 'Tremblez tyrans! Voici les sans-culottes!' From mid-1791 active democrats among the *menu peuple* commonly became known by this new term *sans-culottes*, which was both a political label for a militant patriot and a social description signifying men of the people who did not wear the knee-breeches and stockings of the upper classes. In time radical women of the people, who did not wear petticoats like upper-class women, became known as *sans-jupons*. These were the politically active among the *menu peuple*: not a working class defined by wage-earning but an amalgam of artisans, shopkeepers and labourers. It was at this time, too, that the use of 'citizen' and 'citizeness' became a mark of patriotic zeal. One Jacobin versifier defined the *sans-culottes* as:

Partisans of poverty,
Each of these proud warriors,
Far from enjoying an excess
Has scarcely more, through civic virtue,
Than the honour of being almost naked.
With this name of 'patriots'
A glorious name that pleases them so,
They console themselves readily
For being without hose and without breeches.

Such a sturdy physical image was in stark contrast to the scurrilous mockery of the king and queen. As Antoine de Baecque has argued, the new man of the Revolution was imagined to be politically and physically virile, the opposite of the derisive image of the aristocracy as physically and morally decadent.[10]

In newspapers, songs, plays, and broadsheets, the period 1789–92 was the great age of savage satire, especially licentious attacks on political opponents, because of the ending of political censorship at a time when popular literature was already distinguished by its mix of obscene mockery, anticlericalism and political slander. It was not only revolutionaries who used the new freedoms. Royalist writers, such as Gautier, Rivarol, Suleau, and Peltier, took this abuse to extremes, dismissing Brissot as 'black Bis-sot' (a doubly-stupid friend of blacks), mocking the homosexuality of the pro-revolutionary Marquis de Villette, and lampooning Pétion as 'Pet-hion' (Donkey-fart) and Théroigne de Méricourt as a prostitute whose 100 lovers a day each paid 100 sous in 'patriotic contributions'.[11]

In this febrile world of satirical and pornographic attack, the king and queen were the most vulnerable of targets for revolutionaries. In particular, Marie-Antoinette was relentlessly attacked for her alleged sexual depravities and maleficent political power which had emasculated the monarchy. In such a situation, the military crisis made the king's position impossible. In using his suspensive veto to block critical pieces of legislation (ending pay for non-jurors, ordering émigrés to return and non-jurors to leave, seizing émigré property and calling volunteers to Paris), the king seemed to be acting in the interests of his wife's nephew, the emperor of Austria. Could not the military defeats since April be seen as proof of this, as well as, from hindsight, his attempted flight in June 1791?

On 11 July the Assembly was forced to declare publicly to the nation that 'the homeland is in danger' and appealed for total support in a spirit of self-sacrifice:

Would you allow foreign hordes to spread like a destroying torrent over your countryside! That they ravage our harvest! That they devastate our fatherland through fire and murder! In a word, that they overcome you with chains dyed with the blood of those whom you hold the most dear.[12]

Early in August Parisians learnt of a manifesto issued by the commander-in-chief of the Prussian armies, the Duke of Brunswick. Its language provoked both anger and resolve, threatening as it did summary justice on the people of Paris if Louis and his family were harmed:

they will wreak an exemplary and forever memorable vengeance, by giving up the city of Paris to a military execution, and total destruction, and the rebels guilty of assassinations, to the execution that they have merited.[13]

The threat added to the popular conviction that Louis was complicit in the defeats being suffered by the army. In response, all but one of the forty-eight sections of Paris voted to form a Commune of Paris to organize insurrection and an army of 20,000 *sans-culottes* from the newly democratized National Guard. Joined by *fédérés*, volunteers from the provinces on their way to the front, these *sans-culottes*, led by Santerre and other sectional commanders, assaulted and took the Tuileries palace on 10 August. Among the women involved in the fighting was Théroigne de Méricourt, well known with Pauline Léon for advocating women's right to bear arms.[14] After Louis took refuge in the nearby Assembly, 600 Swiss guards, the palace's main defenders, were killed in the fighting or subsequently in bloody acts of retribution.

Louis might have saved his throne had he been willing to accept a more minor role in government or had he been less prone to vacillation. However, his downfall was also caused by the intransigence of most nobles and the logic of popular politicization at a time of dramatic change and crisis. The declaration of war, and subsequent military defeats, had made his position impossible. The crisis of the summer of 1792 was a major turning-point of the Revolution. By overthrowing the monarchy, the popular movement had effectively issued the ultimate challenge to the whole of Europe; internally, the declaration of war and overthrow of the monarchy radicalized the Revolution. The political exclusion of 'passive' citizens now called to defend the Republic was untenable. If the Revolution was to survive it would have to call on all the nation's reserves.

The military defeats of the summer of 1792 again confronted priests with the most fundamental of questions about their loyalties. Many accepted their new role as citizen priests whose task it was to strengthen the resolve of their fellow villagers. However, the position of the non-juring clergy was now impossible. On 23 August the

Assembly required all non-juring clergy to leave the kingdom within seven days, 'considering that the unrest excited in the kingdom by priests who are not under oath is one of the major causes of danger to the fatherland'.[15]

Then, on 2 September, word reached Paris that the great fortress at Verdun, just 250 kilometres from the capital and the last major obstacle to invading armies, had fallen to the Prussians. The news generated an immediate, dramatic surge in popular fear and resolve. Convinced that 'counter-revolutionaries' (whether nobles, priests, or common law criminals) in prisons were waiting to break out and welcome the invaders once the volunteers had left for the front, hastily convened popular courts sentenced to death about 1,200 of the 2,700 prisoners brought before them. Among them were about 240 priests. This was the final proof for non-juring clergy that the Revolution had become godless and anarchic. On the other hand, those who 'tried' the prisoners were plainly convinced of the necessity and even justice of their actions. One of them wrote home on the 2nd that 'necessity has made this execution inevitable . . . It is sad to have to go to such lengths, but it is better (as they say) to kill the devil than to let the devil kill you.' Another of them, who had stolen a handkerchief from a corpse's clothing, was himself put to death by the killers for this 'uncivic act'.[16]

The killings were witnessed by Restif de la Bretonne, perhaps the most acute and informed observer of revolutionary Paris. Restif was aghast at what he saw, and tried to convince himself that the 'cannibals' were not residents of his beloved city. He found it difficult to describe the death of the Princess de Lamballe, a close confidante of Marie-Antoinette and detained with her in La Force prison:

Finally, I saw a woman appear, pale as her underclothing, held up by a counter-clerk. They said to her in a harsh voice: 'Cry out: Long live the nation!—No! no!' she said. They made her climb onto a heap of corpses. . . . They told her again to cry out 'Long live the nation!' She refused disdainfully. Then a killer seized her, tore off her dress and opened her belly. She fell, and was finished off by the others. Never had such horror offered itself to my imagination. I tried to flee; my legs failed. I fainted.

On reflection, Restif was quite clear about the impulse behind the killings; it was not simply mindless bloodlust:

What is, therefore, the true motive for this butchery? Several people think that it was actually so that volunteers, departing for the frontiers, would not leave their wives and children to the mercy of brigands, that the courts could discharge with a pardon, that malevolent people could help escape, etc. I wanted to know the truth and I have finally found it. They only wanted one thing: to get rid of non-juring priests. Some even wanted to get rid of all of them.[17]

Prominent revolutionaries, notably Danton and Marat, excused the killings, as did the Paris Commune: thereafter, they would be derided by their opponents as 'septembriseurs'. Never before had the Revolution seen such horrifying bloodshed. To historians such as Simon Schama, Norman Hampson, and François Furet, the escalation of punitive violence was the result of a revolutionary intolerance already discernible in 1789: the counter-revolution was essentially a creation of revolutionary paranoia and popular bloodlust. The September massacres have been described by Schama as 'the central truth of the Revolution'. An alternative explanation, that of Hampson, has emphasized 'millenarial' ideologies rather than social conflict as the cause of the collapse of consensus. That is, the revolutionaries were obsessed with their vision of a regenerated, purged society.[18]

Such arguments minimize the extent of the internal and external enemy republicans were facing, and ignore the violent threats made by royalists. Well before 10 August, the right-wing press had been publishing lists of 'patriots' the Prussians would execute when they reached Paris, coupled with lurid images of the Seine choked with Jacobins and streets red with the blood of *sans-culottes*. By the summer of 1792, the stakes being fought for in France and western Europe were so high that a thorough purge of their enemies seemed to both sides the only way to secure or overturn the Revolution.[19]

The radicalization of the Revolution also encouraged the Assembly to finally resolve the matter of compensation for seigneurial dues. From the outset of the pre-revolutionary debate questions, pertaining to the control of resources in the countryside and whether they would be unencumbered by seigneurial dues had been central to politics in the countryside. Across most of rural France the response to the National Assembly's prevarication in August 1789 over the final abolition of seigneurialism had been an extension of non-compliance and rebellion against those practices which the Assembly seemed hesitant to abolish. This lasted until the final abolition of seigneurialism in 1792–3.

Successive assemblies' hesitations about outright abolition of seigneurialism had fuelled a complex dialogue between peasant and legislator, in which rural communities, by legal and illegal means, pressured and responded to successive assemblies and made political choices about the means to do so. It was a two-way process, in John Markoff's words: 'as peasant rebellions were an essential context for anti-feudal legislation, anti-feudal legislation was an essential context for peasant action'. Markoff has calculated that there were 4,689 protests or 'incidents' between 1788 and 1793, of which anti-seigneurial protests made up 36 per cent of the total. In April 1792 alone, at least 100 peasant attacks on chateaux were recorded in the department of the Gard. On 25 August, a motion to end seigneurialism was passed by the Legislative Assembly. Seigneurial dues were abolished without compensation, unless they could be proven to be derived from concession of land, with a legally valid contract. In essence, the feudal régime was dead.[20]

By the autumn of 1792, then, the Revolution had been through a radical, second Revolution. It was now armed, democratic, and republican. Nevertheless, the exhilarated sense of regeneration and resolve by which these months are characterized was, in stark contrast with 1789, muted by the horrors of September and the desperate military situation.

Some two weeks after the massacres, revolutionary armies won their first great victory, at Valmy, 200 kilometres east of the capital. As news arrived, the new National Convention, elected by universal manhood suffrage (although still in a two-stage voting process), was convening in Paris. The military crisis was the major issue confronting these 750 deputies, but they also had to resolve the fate of Louis and work towards new constitutional arrangements now that the Constitution of 1791 was inoperable. The men of the Convention were united by social background and political assumptions. Overwhelmingly bourgeois by social origin, they remained committed to the desirability of economic liberalism and safeguards for private property. They were also democrats and republicans: immediately on convening, they abolished the monarchy and proclaimed France a republic. Across much of the country the news was the occasion of celebration, tempered always by the knowledge of the nation's parlous military position. At Villardebelle, in the foothills of the Pyrenees, the constitutional priest Marcou celebrated the proclamation of the Republic on 21 September by planting a liberty tree, still standing today. In the port of Brest, liberty caps 80 cm in diameter were mounted on poop decks while others in wood were raised to mastheads.

The composition of the Convention testifies to the social transformation wrought by the Revolution. Former nobles (23) and Catholic clergy (46) were conspicuously few; instead the Convention was composed of professional men, officials, landowners, and businessmen, with a sprinkling of farmers and artisans. One of the very few workers was Jean-Baptiste Armonville, a weaver from Reims who made a point of attending the Convention in his working clothes. Although comparatively young (two-thirds of them were under 45 years old), the deputies were experienced in local and national politics after three years of revolution. Municipal councils were somewhat more democratic in composition. In major provincial towns such as Amiens, Nancy, Bordeaux, and Toulouse, bourgeois men still predominated, but artisans and shopkeepers were 18–24 per cent in all four cities. In small rural communities, too, the years 1792–4 were a time of social levelling with poorer peasants and even labourers represented for the first time on councils.

It was at this time that Rouget de Lisle's 'Chant de guerre pour l'armée du Rhin' became popular. Composed for the king's armies by this royalist army officer in Strasbourg, the song had travelled south and become adopted by republican patriots in Marseilles and Montpellier. The soldiers of Marseilles brought the song—now known as the 'Marseillaise'—with them to the capital in August. In late September the *Révolutions de Paris* reported:

The people's spirits are still extremely good . . . one must see them, one must hear them repeating in chorus the refrain of the war song of the Marseillais, which the singers in front of the statue of Liberty in the Tuileries gardens are teaching them every day with renewed success.

> Forward children of the homeland!
> The day of glory is upon us;
> Against us, the bloody standard
> Of tyranny is raised.
> Do you hear these ferocious soldiers

> Bellowing in the fields?
> They come into your very midst
> To slaughter your sons, your wives!
> To arms, citizens, form your battalions,
> March on, march on,
> That impure blood will water our furrows.[21]

Outside Paris, the 'Marseillaise' was used for wider purposes. On 21 October the Jews of Metz in eastern France joined with their Gentile neighbours to celebrate the victory of French armies at Thionville. One of them, Moise Ensheim, a friend of the Abbé Grégoire, had composed a Hebrew version of the 'Marseillaise' which used biblical imagery linking Jewish history to the Revolution:

> O House of Jacob! You have suffered abundant grief.
> You fell through no fault of your own . . .
> Happy are you, O Land of France! Happy are you!
> Your would-be destroyers have fallen to the dust.

In such a way the emancipation of Orthodox Jews a year earlier could be celebrated at the same time as a republican victory.[22]

The most important organized form of popular leisure in revolutionary Paris was theatre. A rich example of this theatre—and the political ideology which pervaded it—in the autumn of 1792 is a play written by the 'citizen Gamas'. *Emigrés in the Austral Lands or the Last Chapter of a Great Revolution, a Comedy*, was performed for the first time in the Théâtre des Amis de la Patrie in Paris in November 1792.[23] Before this time there had been two centuries of European utopian literature about the 'Austral Lands', an ideal place for authors to locate an imaginary world turned upside down. In France this interest had been heightened by the tales of the Pacific brought back by Bougainville. This was a literature which was more about France and its discontents than any real southern land. Marin Gamas's short play, while within this genre, is of particular interest because it was the first play in any language about the new British colony of New South Wales. It was located at Botany Bay, described in the play as 'an uncultivated landscape' strewn with 'rocks and a few tents'.

The play is redolent of the heady mix of patriotic virtues and hatred for the old Europe of the aristocracy so typical of these months. It depicts the struggle of a group of anti-revolutionary *émigrés* exiled to

Australia to come to terms with life in a 'state of nature'. The characters are stereotypes, including Truehart, Captain of the National Guard, and the *émigrés* Prince Braggart, Baron Swindle, Judge Blunder, the abbot Smarmy, the financier Leech, and the monk Greedy. The noble and clerical *émigrés*, still dressed in their finery and utterly unreconstructed in their prejudices, have to come to terms with life in a state of nature. Oziambo, chief of the Aborigines, is an idealized child of nature, who worships a Supreme Being but has no need of priests: indeed, he expresses some good Parisian anticlericalism when he mistakes the abbot Smarmy in his cassock for a woman. Oziambo is eager to learn from Mathurin the ploughman, the 'benefactor of humanity', and speaks perfect French. Mathurin, one of 'those really useful men who used to be despised in Europe', is the hero of the play. Oziambo announces him the leader of the colony: 'Love of fellow man, courage, integrity, these are his obligations. There are none more sacred . . . The idle man is the greatest scourge of any society, and will forever be banished from ours.' The abbot Smarmy is thereby thwarted in his machinations to place himself at the head of the local people, turning the natives into a new Third Estate, and he and the other *émigrés* are condemned to a life of having to earn their keep. The play ends with a rousing song castigating 'the hideous hydra of despotism' and promising that 'our strong arms may set free the universe', sung to the tune of the 'Marseillaise' first heard in Paris only a few months earlier.

The Convention's sense that it was at the heart of a struggle of international significance was personified by the presence, as elected deputies, of two foreign revolutionaries, Tom Paine, and Anacharsis Cloots. Joseph Priestley was elected in two departments, but declined to take his seat. They were three of eighteen foreigners 'who in various countries have brought reason to its present maturity' who had already been made honorary French citizens—among the others were heroes of the American Revolution and Republic (James Madison, Alexander Hamilton, George Washington), British and European radicals (William Wilberforce, Jeremy Bentham, Thaddeus Kosciuszko) and the German and Swiss educators Campe and Pestalozzi:

those men who, through their writings and through their courage, have served the cause of liberty and prepared the emancipation of peoples, cannot be seen as foreigners by a nation that has been made free by their knowledge and their courage.[24]

Despite the considerable consensus in the Convention, in the autumn and winter of 1792–3 it tended to divide into three roughly equal voting blocs. Paris was dominated by Jacobins (20 of its 24 deputies) of the renown of Robespierre, Danton, Desmoulins, and Marat, which resulted in a tendency to see Jacobins and Paris as synonymous. However, like their antagonists, the 'Girondins', they were above all a nationwide political tendency. In social and political terms, Jacobins were somewhat closer to the popular movement, and their habit of sitting together on the upper left-hand benches in the Convention quickly earned them the epithet of 'Mountain' and an image of uncompromising republicanism. The label 'Girondins' denoted men closer in sympathy to the upper bourgeoisie of Bordeaux, capital of the Gironde, whence the deputies Vergniaud, Guadet and Gensonné had been elected, and whose colonial and slave trade had been unsettled by revolution and war. A large group of uncommitted deputies, dubbed the 'Plain' or 'Marsh', and including Sieyès and Grégoire, swung their support behind the two groups depending on the issue.

From the outset, political practice and attitudes on a number of critical issues divided the deputies. The first of these issues was the trial of the king. Louis himself was dignified and clear during his trial. Again and again, as his accusers went over the list of crises faced by the Revolution since 1789, such as the killings on the Champ de Mars on 17 July 1791, Louis simply replied: 'What happened on July 17th can have nothing to do with me.' While the deputies present during the king's trial agreed on his guilt, Girondins were particularly likely to argue that his fate should be decided by referendum, that he should not be sentenced to death or that he should be reprieved. Specific provisions of the Constitution of 1791 seemed to support their legalistic position:

The king's person is inviolable and sacred; his sole title is *king of the French*. . . .

If the King places himself at the head of an army and directs the forces thereof against the nation, or if he does not, by formal statement, oppose any undertaking carried out in his name, he shall be deemed to have abdicated the throne. . . .

After express or legal abdication, the King shall be classed as a citizen, and as such he may be accused and tried for acts subsequent to his abdication.[25]

In contrast, the great strength of the Jacobin argument during this dramatic and eloquent debate was that to spare Louis would be to admit his special nature: was not Louis Capet a citizen guilty of treason? Robespierre, Marat, and Saint-Just argued that, as an outlaw, he should simply be summarily executed: 'the people' had already judged him. However, most Jacobins argued for a full trial: the king's flight had effectively nullified any constitutional protection and now he should be tried like any other alleged traitor. On 16–17 January 361 deputies voted for death; 360 voted instead for other punishments. The Jacobins then successfully defeated the Girondins' final appeal for clemency, by 380 votes to 310. Many people agreed with the Jacobins: from Bordeaux, capital of the Gironde itself, the Citizenesses' Society of the Friends of Liberty accused Louis of

striking down his enemies in secret, with the same gold that he had from his fortune, protecting factious priests, who sowed trouble and discord in the interior . . . he who turns his army against the fatherland! . . . he who orders the carnage of his subjects! . . . and was reclusion or banishment enough for the one who made so much blood flow? . . . No: his head had to fall; Representatives, you have fulfilled the wish of the Republic, you have been just . . .[26]

Louis went to the scaffold on 21 January, evidently with courage. He strode to the edge of the platform and attempted to silence a drum-roll so he could address the crowd. We do not know how effectively he did so, but one account recalls him stating:

I die perfectly innocent of the so-called crimes of which I was accused. I pardon those who are the cause of my misfortunes. Indeed, I hope that the shedding of my blood will contribute to the happiness of France . . .[27]

The Girondins were further embarrassed by the deterioration of a war they, as followers of Brissot, had so vehemently urged in 1792. The 'nation in arms' had occupied the Low Countries, the Rhineland, and Savoy (which agreed to become a department of France) by Christmas, but the execution of Louis on 21 January 1793 expanded the war to include Britain and Spain and altered the fortunes of battle. A series of defeats in the southeast, southwest, and northeast resulted in foreign forces crossing well into France in March. Suspicions that the Girondins were incapable of leading the Republic through military crisis seemed proven by the defection on 5 April of a leading Girondin sympathizer, General Dumouriez, who had been the hero of the first great victories at Valmy and Jemappes.

The deteriorating military situation called for desperate measures. In border areas in particular, the Convention's appeal for volunteers was accompanied by the local organization of battalions of volunteers outfitted by local communities. The records of the formation of these battalions are eloquent testimony to the revolutionary change wrought in political culture. While principles of popular sovereignty were never applied in the professional army, the local units of volunteers chose their own officers of all levels in ceremonies of exuberant patriotism. Their revolutionary zeal was not always a substitute for military training. In the south of the department of the Aude, from where the fighting with the Spanish army around Perpignan could be seen and heard, the former seigneur turned 'patriot' Antoine Viguier was unimpressed by the volunteers: 'The officers who have been chosen by their companies know no more about military matters than they do the Koran. The soldiers have no experience, they spend the whole day scouting the river-banks for frogs.'[28] The enthusiasm of the volunteers of 1792–3 was soon to be sorely tested.

Notes

1. *Archives parlementaires*, 21 June 1791, 378–83. Two very different, but equally brilliant, cinematic presentations of the king's flight are Ariane Mnouchkine's 1974 film of *1789*, a Théâtre du Soleil play, and Ettore Scola's *La Nuit de Varennes* (1982).

2. *Archives parlementaires*, 15 July 1791, 326–34. In 1792–3, Barnave wrote the first class-based analysis of the Revolution: see Emanuel Chill (ed. and trans.), *Power, Property and History: Barnave's Introduction to the French Revolution and other Writings* (New York, 1971). On this *journée*, see Rudé, *Crowd in the French Revolution*, ch. 6.

3. *Les Révolutions de Paris*, 16–23 July 1791, 53–4, 60–1, 64–5.

4. *Moniteur universel*, no. 201, 20 July 1791, vol. 10, 170.

5. William Murray, *The Right-Wing Press in the French Revolution, 1789–1792* (London, 1986), 126–8, 289; Thomas F. Sheppard, *Lourmarin in the Eighteenth Century: A Study of a French Village* (Baltimore, 1971), 186.

6. *Moniteur universel*, no. 313, 9 November 1791, vol. 10, 325; Timothy Tackett, 'Conspiracy Obsession in a Time of Revolution: French Elites and the Origins of the Terror', *American Historical Review*, 105 (2000), 691–713. On slavery and the colonies, see the chapters by Carolyn Fick and Pierre Boulle in Frederick Krantz (ed.), *History from Below: Studies in Popular Protest and Popular Ideology in Honour of George Rudé* (Montreal, 1985).

7. *Procès-Verbal (Assemblée législative)*, vol. 7, 355; *Moniteur universel*, no. 143, 23 May 1790, vol. 4, 432.

8. Elizabeth Rapley, ' "Pieuses Contre-Révolutionnaires": The Experience of the Ursulines of Northern France, 1789–1792', *French History*, 2 (1988), 453–73.

9. Elisabeth Roudinesco, *Madness and Revolution: The Lives and Legends of Théroigne de Méricourt*, trans. Martin Thom (London, 1991), 95.

10. Rose, *Making of the 'sans-culottes'*, 106; Antoine de Baecque, *The Body Politic: Corporeal Metaphor in Revolutionary France, 1770–1800* (Stanford, Calif., 1997). The origins of the vituperative attacks on Marie-Antoinette are studied by Lynn Hunt, *The Family Romance of the French Revolution* (London, 1992); Chantal Thomas, *The Wicked Queen: The Origins of the Myth of Marie-Antoinette*, trans. Julie Rose (New York, 2000); and Thomas E. Kaiser, 'Who's Afraid of Marie-Antoinette? Diplomacy, Austrophobia and the Queen', *French History*, 14 (2000), 241–71.

11. Murray, *Right-Wing Press*, chs. 11–12; Kennedy, *Cultural History*, chs. 5, 9–10; Mason, *Singing the French Revolution*.

12. *Moniteur universel*, no. 194, 12 July 1792, vol. 13, 108.

13. *Moniteur universel*, no. 216, 3 August 1792, vol. 13, 305–6.

14. Rudé, *Crowd in the French Revolution*, ch. 7.

15. *Moniteur universel*, no. 241, 23 August 1792, vol. 13, 540.

16. Colin Lucas, 'The Crowd and Politics between *Ancien Régime* and Revolution in France', *Journal of Modern History*, 60 (1988), 438; M. J. Sydenham, *The French Revolution* (New York, 1966), 122.

17. Restif de la Bretonne, *Les Nuits de Paris*, part XVI (Paris, 1794).

18. Schama, *Citizens*, 637; Norman Hampson, *Prelude to Terror: The Constituent Assembly and the Failure of Consensus, 1789–1791* (Oxford, 1988); François Furet, *The French Revolution 1774–1884* (Oxford, 1992).

19. In different ways, the potency of the counter-revolution is stressed in D. M. G. Sutherland, *France 1789–1815: Revolution and Counterrevolution* (London, 1985), chs. 4–6; Murray, *Right-Wing Press*, chs. 9, 12. See, too, the discussion by Mona Ozouf, 'War and Terror in French Revolutionary Discourse (1793–1794)', *Journal of Modern History*, 56 (1984), 579–97.

20. Markoff, *Abolition of Feudalism*, 426, 497–8, ch. 8; Jones, *Peasantry*, 70–4; Anatoli Ado, *Paysans en Révolution* (Paris, 1996), ch. 2. According to Markoff, the August decree effectively ended anti-seigneurial protest. On the June decree, see C. J. Mitchell, *The French Legislative Assembly of 1791* (Leiden, 1989), ch. 5.

21. Mason, *Singing the French Revolution*, 93–103.

22. Ronald Schechter, 'Translating the "Marseillaise": Biblical Republicanism and the Emancipation of Jews in Revolutionary France', *Past & Present*, 143 (1994), 128–55.

23. We know virtually nothing about Gamas except that he wrote three other plays around this time. The text was published by the citizeness Toubon in 1794. The play has been edited and translated by Patricia Clancy, *The First 'Australian' Play: Les Emigrés aux terres australes (1792) by Citizen Gamas* (Melbourne, 1984).

24. *Moniteur universel*, no. 241, 23 August 1792, vol. 13, 540–1. There were no political parties in the modern sense during the Revolution, and the identification of political and social tendencies within the Convention has long aroused debate: see Alison Patrick, *The Men of the First French Republic: Political Alignments in the National Convention of 1792* (Baltimore, 1972); Michael Sydenham, *The Girondins* (London, 1961); and the forum in *French Historical Studies*, 15 (1988), 506–48.

25. *Moniteur universel*, no. 218, 6 August 1791, vol. 9, 312–20, no. 348, 13 December 1792, vol. 14, 720–1. On the king's trial, see Patrick, *Men of the First French Republic*, chs. 3–4; David Jordan, *The King's Trial: The French Revolution versus Louis XVI* (Berkeley, Calif., 1979); Michael Walzer (ed.), *Regicide and Revolution: Speeches at the Trial of Louis XVI* (Cambridge, 1974).

26. Archives départementales de la Gironde. On provincial women's clubs, see Suzanne Desan, ' "Constitutional Amazons": Jacobin Women's Clubs in the French Revolution', in Ragan and Williams (eds.), *Re-creating Authority*.

27. John Hardman, *Louis XVI* (New Haven, 1993), 232. Louis is described in this fine and sympathetic biography as 'fairly intelligent and fairly hard-working': 234.

28. McPhee, *Revolution and Environment*, 97.

6

The Revolution in the Balance, 1793

Before August 1792 the Girondins had been able to blame Louis for military reverses; whom could they accuse now? They rounded on a new scapegoat, the *sans-culottes* and their Jacobin allies, whom they attacked as 'anarchists' and 'levellers'. Towards the end of the year, the brilliant Girondin journalist and deputy Antoine-Joseph Gorsas used a parody of the 'Marseillaise' as a 'Christmas carol' attacking the Jacobins:

> Forward children of anarchy,
> The shameful day is upon us . . .
> The people blinded by rage,
> Raise the bloody knife.
> In this time of horror and crimes,
> To serve iniquitous designs,
> They count neither their infamies,
> Nor the number of their prey.

For Vergniaud, 'equality for man as a social being consists solely in the equality of his legal rights'; and Brissot issued an *Appel à tous les républicains de France* in October warning against 'the hydra of anarchy', castigating Jacobins as 'disorganizers who wish to level everything: property, leisure, the price of provisions, the various services to be rendered to society'.

While Brissot exaggerated the 'levelling' impulses of the Jacobins, they were certainly more flexible in their willingness to temporarily control the economy, particularly the price of foodstuffs. In late 1792 Robespierre had responded to food-rioting in the department of the Eure-et-Loire by insisting that 'The most fundamental of all rights is the right of existence. The most fundamental law of society is, therefore, that which guarantees the means of existence to every person; every other law is subordinate to this.' Similarly, his young ally, Louis-Antoine de Saint-Just, elected to the Convention at age 25 from the northern frontier department of the Aisne, asserted that 'In a single instant you can give the French people a real homeland, by halting the ravages of inflation, assuring the supply of food, and intimately linking their welfare and their freedom.'[1]

By early 1793, Girondin rhetoric sounded increasingly hollow in the context of external military crisis, and most of the deputies of the 'Plain' swung behind the Jacobins' emergency proposals. In particular, the Convention responded to the crisis by ordering a levy of 300,000 conscripts in March. This levy was easily implemented only in the southeast and east—two frontier regions—and around Paris. In the west it provoked massive armed rebellion and civil war, known, like the region itself, as 'the Vendée' (see Map 5). Erupting as it did at a desperate time for the young Republic, and resulting in terrible loss of life, the insurrection left permanent scars on French society and politics. It continues to divide historians: for some the repression of the rebellion amounts to 'genocide', to others it was a regrettable but necessary response to a 'stab in the back' at the moment of the Revolution's greatest crisis.

The origins of the rebellion are to be found in the region's distinctive characteristics and the specific impact the Revolution had had there since 1789. The departments south of the Loire where violence flared were in a region of *bocage* (scattered farms separated by high hedgerows), poor communications with the outside, and a mix of subsistence farming and cattle raising, with textile production based in small village centres (*bourgs*). The large holdings of nobles and religious orders were rented on secure leases to relatively prosperous farmers through bourgeois middlemen. The exactions of seigneurs and the state before 1789 had been comparatively light. A numerous, locally recruited and active clergy played a pivotal social role, with the wealth to do so: as in other dioceses of the west, most priests directly collected the tithe rather than being allotted a *portion congrue* by the cathedral. For the majority of people who lived on scattered farms and hamlets, Sunday mass was the occasion when, on coming to the *bourg*, the community felt its parochial identity, made decisions, and heard news conveyed by the priest.

The *cahiers* of the region expressed many of the hopes of rural people elsewhere, calling for an end to privilege and for a sharing of political power. Only in their lack of criticism of the Church were the *cahiers* unusual. The Revolution brought the peasants of the Vendée no obvious benefits. Heavier state taxes were collected more rigorously by local bourgeois who also monopolized new offices and municipal councils, and bought up church lands in 1791: in the district of Cholet, nobles bought 23.5 per cent of such land, bourgeois 56.3 per cent, but peasants only 9.3 per cent. The collapse of demand for textiles, following the free trade treaty with England in 1786 and the economic difficulties of the revolutionary period, alienated textile workers. Similarly, by assuming the distinctive long-term tenancies of the west to be only one more form of rental agreement, revolutionary governments made the rural middle class more vulnerable rather than recognizing them as *de facto* landowners.

Priests in the west were hostile to the abolition of the tithe and the imposition of an urban, civic concept of priesthood. They were supported by their communities, disappointed with the outcomes of the Revolution and irritated by the zealous enforcement of church reform by bourgeois officials. In Angers, for example, the new bourgeois administrators had long been characterized by their hostility to clerical wealth and values. In the district of La Roche-sur-Yon, too, administrators had few hesitations about closing nineteen parish churches (out of a total of fifty-two) deemed to be surplus according to the provisions of the Civil Constitution of the Clergy. All too rare was the official at Vitré (department of Deux-Sèvres) who, while believing that 'unfortunately, fanaticism is deep-rooted in this district', advised that 'we must not confront it directly [for fear of] shedding too much blood. Let us educate, let us be persuasive and we will bring everyone round.'[2]

The rural community responded to these accumulating grievances in 1790–2 by humiliating constitutional clergy elected by 'active' citizens, by boycotting local and national elections, and by repeated instances of hostility to local office-holders. More than anything else, the conscription decree focused their hatreds, for the bourgeois officials who enforced it were exempt from the ballot. Whereas the republicans or 'blues' were largely bourgeois, artisans, and shop-keepers, the rebels represented a cross-section of rural society. Women played a vital role in the rebellion, as intermediaries between ecclesiastical and secular communities and in sustaining households during the fighting. Republicans dismissed the rebels as superstitious and ignorant peasants under the sway of 'fanatical' priests. In turn, the slogans of the insurgents expressed support for the 'good priests' as the essence of a threatened way of life, and hatred for bourgeois:

> You'll perish in your towns
> Cursed *patauds* (bourgeois patriots)
> Just like caterpillars
> Your feet in the air.[3]

Accordingly, the first targets were local officials, who were assaulted and humiliated, and small urban centres such as Machecoul, where about 500 republicans were tortured and killed in March.

The Vendée was not initially counter-revolutionary so much as anti-revolutionary: the Revolution, so welcomed at the outset, had brought nothing but trouble. The later entry of nobles and refractory clergy gave it a counter-revolutionary hue, but most peasants were unwilling to form an army to march on Paris or to recommence paying dues and tithes. The terrain suited guerrilla-type ambushes and retreat, and exacerbated a vicious cycle of killing and reprisals by both sides convinced of the treachery of the other. For the republican troops, the rebels were superstitious and cruel, manipulated in their ignorance by malevolent priests and nobles. For the rebels, the extent of the reprisals—which some historians continue to describe, quite incorrectly, as 'genocide'—reinforced a bloody image of Paris which was to be widely held in many rural areas for the next century.

Ultimately, the civil war was to claim perhaps as many as 200,000 lives on each side, as many as the external wars of 1793–4. The bitterness of the fighting at a time of national military crisis encouraged sweeping repression; when General Westermann reported back to the Convention in December 1793 that 'the Vendée is no more', he admitted that 'we did not take any prisoners: it would have been necessary to give them the bread of liberty, and pity is not revolutionary'. Between December and May 1794, after the insurrection had been crushed, General Turreau's 'infernal columns' conducted a 'scorched-earth' revenge on 773 communes declared outside the law. To the Minister of War he reported that all rebels and suspected rebels of all ages and both sexes would be bayoneted; 'all villages, farms, woods, heathlands, generally anything that will burn, will be set on fire'. It has been estimated that some 117,000 people (15 per cent of the population) died in these communities.[4]

In La Rochelle, on the southern edge of the Vendée, the Revolution had also brought uncertainty and economic difficulty; here, however, frustration was expressed in a very different way. La Rochelle had long lived on its privileged trading relationship with St-Domingue, its commerce with northern Europe and the coast, the sale of African slaves, and its export of salt, wine, and wheat. The war was a disaster for the slave trade: from twenty-two slave expeditions in 1786, the number fell to two in 1792. The sugar refineries closed with the collapse of colonial trade. By June 1792, five of the wealthiest merchants were bankrupt, including Daniel Garesché, the mayor.

Despite these vicissitudes, La Rochelle was staunchly pro-revolutionary, especially its Protestant elite. On 16 January 1793 seven boys and eight girls aged about 13 years appeared before the municipal council of La Rochelle to present clothing for soldiers which they had bought by pooling their savings. One of them, Nanine Weis, from one of the wealthy Protestant families of the town, made this statement on their behalf:

Citizen magistrates, you see before you a little society of young patriots, often brought together by the need our age has of fun, under the auspices of the friendship which unites our parents. Love of the homeland is already growing in our young hearts and we were worried to learn that the brave volunteers from our department who have leapt to our defense lack some of the necessities of their equipment. We took up a collection among ourselves, using our modest savings; we don't have much to offer. Our efforts have so far only been able to extend to the purchase of 26 pairs of shoes and 29 pairs of socks, that we ask you to send to our generous compatriots on the frontiers. We will not stop offering prayers to Heaven for the success of our arms against the enemies of our Republic.[5]

A fortnight later, following the execution of Louis XVI, France and England were at war. The coastal trade, always more important than the slave and colonial trade, now went into decline. The English naval blockade spelt the ruin of Protestant families whose wealth had been based on overseas trade, particularly in slaves and colonial produce. Among them were the Weis family, who left for Paris having lost three-quarters of their wealth.

When Rochelais explained their misfortunes, non-juring priests were the most obvious scapegoats, just as in Lille in April 1792 and Paris in September. They not only personified the difficulties faced by the Revolution but, at least for some of the men of the city, it seems as though they were also blamed for sexual frustrations: men in a crowd of 400 which smashed furniture in monasteries and convents in May 1792 on the pretext of looking for non-jurors were heard to shout 'We'd rather smash chairs and windows than our wives' arms and legs, we haven't had our pleasure for four months, it's the devil we have at home.' This suggests that non-juring clergy had counselled women to deny sex to patriot husbands. By May 1792, of course, France was at war, and the non-juring clergy were on the run.

By the time rebellion erupted in the Vendée, the town was in a state of hunger, despair, and resentment. The Vendéan rebels were hated as the personification of old Catholic France and Europe which, by repudiating the Revolution, had brought on sharp misery and the crushing of hopes. A band of 2,000 volunteers sent to the Vendée on 19 March was quickly routed; on their return to La Rochelle, the wounded and humiliated remnants found an outlet for their rage. On the morning of the 21st, four refractory priests were to be moved for their own safety from the city prison to an offshore prison. In the words of the justice of the peace:

The people, assembled in very large numbers, were opposed to their embarcation near the Tour de la Chaine—the effervescence became much greater when suddenly arrived a large number of citizens of this town wounded during the unfortunate expedition to the Vendée on the 19th of this month.

The priests were surrounded and stabbed to death. Then, reported the justice of the peace, 'the people seized the bodies and after having decapitated them began to parade them through various parts of the town'. This was a sanitized summary of the extraordinary acts of mutilation committed on the bodies, repeated the next afternoon when two other priests had the misfortune to arrive in La Rochelle from the Île-de-Ré. The bodies were literally torn to pieces; genitals were brandished on the end of sticks.

Yet another different response to the crisis of spring 1793 occurred at the farthest extremity from Paris, in the small Pyrenean town of St-Laurent-de-Cerdans. Here the Revolution, initially welcomed by an impoverished majority as promising the end of privilege, had quickly soured for Laurentins with the increased difficulties of legal and illegal trade across the Pyrenees and, especially, with ecclesiastical reforms perceived as an urban, secular outrage against orthodox Catholicism. On 17 April 1793 Laurentins welcomed royal Spanish troops into their village and the local National Guard fired on retreating French volunteers. The Spanish troops were welcomed with a song in Catalan asking them for 'good laws', code for the Catholic Church they had known:

> La bonica mozardalla es la dels fusillers bermels,
> Ni ha pas en tot França de comparables a els,
> Tots volem ser ab vosaltres,
> Mentres nos dongueu bonas leys.

> What fine soldiers are these red-coated fusiliers!
> There are none in all of France which are their equals.
> We all want to join with you,
> Provided you give us good laws.

Several hundred men fought alongside Spanish troops for a year until Jacobin armies retook the upper reaches of the Vallespir in May 1794.[6]

An even more severe body blow to the Republic was the anti-Jacobin insurrection of April in Corsica, important to the Revolution because of Paoli's popularity and the island's long republican tradition. As General-in-Chief of the island, Paoli had had a liberal democratic constitution adopted at the Consulte Generale di Corti in 1755. Then, in 1768, the French troops of Louis XV had invaded the island and ended self-rule. Not surprisingly, from 1789 Paoli was celebrated as a hero by the National Assembly. With the overthrow of the monarchy and the defeat of Federalism in mid-1793, however, Paoli became increasingly concerned at the centralizing imperatives of the National Convention. Corsican society effectively divided between supporters of Paoli and of the Bonaparte clan, the latter forced to flee to the mainland and denounced by the Corsican Assembly as 'traitors and enemies to the fatherland, condemned to perpetual execration and infamy'.[7]

The civil war in the Vendée, military losses on the frontiers, and the increasingly desperate rhetoric of the Girondins pushed the Plain into supporting Jacobin proposals for emergency wartime measures. Between March and May 1793 the Convention placed executive powers in a Committee of Public Safety and policing powers in a Committee of General Security, and acted to supervise the army through 'deputies on mission'. It passed decrees declaring *émigrés* 'civilly dead', providing for public relief and placing controls on grain and bread prices.

The Girondins were stung by their loss of power in the Convention and the increasing attacks on them by the *sans-culottes*. They countered by seeking to impeach 'the people's friend' Marat, by threatening to move the capital to Bourges, and by attacking the municipal government of Paris, the Paris Commune. 'I tell you in the name of France', Isnard warned the *sans-culottes*, 'that if these perpetually recurring insurrections ever lead to harm to the parliament chosen by the nation, Paris will be annihilated, and men will search the banks of the Seine in vain for traces of the city'. Such threats, in the context of military crisis and rapid inflation, sounded eerily like the Duke of Brunswick's manifesto of July 1792, and outraged Parisian working people. Market-women began the call for a purge of such unrevolutionary 'people's mandatories': by mid-April thirty-five sections had agreed on a list of Girondins to be expelled from the Convention and established a Central Revolutionary Committee. The Paris Commune ordered the formation of a paid militia of 20,000 *sans-culottes* which surrounded the Convention at the end of May and compelled the reluctant deputies to meet its wishes. Twenty-nine Girondin deputies were arrested.[8]

Initially the Convention hesitated: was not the purging of the Convention an inexcusable affront to the principle of national sovereignty? However, it then acted to meet the crisis of a nation in danger of internal collapse and external defeat. In the summer of 1793 the Revolution faced its greatest crisis, which was at the same time military, social, and political. Enemy troops were on French soil in the northeast, southeast, and southwest and, internally, the great revolt in the Vendée absorbed a major part of the Republic's army. These threats were aggravated by the hostile response of sixty departmental administrations to the purge of the Girondins. The largest provincial cities fell to a coalition of conservative republicans and royalists, and on 29 August the key Mediterranean naval arsenal of Toulon was handed over by its officers to the English navy blockading the coast.

These so-called 'Federalist' revolts were united only by the coincidence of their timing. However, they all drew on strong regional traditions. The 'Federalist' revolt was particularly powerful in the large cities of the south (Bordeaux, Lyons, Toulouse, and Marseilles) and in Normandy (centred on Caen). Above all, at the heart of Federalism was the anger of the upper bourgeoisie, especially those in commercial towns, at the radical direction the Revolution had taken; the purging of their elected representatives was the last straw. The immediate targets of the revolts were local Jacobins and militants, reflecting the class-based nature of local divisions. In Toulon the Comité Général which seized power included 16 merchants, 8 lawyers, 6 *rentiers*, 11 naval officers and navy engineers, 3 officials, 3 priests, and 3 artisans. It insisted that 'We want to enjoy our goods, our property, the fruits of our toil and industry in peace . . . Yet we see them incessantly exposed to threats from those who have nothing themselves.' In Lyons, too, the Jacobin–Girondin struggle was linked to the political and workplace militancy of silk-weavers, expressed through Jacobin clubs, in the years since 1789. Nowhere, however, could 'Federalists' muster a sufficiently powerful military force to pose a serious threat to national armies.[9]

The threat reached the heart of the Convention on 13 July when Charlotte Corday assassinated Marat. Corday, from the Federalist stronghold of Caen, was a Girondin supporter for whom Marat was the personification of the Revolution's excesses. She was tried on the 17th and executed the same day. With Le Peletier, murdered by a royalist the night the Convention voted the death of Louis, and Joseph Chalier, the Jacobin leader in Lyons killed by Federalists on 17 July, Marat formed a triumvirate of revolutionary martyrs. Economically, the plight of wage-earners in particular continued to deteriorate: by August purchasing power of the *assignat* had fallen to 22 per cent of its face value, from 36 per cent in June. By then the Revolution, indeed France itself, was in danger of falling apart.

The prime objective of the Jacobin Committee of Public Safety elected by the Convention on 27 July was to implement the laws and controls necessary to strike 'Terror' into the hearts of counter-revolutionaries. The Convention acquiesced in draconian measures—such as surveillance committees, preventive detention and controls on civil liberties—necessary to secure the Republic to a point where the democratic, libertarian Constitution of June 1793 could be implemented. The Constitution, largely the work of Robespierre, was remarkable for its guarantees of social rights and popular control over an assembly elected by direct, universal male suffrage:

Article 21. Public aid is a sacred debt. Society owes subsistence to unfortunate citizens, either by obtaining work for them, or by providing means of existence to those who are unable to work.

Article 22. Instruction is the need of all men. Society must further the progress of public reason with all its power, and make instruction available to all citizens. . . .

Article 35. When the government violates the rights of the people, insurrection is the most sacred of rights and the most indispensable of duties for the people and for each portion of the people.[10]

The results of a referendum on its acceptance (officially 1.8 million 'yes' votes to 11,600 against) were announced at the 'Fête de l'Unité' on 10 August, the first anniversary of the overthrow of the monarchy. The final figure for 'yes' votes was probably closer to two million of the approximately six million eligible males. Participation rates ranged from fewer than 10 per cent in much of Brittany to 40–50 per cent along the Rhine and parts of the Massif Central. In some areas the voting was a festival: at St-Nicolas-de-la-Grave (department of Haute-Garonne) some of those present were moved by a speech into 'transports of the most sublime enthusiasm . . . their eyes swimming with tears of joy, threw themselves into each others' arms to share a fraternal kiss'. At Lamballe (Côtes-du-Nord), similarly, 'women swarmed into the assembly to offer their assent to the Constitution'.[11] Elsewhere, 343 women voted at Laon and 175 women and 163 children at Pontoise. Such was the degree of individual freedom guaranteed in the constitution, however, that it was suspended until the peace, lest counter-revolutionaries abuse its freedoms.

By mid-1793, the Republic was at war with most of Europe, and foreign troops were on its soil in the southwest, southeast and northeast. The military challenge was met by an extraordinary mobilization of the nation's resources and repression of opponents. Essential to this mobilization was the creation by the Jacobin government of a rural-urban alliance by a mixture of intimidation, force, and policies aimed both to meet popular grievances and to place the entire country on a war footing.

The Convention had to overcome the odds of fighting on numerous fronts at a time of internal division and civil war, and a good deal of despair: perhaps 35,000 soldiers (6 per cent of the total) had deserted in the first half of 1793, and many others reacted to deficiencies in supplies by theft of local produce. During the winter of 1793 a soldier wrote from the southeast that his battalion 'is in the greatest need, just like real *sans-culottes*, since from first to last we are without shoes, tormented by scabies, and eaten by vermin'. A nearby battalion reported that it was surviving by eating roots.[12]

Desertion was cut to a minimum in the year 1793–4 as the result of a mixture of coercion, propaganda, and the effectiveness of the Jacobin Committee of Public Safety and its officials in supplying an army of nearly one million men. Sustaining the energies of the Convention and its committees was the demand of the *sans-culottes* that only total mobilization of rich and poor alike could save the Republic: on 23 August all single males of 18–25 years were conscripted by a *levée en masse*:

The young men will go forth to fight; married men will forge weapons and transport provisions; the women will make tents and uniforms; the old men will be carried to public places to rouse the warriors' courage, to preach hatred for kings and to uphold the unity of the Republic.[13]

National Guard units were charged with hunting down those who evaded conscription or deserted. Conscripts from non-French-speaking regions were given basic instruction in French and scattered through the army to reduce the temptation of collective flight; mass propaganda, such as Hébert's earthy, obscene paper *Le Père Duchesne*, was distributed, and 'deputies on mission' from the Convention guaranteed swift retribution to hesitant officers and unwilling rank-and-file. The building of a new spirit in the army was not the result of coercion alone: soldiers' letters home are also full of remarks about revolutionary zeal and their commitment to the *patrie*. The volunteer Pierre Cohin wrote to his family from the Armée du Nord:

The war which we are fighting is not a war between king and king or nation and nation. It is the war of liberty against despotism. There can be no doubt that we shall be victorious. A nation that is just and free is invincible.

The political culture of the Republic implied new relationships with authority. The creation of mass republican armies, with 'line' and volunteer units now fused, had engendered a new military culture which was a microcosm of the 'regenerated' society the Convention anticipated.[14]

The 'Law of Suspects' (17 September) was designed to expose the unpatriotic to detention or to intimidate them into inaction. The arrest of 'suspects' by surveillance committees was directed at those who, by word, action or status, were associated with the *ancien régime*. In Rouen 29 per cent of the 1,158 suspects arrested were nobles, 19 per cent clergy, and 7.5 per cent former office-holders; such people were arrested because of who they were, coupled with suspicions of *incivisme*. They were not the only ones arrested: bourgeois were 16.8 per cent of 'suspects' and working people 27 per cent. While many of these commoners had worked for the *ancien régime*, those arrested were also charged with anti-revolutionary words and acts; among shopkeepers, such acts often concerned speculation and stockpiling of goods. Significantly, 39.4 per cent of all 'suspects' were women, particularly among the nobility and clergy, reflecting the tendency for males in these groups to emigrate, leaving women as the focus of suspicion because of their family name and support for non-jurors.[15]

These months were the pinnacle of popular involvement in the Revolution, and of popular opposition to it. Ever since 1789 the symbolic representation of liberty, then of the Republic itself, had been a female figure, probably because the classical virtues and qualities are female in French and in unconscious imitation of the representation of the Catholic virtues by Mary. Late in 1793 the goddess of the Republic, even the Republic itself, came to be referred to derisively by opponents as 'Marianne', a common peasant name that denoted 'of the people'. As had been the case with the epithet *sans-culottes*, republicans then adopted the name Marianne with pride. On 14 November 1793 an official reported from Narbonne:

The churches, with the exception of two, have been done away with and this reform has made only a few zealous women complain. They persist in refusing to believe in the God that the constitutional priests have brought down to us. They are particularly amusing to see when they meet and inquire after news of the Revolution. They adopt an elegiac tone and contort their eyes and lips in a pious grimace: How is *Marianno*—Ah, she's not well, she won't last long—or—she's getting better, she's convalescent.[16]

Many rural communities and urban neighbourhoods used a rich variety of strategies to sidestep or openly oppose the demands of central government and its local agents. Resistance to the exactions of the revolutionary government was manifested through the non-payment of taxes, the avoidance of the *maximum* levied on prices of essential consumer items and wages, and an unwillingness to use *assignats*. However, political opposition at a time of war implied the threat of capital punishment for treachery. In Nantes, Carrier was supported by furious and vengeful local republicans when he ordered the mass drowning of perhaps 1,800 Vendéan rebels, including priests.

As in the Vendée, the repression of the Federalist revolts was uncompromising. While many leading Federalists were committed republicans, they were doubly compromised: first, because they had repudiated the Convention's authority at a time of the Republic's gravest military crisis; and, secondly, because the support given them by royalists, nobles and priests tarnished them by association. It was easy for Jacobins in the Convention to paint the Federalists as in league with the armies of old Europe. In Marseilles, 499 of the 975 suspects tried by the Revolutionary Tribunal were found guilty, and 289 were executed; in Lyons, in contrast, 1,880 were condemned by a less punctilious tribunal. Collot d'Herbois, from the Committee of Public Safety, ordered executions by firing squad, to purge the renamed 'Ville Affranchie'. Among those executed was Antoine Lamourette, the constitutional bishop of Lyons who had convinced all parties in the Legislative Assembly to embrace (the *baiser Lamourette*) at a famous session on 7 July during the first military crisis.

In its declaration on revolutionary government of 10 October, the Committee of Public Safety announced that 'The provisional government of France is revolutionary until the peace'; all government bodies and the army were now placed under the control of the Committee, which had to report weekly to the Convention. The same month, Marie-Antoinette was followed to the guillotine by 21 Girondin deputies expelled in June, then by Bailly and Barnave.

Among the Girondins executed was the journalist and deputy Gorsas, who had fled the capital on 2 June. He had organized armed insurrection in Normandy, then gone into hiding when it failed; he was arrested when he returned to Paris to visit his mistress. Whereas, from the inception of the Paris Revolutionary Tribunal in March 1793 until September, only 66 of 260 'suspects' had been found guilty of a capital offence, in the final three months of the year this was the fate of 177 of 395 accused. However, until June 1794, most 'suspects' never appeared before the Tribunal and, of those who did, 40 per cent were acquitted. Those who were not faced the finality of premature death and farewells to loved ones. In October Marie-Madeleine Coutelet, who worked at a hemp-spinning mill in Paris, was arrested because of letters found in her room which criticized the Terror's restrictions (Coutelet insisted in vain that they were ironic mockery). Her last letter was to her parents:

Farewell, I embrace you for the last time, I that am the most loving of daughters, the most affectionate of sisters. I find this day the most beautiful given me by the Supreme Being. Live and think of me only to rejoice in the happiness that awaits me. I embrace my friends and am grateful to all those who have been so good as to speak in my defence.

Farewell for the last time, may our children be happy, that is my last wish.

More fortunate was the 26-year-old clerk Jean-Louis Laplane, who fled Marseilles into exile in mid-September 'pursued', in his words, 'by this barbarian horde who then covered France with blood and mourning'.[17]

The mass mobilization of the whole nation required the Convention to take steps to forge a new unity by positive measures as well as by intimidation. On 5–6 September thousands of *sans-culottes*, now at the peak of their power, invaded the National Convention to insist that their 'mandatories' impose radical military and economic measures. The Convention acted to meet the demands of this *journée* or insurrection by decreeing the 'general maximum' of 29 September which pegged the prices of thirty-nine commodities at 1790 levels plus one-third, and set wages at 150 per cent of 1790 levels.

The Convention was also impelled to respond to the waves of rural unrest which had affected two-thirds of all departments since 1789. While advocating the subdivision of large estates, or the 'agrarian law', was made a capital offence in March 1793, Jacobins later took a series of measures designed to win over the rural masses, the indispensable condition for military success. On 14 August 1792 the Legislative Assembly had issued a brief, radical decree directing communes to divide non-forested common land. On 10 June 1793 the Convention replaced this law with one which was even more radical and contentious, one of the most ambitious attempts of the revolutionary government to meet the needs of the rural poor. The legislation required communes to proceed to a division if this was the wish of one-third of adult men; the land was then to be divided on the basis of an equal share to every man, woman, and child. However, the cost of surveyors' fees reduced the use made of this law as a way of resolving an issue which had long divided rural people: would the interests of the rural poor best be secured by dividing common lands or by preserving them? A series of measures pushed the decree of 25 August 1792 further in the direction of the complete abolition of seigneurialism. From 17 July 1793, former seigneurs were left with only those 'rents and charges which are purely on land and non-feudal'. The feudal regime was dead by the middle of 1793, not because successive assemblies had launched a series of ever bolder attacks on the complex accretions of a centuries old social order, but because they had been forced to respond to a series of waves of anti-seigneurial actions from country regions.

The protracted rural revolution against seigneurialism had bonded rural communities together. Now that the feudal regime was dead, internal divisions began to surface within rural society. From the outset of the Revolution, the friction over the anti-seigneurial legislation of 1789 had been embedded in more general conflict over ownership and control of the 'wastelands'. The seigneurial regime had been finally abolished, but it was to take far longer to resolve the associated questions of control of collective economic resources, land-hunger and clearances. Despite the Jacobins' willingness to restrict individual freedoms in the national interest, in the end they had had no more success than their liberal predecessors. In a report written from Lagrasse on 8 December 1793, the Jacobin official Cailhava reported in his characteristically blunt fashion that the district 'was formerly covered in coppices, mostly in green oak; but with the Revolution every individual treated them like the cabbages in his garden'.

Cailhava explained this by the attractions of the high price of charcoal and bark, but also because shepherds habitually took their flocks to the youngest, most succulent plants, felling larger trees for winter feed. One noble 'had the goodness to leave 760 *sétérées* [about 300 hectares] of woods when he emigrated; well, they've been uprooted, destroyed, pillaged, goats graze there every day'. In the district of Narbonne there was a terrible shortage of wood 'because of the disdain the inhabitants show for trees which give only shade'. As for oaks,

war is made on them continually, the bark on their roots being the best tan for the preparation of leather. . . . People are ready to undertake new clearances, and there is much to fear from this thoughtless passion of turning all the land into fields.[18]

The legislators' hesitations about seigneurialism and access to land fuelled rural politics in the years 1792–4, exacerbating divisions caused by the reforms to the Church. The rural revolution had its own rhythms and inner dynamic, generated by the specific nature of the locality. The precise form which rural politics took was a function of perceptions of the benefits and hardships brought by the Revolution, attitudes to the Church, and local social structures. While political attitudes therefore varied across the countryside, underpinning attitudes everywhere was hostility both to the *ancien régime* and to bourgeois concepts of the rights of private property. To calls for the 'agrarian law' in the northeast corresponded anti-bourgeois risings in the west, Brittany and elsewhere. In Neulisse (Loire), armed youths who gathered for the conscription ballot of 1793 conducted their own choice for the fifteen men the commune had to supply: the constitutional priest and fourteen bourgeois 'patriots' who had profited most from the Revolution. In contrast, the distinctive mix of civic virtues which should identify true *sans-culottes* was articulated by Antoine Bonnet, a café-owner and secretary to the surveillance committee in Belley (department of the Ain):

Men with more commonsense than education, virtuous, sensitive, humane; men outraged by the slightest whisper of injustice; intrepid, energetic men who desire the common good, Liberty, Equality or death . . .[19]

Every rural district had its share of ardent Jacobins who read

Parisian and local papers or belonged to Jacobin clubs and popular societies. Cerutti's *La Feuille villageoise*, aimed specifically at a rural audience, sold 8,000–16,000 copies. It is estimated that, because copies of newspapers were commonly passed around or read aloud in rural communities, its audience may have been 250,000 people in 1793. The administration of the Gers subscribed to a copy for each of its 599 communes. Nationally there were perhaps 6,000 Jacobin clubs and popular societies created during the Terror, short-lived though many of them were. Though most common in small towns, in Provence 75–90 per cent of all villages had one, symptomatic of the lively political life of the southeast which also sustained active counter-revolutionaries.

Paris in 1792–4 was the pulsating, tumultuous centre of the Revolution, where huge numbers of civilians and soldiers on the move coexisted uneasily with long-established neighbourhood communities. The chaos of a city at the heart of the Revolution was barely contained by vigorous policing. In such a situation the news spread by 1,000 newspaper street-sellers was embellished by word of mouth, creating a city crackling with a potent mixture of rumour, optimism, and suspicion. The Law of Suspects was designed to quell such insecurity; in its implementation, sections, and their thousands of police, drawn from fortnightly service by all able-bodied men, played the grass-roots role. Lies, personal feuds, and denunciations found a fertile atmosphere, yet the activities of section authorities were self-consciously legal and 'correct'.

In the eighteen months between August 1792 and early 1794, the political participation of Parisian working people reached its zenith. While it is true that only about 10 per cent of men regularly attended section meetings and that many *sans-culottes* militants were bourgeois by occupation, this remains a remarkable level of popular participation at a time of long working days, food queues, and worries about survival. It was reflected in an unprecedented levelling in the social composition of local government: in Paris, for example, one-third of the Commune councillors were from the *menu peuple*, as were four-fifths of the 'revolutionary committees' elected in each of the 48 sections of the city. The *sans-culottes'* political and social goals were also expressed through more than forty popular societies (with some 6,000 members, of whom 86 per cent were artisans and wage-earners), and above all in local section meetings.[20] An analysis of provincial Jacobin Clubs in 1789–91 compared with 1793–5 shows that the number of artisans and shopkeepers had increased from 38.6 to 45 per cent and farmers from 1.1 to 9.6 per cent. The percentage of merchants and businessmen had declined from 12.1 to 8.2, while clergy had declined from 6.7 to 1.6 per cent. Nobles, 0.6 per cent early in the Revolution, had disappeared altogether.

Despite the difficulties faced by administrators in organizing and conscripting an army in the countryside, the successes outweighed the failures: volunteers and conscripts entered the armies in huge numbers, quotas of food and carts were met. The Jacobin Republic of 1793–4 was, however, a demanding regime: the language of patriotism, Jacobinism and citizenship was mixed with one of sacrifice, requisitioning and conscription. It was a regime in which its local representatives refused anything smacking of *ancien régime* pretensions and threatened the recalcitrant. In the words of one southern official: 'The time of ridiculous pretensions has passed . . . The Convention honours and recognizes talents and virtues . . . The tree of the Republic will be shaken and the caterpillars which are gnawing it will fall down.'[21]

The two villages with which this book began were typical of those which sustained the extraordinary war effort of 1793–4. Menucourt was also one of thousands of villages where the years of Revolution passed comparatively peacefully: the reforms of the National Assembly were welcomed and supported, the requisitioning of men and supplies during the years of war was reluctantly accepted; the news of revolution and Terror reached the village quickly, but Parisian political divisions were not reflected there and no one was guillotined. The only local political incident of consequence occurred on 20 September 1792. On the very day that revolutionary armies were fighting for their first decisive victory, at Valmy in eastern France, and the National Convention was convening in Paris, Prosper Vacher, the gardener at the chateau, responded to the greeting of 'Vive la Nation!' proffered by a group of fifty 'Volontaires de Mort' by retorting 'Vive le Roi!' (It says something of the tenor of village life, however, that Vacher was soon released once he had apologized.) Menucourt was small and just distant enough to avoid the most divisive episodes of the Revolution. Some of the responsibility for this rests with the priest, the Abbé Thomas Duboscq, who had only arrived in Menu-court in February 1789, aged 39, but became a source of stability as a constitutional priest (like 70 per cent of the priests of the department) and an elected public official. In January 1794 he renounced his priestly status; the following month his former parishioners sang patriotic songs he had written for the planting of a liberty tree.

In Gabian, the revolutionary years were less peaceful than in Menu-court, but the village became renowned for its republicanism. One reason for this was that the abolition of seigneurialism had alleviated a major burden; another was that, unlike most of the priests of the district of Béziers, Pierre Blanc, the *curé* of Gabian, took the oath of loyalty on New Year's Day 1791 and stayed in the village. It seems that anger at Blanc's support for the Revolution may have been one reason for a protracted episode of law-breaking which developed into counter-revolution. In 1791–3 a group of local men and women committed thirty thefts, often with violence, as they lived on the run. They enjoyed taunting the revolutionary officials who attempted to arrest them. After the execution of Louis XVI and the invasion of the south by the Spanish army in 1793 they openly threatened that the latter 'would make the patriots of Gabian dance . . . that they would join the Spaniards to help them make them dance and cut their throats . . . things are going well in the Vendée'. Several of these 'brigands' would be guillotined in 1794. However, the Surveillance Committee of Gabian was confident that it had had no choice at a time of crisis but to arrest them:

We have done the right thing as much as we could; it is sweet and glorious for us to be part of society with the certainty of having public esteem and the confidence of feeling no remorse.[22]

The two villages were fortunate that their priests stayed in the par-ishes. For the role of the Catholic Church in the counter-revolution inevitably called into question the survival of religious structures inside France. Deputies sent to the provinces as 'deputies on mission' to implement the Terror, such as Fouché in the Nièvre and Javogues in the departments around Lyons, took the initiative in closing churches and emptying them of metal for the war effort. There were parts of the country where local people were predisposed to join in this 'dechris-tianization', or even to initiate it; elsewhere, however, it was bitterly resented. The dechristianization campaign coincided and was often identified with the activities of forty-five *armées révolutionnaires* (in all, 30,000–40,000 men) active in fifty-six departments in the autumn of 1793. These bands of *sans-culottes* militants, mixed with men on the run from the law and others who seemed simply to enjoy the rough camaraderie, had as their mission the requisitioning of food for cities and the armies, the payment of taxes, the purging of counter-revolutionaries, the seizure of metals from churches for the war effort, and the maintenance of revolutionary zeal. Their size ranged from small groups of ten to democratically run armies of up to 7,000 in the Aveyron and Lozère and from Paris.[23]

By the late autumn of 1793, the military tide seemed to be turning. Victories in September and October over the English at Hondschoote near Dunkerque and over the Austrians at Wattignies stemmed the tide of invasion in the north. Then the crushing by Westermann's armies of the remnants of the Vendéan rebellion at Savenay on 23 December convinced many that some at least of the Terror's controls could be released.

The response of the government, however, was contradictory. On the one hand, a decree of 6 December affirmed the principle of free-dom of worship: dechristianization was seen as a needless affront to the religious. On the other, a most important law on local govern-ment passed two days earlier asserted the pre-eminence of central government at the expense of popular participation and initiative. Article I of the Law of 4 December insisted that 'the National Conven-tion is the sole centre of government initiative'. For many people, that central government now represented increasingly arbitrary repression, whatever its role in securing military victories. The jour-nalist Louis-Sébastien Mercier, elected like Antoine-Joseph Gorsas from the department of Seine-et-Oise near Paris, was imprisoned in October 1793 for speaking out against the purging of the Girondins. For Mercier, 'God preserve me from ever inhabiting this Mountain, or rather this sulphurous and fetid crater where sit men of blood and mud, stupid and ferocious beasts.'[24] The Jacobins whom he detested, however, did not see themselves as men of 'blood and mud', but rather the people's representatives entrusted with saving the Republic and creating a society worthy of it.

Notes

1. These statements of Girondin and Jacobin attitudes are taken from Mason, *Singing the French Revolution*, 82; Albert Soboul, *A Short History of the French Revolution 1789–1799*, trans. Geoffrey Symcox (Berkeley, Calif., 1977), 86–90; Soboul, *The French Revolution*, 273–82, 303–13.

2. Michel Ragon, *1793: l'insurrection vendéenne et les malentendus de la liberté* (Paris, 1992), 180. Among the major studies of the Vendée are Charles Tilly's pathbreaking *The Vendée* (Cambridge, Mass., 1964); Timothy Tackett, 'The West in France in 1789: The Religious Factor in the Origins of the Counterrevolution', *Journal of Modern History*, 54 (1982), 715–45. A useful review essay is by Claude Petitfrère, 'The Origins of the Civil War in the Vendée', *French History*, 2 (1988), 187–207.

3. Charles Tilly, 'Local Conflicts in the Vendée before the Rebellion of 1793', *French Historical Studies*, 2 (1961), 231.

4. Cobb and Jones (eds.), *Voices of the French Revolution*, 206; Reynald Secher, *Le Génocide franco-français: la Vendée-vengé* (Paris, 1986). Secher's claim of genocide is contested by Hugh Gough, 'Genocide and the Bicentenary: The French Revolution and the Revenge of the Vendée', *Historical Journal*, 30 (1987), 977–88.

5. The account which follows draws on records in the Archives Municipales de La Rochelle and the Archives Départementales de la Charente-Maritime; and Claudy Valin, *Autopsie d'un massacre: les journées des 21 et 22 mars 1793 à La Rochelle* (St-Jean-d'Angély, 1992).

6. Peter McPhee, 'Counter-Revolution in the Pyrenees: Spirituality, Class and Ethnicity in the Haut-Vallespir, 1793–1794', *French History*, 7 (1993), 313–43.

7. Dorothy Carrington, 'The Corsican Constitution of Pascal Paoli', *English Historical Review*, 88 (1973), 481–503; Jean Defranceschi, *La Corse française, 30 novembre 1789–15 juin 1794* (Paris, 1980).

8. Soboul, *French Revolution*, 309. On this *journée*, see Rudé, *Crowd in the French Revolution*, ch. 8; Morris Slavin, *The Making of an Insurrection: Parisian Sections and the Gironde* (Cambridge, Mass., 1986).

9. Malcolm Crook, *Toulon in War and Revolution: From the Ancien Regime to the Restoration, 1750–1820* (Manchester, 1991). Among the many studies of 'Federalism', see Alan Forrest, *Society and Politics in Revolutionary Bordeaux* (Oxford, 1975), ch. 5; Bill Edmonds, *Jacobinism and the Revolt of Lyon, 1789–1793* (Oxford, 1990); Paul Hanson, *Provincial Politics in the French Revolution: Caen and Limoges, 1789–1794* (Baton Rouge, La., 1989).

10. *Archives parlementaires*, 24 June 1793, vol. 67, 143–50.

11. Crook, *Elections in the French Revolution*, ch. 5.

12. Alan Forrest, *Conscripts and Deserters: The Army and French Society during the Revolution and Empire* (Oxford, 1989), 94–5.

13. *Moniteur universel*, 25 August 1793, vol. 17, 478.

14. Forrest, *Soldiers of the French Revolution*, 160; see, too, Bertaud, *Army of the French Revolution*; John A. Lynn, *The Bayonets of the Republic: Motivation and Tactics in the Army of Revolutionary France, 1791–4* (Urbana, Ill., 1984). A taste of *Le Père Duchesne* may be found in Cobb and Jones (eds.), *Voices of the French Revolution*, 184–5, and J. Gilchrist and W. J. Murray, *The Press in the French Revolution* (Melbourne, 1971).

15. Gilles Fleury, 'Analyse informatique du statut socioculturel des 1,578 personnes déclarées suspectes à Rouen en l'an II', in *Autour des mentalités et des pratiques politiques sous la Révolution française* (Paris, 1987), vol. 3, 9–23. The history of the Terror is recounted in Soboul, *French Revolution*, 259–415; Hugh Gough, *The Terror in the French Revolution* (Basingstoke, 1998); and the classic study by R. R. Palmer, *Twelve who Ruled: The Year of the Terror in the French Revolution* (Princeton, 1941).

16. Maurice Agulhon, *Marianne into Battle: Republican Imagery and Symbolism in France, 1789–1880*, trans. Janet Lloyd (Cambridge, 1979), 32–3.

17. Olivier Blanc, *Last Letters: Prisons and Prisoners of the Revolution, 1793–1794*, trans. Alan Sheridan (New York, 1987), 134; Jean-Louis Laplane, *Journal d'un Marseillais 1789–1793* (Marseilles, 1989), 177. Laplane returned in 1795, and died in 1845. The standard statistical survey of the Terror remains Donald Greer, *The Incidence of the Terror during the French Revolution: A Statistical Interpretation* (Cambridge, Mass., 1935).

18. McPhee, *Revolution and Environment*, 134.

19. Giles MacDonogh, *Brillat-Savarin: The Judge and his Stomach* (Chicago, 1992), 103; Jones, *Peasantry*, 225. On rural political tendencies, see David Hunt, 'Peasant Politics in the French Revolution', *Social History*, 9 (1984), 277–99; Jones, *Peasantry*, 206–40; R. B. Rose, 'The "Red Scare" of the 1790s: The French Revolution and the "Agrarian Law"', *Past & Present*, 103 (1984), 113–30.

20. The classic study of the *sans-culottes* is Albert Soboul, *Les Sans-culottes parisiens de l'An II* [1958], sections of which were translated by Gwynne Lewis as *The Parisian Sans-Culottes and the French Revolution, 1793–4* (Oxford, 1964).

21. McPhee, *Revolution and Environment*, 111.

22. Peter McPhee, *Une communauté languedocienne dans l'histoire: Gabian 1760–1960* (Nîmes, 2001), ch. 2.

23. These armies are the subject of one of the classics of French revolutionary historiography, Richard Cobb, *The People's Armies*, trans. Marianne Elliott (New Haven, 1987).

24. Ribeiro, *Fashion in the French Revolution*, 143.

7

The Terror: Revolutionary Defence or Paranoia?

The central purpose of the Terror was to institute the emergency and draconian measures necessary at a time of military crisis. By the end of 1793, the threat of civil war and invasion had at least been countered. However, decrees were passed by the Convention and Committee of Public Safety which went well beyond national defence and revealed a Jacobin vision of a regenerated society worthy of the grandeur of the Enlightenment and the Revolution. This was to be created, for example, by a secular and republican education system and a national programme of social welfare.

Jacobin education policy, particularly the Bouquier Law of 19 December 1793, envisaged a system of free, compulsory education for children of 6–13 years with a curriculum emphasizing patriotism and republican virtues, linguistic uniformity, the simplification of formal French, physical activity, field-study and observation, and a role for schools in civic festivals. Bouquier and his committee had no time for the relaxed attitude to instruction permitted by the parish priests under the *ancien régime*:

Those fathers, mothers, guardians or trustees who have neglected to have their children or wards enrolled, will be punished, on the first occasion, with a fine equal to a quarter of their taxes, and on the second occasion, relieved of their citizen's rights for ten years. . . .

Those young people who, reaching the age of twenty, have not learnt a science, art or trade useful to society, will be deprived for ten years of citizen's rights.[1]

The collapse of primary education provided by the Church under the *ancien régime* accelerated the demand for new reading materials: some

700 new titles were produced across the revolutionary decade, with 41 per cent of them in 1793–4. In the first half of 1794, five issues of 'Collections of Heroic and Civic Acts of French Republicans', the third in 150,000 copies, were sent to schools to replace catechisms. However, the Jacobins never had the time or money to implement their education policy, let alone to train lay teachers to replace priests, and few children attended school during the Terror. In the city of Clermont-Ferrand, for example, only 128 pupils attended school from a population of 20,000 people.

The imperatives of reason and regeneration impelled the Convention to accept proposals for sweeping reform of the systems of measuring weight, distance, and volume. Previous systems were condemned as both bewilderingly irrational and tainted by their origins in the mists of *ancien régime* time. A uniform, decimal system of weights and measures, announced the Convention on 1 August 1793, would be 'one of the greatest benefits that it can offer to all French citizens'. The 'artists' of the Academy of Science would be responsible for the design and exactitude of the measures, while 'Instructions on the new measurements and their relationship to the most widely used old ones will be inserted into elementary arithmetic textbooks which will be created for national schools.'[2] The new measures would be more successful than the Republic's primary schools.

The Constitution of 1793 had made an unprecedented commitment to social rights and the Convention took several measures to extend the rights of children: on 4 July 1793 abandoned children became a state responsibility and on 2 November 1793 children born outside marriage were guaranteed full inheritance rights. As with education policy, Jacobin commitment to eradicating poverty foundered because of the financial demands of the war and lack of time. Saint-Just's draft laws of February–March 1794, which were to use 'suspects'' property to 'indemnify the poor', and the national programme of social welfare announced on 11 May 1794, were only spasmodically implemented.

During the eighteen months from the overthrow of the monarchy in August 1792 until early 1794, a combination of radical Jacobin reforms such as these and popular initiative created an extraordinary force for republican 'regeneration'. This was one of those rare periods in history when huge numbers of people acted as if they had remade the world, a time of 'cultural revolution'. Its inspiration came from images of the virtues of ancient Greece and Rome, in which middle-class Jacobins had been schooled, and from the practice of huge numbers of working people in town and country living through a radical revolution which was under siege. Jacobin policy and popular action coincided through official and spontaneous use of festivals, plays, songs, broadsheets, decoration, clothing, and leisure. There was often, however, a tension between popular symbolic enaction of total change—the physical destruction of religious statuary, paintings, and other signs of the *ancien régime*—and Jacobin concern for what Grégoire called 'vandalism', leading to protective laws in September 1792. This coincided with the creation of departmental and national public libraries, archives and museums late in 1793. In contrast, the Jacobins were not to have the time to implement their grandiose plans for massive revolutionary monuments to supplant those of the *ancien régime*.

The place of the pope and the refractory clergy in the bitter, bloody internal conflict in the west and in the wars being fought on French soil generated an angry response which called Catholicism, and even Christianity, into question. On 5 October the Convention inaugurated a new 'republican' calendar. The proclamation of the Republic on 21 September 1792 was retrospectively dated the first day of the year I of the republican era. The new calendar combined the rationality of decimal measurement (twelve months of 30 days, each with three *décadi* of 10 days) with a total repudiation of the Gregorian calendar. Saints' days and religious festivals were replaced by names drawn from plants, the seasons, work implements, and the virtues (see Appendix). The calendar was adopted across the country, but coexisted uneasily with the older rhythm of Sunday worship and weekly markets.

Popular festivals expressed hostility to the Church by mockery of priests and other counter-revolutionaries. At Dormans, through which Louis had passed to and from Varennes in 1791, the figure of the English prime minister William Pitt was perched backwards on a donkey and paraded through the town. At Tulle, there was a burial of a coffin containing the remains of 'superstition' and crowned with a pair of ass's ears and a missal; saints' statues were flogged. 'Dechristianization' ceremonies in particular had a carnival and cathartic atmosphere, often utilizing the 'promenade des ânes', used in the *ancien régime* to censure violators of community norms of behaviour, but now with someone dressed as a priest sitting backwards on the donkey. Popular initiative, at times encouraged by 'deputies on mission', closed churches and pressured the constitutional clergy to abdicate and marry as a sign of patriotism.

There were wide variations in the number of such abdications, from only twelve in the Alpes-Maritimes and twenty in the Lozère to 498 in the Saône-et-Loire. In the twenty-one departments of the southeast, there were up to 4,500. In all, about 20,000 priests abdicated their calling and 5,000 of them married. In the Allier, only 58 of 426 priests did not abdicate, and nationally perhaps only 150 parishes out of 40,000 were openly celebrating mass in spring 1794. Some clerics may have felt like the former priest Duffay, who wrote to the Convention in January 1794:

I listened to the voice of nature and exchanged my old prayer book for a young republican woman . . . As I have always regarded the state of priesthood as just as useless as a player of skittles, I have used [my church diplomas] for the fire . . . I am labouring in a factory where, despite the exhaustion to which one is subject, I am very happy if my sweat keeps me from poverty.[3]

However, for many other priests—and their parishioners—these were desperate times, in which the institutional forms of religion collapsed almost completely.

The cultural revolution was not expressed through books: the number of books printed in 1794 was only 371, compared with pre-revolutionary figures of over 1,000 annually, and in the two years 1793–4 only thirty-six new novels were published. One exception was the popularity of Rousseau's *Contrat social*, which went through thirteen editions in 1792–5, including a pocket-sized version for soldiers. Similarly, with the increasing restrictions on press freedom after the declaration of war and the overthrow of the monarchy, the number of new Parisian papers fell from 134 in 1792 to 78 in 1793 and 66 in the year II. Instead, 1792–4 was the great age of political songs: one estimate is that the number of new songs climbed from 116 in 1789 to 325 in 1792, 590 in 1793, and 701 in 1794. Most of these were forgettable exhortations to courage or traded on caricatures of royalty:

They have returned to the shadows,
Those great kings, cowardly and licentious,
Infamous drinkers, famous hunters,
Playthings of the vilest harlots. (*repeat*)
Oh you, who are discouraged by nothing!
True lovers of Liberty!
Establish equality
On the debris of slavery.
Republican Frenchmen, conquerors of your rights,
Strike down (*repeat*) all these tyrants, profaners of the law.[4]

Although most plays performed had been written before 1789, their themes and characters were reworked along revolutionary lines. Others continued to draw their humour from mocking the Church: one of the most popular plays in Paris, running from 1792 to 1794, was Louis-Benoît Picard's *Les Visitandines*, featuring two drunken rogues mistaking a convent for an inn. In January 1794, theatres were subsidized if they gave a free performance each week. Painting was also profoundly affected. Jacques-Louis David was instrumental in opening the previously restricted world of the Salon: whereas 63 invited painters and sculptors had exhibited 289 works at the Salon of 1787, 318 of them displayed 883 works at that of 1793. The government gave 442,000 livres in prizes. David threw himself into the war effort, his ribald cartoons lampooning the counter-revolution being only matched for propaganda effect across the channel by Gilroy's depictions of *sans-culottes'* cannibalism, their children happily munching on priests' entrails.

The triumvirate of 'martyrs of the Revolution' (Marat, Chalier, Le Peletier) was accompanied by the celebration of the heroism of François Bara and Joseph-Agricol Viala, 13-year-old boys killed fighting counter-revolution. It was proposed that the great anniversaries of 14 July, 10 August, 21 January and 21 September would ultimately to be supported by thirty-six national festivals, one each *décadi*. The national festivals were elaborate affairs. On 10 August 1793, for example, the anniversary of the overthrow of the monarchy was celebrated as the Festival of the Unity and Indivisibility of the Republic. Symbols of monarchy were burned on public squares in Paris, then, during an immense republican picnic of loaves and fishes, members of the Convention drank fluid symbolizing the milk of liberty spurting from the breasts of a statue of the goddess of liberty. From the statue were then released three thousand doves, each with tiny banners saying 'We are free! Imitate us!' attached to their feet. The festivals organized by the government were lofty affairs elevating the Revolution with evocations of nature. They were at times only for early risers, as evidenced in the verses penned by the 'deputy on mission' Léonard Bourdon for local patriots who gathered before dawn for the Festival of Nature on a bridge across the Adour at Tarbes:

> Ye of little faith
> Who would see and hear the Supreme Being,
> May do so, with morality in your hearts,
> But you must go out into the fields,
> Two by two, bearing a flower.
> There, by pure waters,
> One hears a God in one's heart,
> As one sees him in Nature.[5]

Four years of revolutionary experience, of boundless hopes, sacrifices, and anxieties, of living within a revolutionary political culture, generated a distinctive *sans-culottes* ideology in cities and towns. This would be a world free of aristocrats and priests, rich men and poverty: in its place would rise a regenerated France of artisans and smallholders rewarded for the dignity and usefulness of their labour, free of religion, the condescension of the high-born, and the competition of entrepreneurs. In these years, collective display also went through what Michel Vovelle has described as a 'creative explosion', as popular initiatives in organizing festivals and remodelling ancient rituals meshed with the Convention's encouragement of civic commemoration. When news arrived, for example, of Louis's execution or of a military victory, whole villages improvised celebrations. Collective celebration drew on pre-revolutionary symbolism, often messianic, and the collective practices of the workplace to visualize a new society.

In towns and cities, club and section meetings often drew on religious forms for their organization, but on revolutionary experience for their content. Members commonly wore the *bonnet rouge* or liberty cap to show they were no longer galley slaves; from late 1793 the slightly different Phrygian cap referring to Greek slaves became more common. Meetings often began with the singing of the 'Marseillaise' or the 'Ça ira' and the reading of letters from the front, followed by discussions of forthcoming anniversaries and processions, the collection of patriotic donations, the denunciation of 'suspects', and orations about 'republican virtues'. To break from a lifetime of socialisation in the vocabulary of inequality, they sought to impose the familiar use of 'tu' in all social dealings (as it was in the Commune and section meetings), dismissing the 'vous' formerly required towards their superiors as intrinsically aristocratic. In the words of a petition of 31 October to the Convention, 'From this will come less pride, fewer distinctions, less ill-feeling, more obvious familiarity, a greater sense of fraternity: consequently more equality.' The section was a microcosm of the one and indivisible Republic, reflected in the practice of *publicité*, whereby votes and opinions were delivered openly and orally. Such a practice was as clearly at odds with bourgeois notions of individual rights and representative democracy as was the imposition of price controls with *laissez-faire*.[6]

The practice of popular sovereignty in the context of war and counter-revolution generated a spate of neologisms and changes to the meanings of existing vocabulary. One study has charted more than 1,350 such innovations in the decade after 1789, and most of these originated in 1792–4. The most famous neologism, of course, was 'sans-culottes'; other political appellations drawn from individuals were more short-lived: 'robespierriste', 'pittiste', 'maratiste'. The proliferation of popular clubs was dubbed 'clubinomanie'; those who frequented them were said to 'clubiner'. Some new words expressed vindictive mockery of the victims of the Terror, who would 'boire à la grande tasse' ('drink a large cup') and be subject to 'déportation verticale', in reference to the mass drowning of priests at Nantes. Others targeted in similar terms those Jacobins deemed to have acquiesced in the September 1792 massacres in Paris as 'buveurs de sang' ('drinkers of blood') or 'septembriseurs'.[7]

The certainty felt by revolutionaries in town and country that they were living on the frontier of social change was expressed in the spontaneous changes of names given to communities themselves and to the newborn. Supporters of the Revolution—'patriots', as they were most commonly called—marked their repudiation of the old world by attempting to eradicate all of its traces. Apart from name changes imposed by Jacobin armies after the defeat of counter-revolution, some 3,000 communes themselves acted to erase Christian connotations: St-Izague became Vin-Bon, St-Bonnet-Elvert became Liberté-Bonnet-Rouge, St-Tropez and Montmartre were renamed Héraclée, and Mont-Marat, while Villedieu took the name La Carmagnole and Villeneuve-St-Georges renamed itself Villeneuve-la-Montagne. In the district of La Rochelle, as elsewhere, villages named after saints were renamed to remove traces of the Church: St-Ouen became Marat, St-Rogatien was changed to Égalité, St-Soule to Rousseau, and St-Vivien to Sans-Culottes. The inhabitants of Montroy themselves repudiated its royal connotations and asked that it be renamed Montagne. All the streets of La Rochelle were renamed, honouring heroes such as Benjamin Franklin or Jean Calas.

It is impossible to estimate how many parents gave revolutionary names to babies in these years: in Poitiers, for example, only 62 of 593 babies born in the year II were named after saints in the *ancien régime* manner. Instead, they were given names reflecting the contrasting sources of political inspiration. A study of 430 names adopted in the Seine-et-Marne shows that 55 per cent drew on nature or the new calendar (Rose, Laurier, Floréal), 24 per cent on republican virtues (Liberté, Victoire, La Montagne), 12 per cent on antiquity (Brutus, Mucius Scaevola), and 9 per cent on new heroes (Le Peletier, Marat). One little boy was called Travail, another Fumier. In the Hautes-Alpes the Lacau parents gave their daughter the name Phytogynéantrope, Greek for a woman giving birth only to warrior sons.

The practice of giving revolutionary names varied enormously across the country, however, and, in any case, is difficult to ascertain precisely. For example, in the districts immediately south of Paris, Rose accounted for 226 of the 783 first names drawn from 'nature' in the Year II, but how deliberately political was such a choice? Some leave us in no doubt, such as the little boy named Faisceau Pique Terreur from Châlons-sur-Marne. In many rural areas the phenomenon was infrequent: only 20 per cent of the 133 communes of the district of Villefranche-en-Beaujolais had any such first names at all. There was also great variation between cities: in the winter and spring of 1794 at least 60 per cent of children received revolutionary names in Marseilles, Montpellier, Nevers, and Rouen, but not a single child in Riom and virtually none in St-Étienne. In Rennes, the first revolutionary name was as early as April 1791 (Citoyen Français), but even at its peak in February–August 1794 the practice touched only one-tenth of infants.[8]

The enthusiasm of most people in Gabian (see Chapter 6) for the Revolution was reflected in the choice many parents made of names for their children, taken from nature rather than from the saints: in 1792–3 the births were registered at the town hall of François Abricot Alengri, Jean-Pierre Abeille Canac, Rose Eléonore Jonquille Couderc, André Aubergine Foulquier, Rose Tubéreuse Jougla, Catherine Laurier Thim Latreille, and Marie Étain [Pewter] Salasc. In La Rochelle, too, parents expressed their values in the names they gave their children. Between 1 January 1793 and 21 September 1794, 981 children were born, and 135 were given revolutionary names. Victoire and Égalité were especially popular, but others were more imaginative: Décadi, Minerve, Bara, Humain, Ail, Carotte, and Cresson.

The revolutionary armies could not have triumphed—nor could the rising in the Vendée have been so powerful—without the active support of women. In urban centres, the collapse of women's work in luxury industries (especially lace) and domestic service was partly met by the temporary availability of work as scores of thousands of men left for the front. In town and country, women's work became more important than ever before in keeping the household together, though in the years 1792–4 perhaps one family in ten was economically and emotionally drained by the death or wounding of a husband, son, or father.

The repudiation of the most fundamental sources of authority in the *ancien régime* inevitably called into question the position of women within the family and society. A number of pieces of legislation were designed to regenerate family life, deemed to have been hitherto cruel and immoral, like the *ancien régime* itself. Family courts were instituted to deal with family conflict, penalties for wife-beating were introduced which were twice as heavy as for assaulting a man, and the age of majority was reduced from 25 to 21. It is doubtful, however, whether patterns of male violence changed, despite the exhortations of revolutionary legislators to a peaceful, harmonious family life as the basis of the new political order.

What did change was the possibility of women protecting their rights within the household. The divorce law voted at the last session of the Legislative Assembly, on 20 September 1792, gave women remarkably broad grounds for leaving an unhappy or meaningless marriage: the couple could agree to separate because of mutual incompatibility, or either spouse could initiate divorce on grounds such as the protracted absence or cruelty of their partner. It was working women above all who used this law: in Rouen, for example, 71 per cent of divorce proceedings were initiated by women, 72 per cent of them textile workers with some economic independence, unlike most rural women. Nationally, perhaps 30,000 divorces were decreed under this legislation, especially in towns: in Paris, there were nearly 6,000 in 1793–5.

For every eight marriages in Rouen, one divorce was decreed and an equal number were resolved by family mediation. Although violence was a common cause cited by women, the customary power of men to humble their wives by physical abuse (called *correction modéré* under the *ancien régime*) would have been called into question in every household. The divorce law could challenge domestic relationships at a fundamental level. The family court sought to mediate in potential divorces, but it did not always succeed. For example, Jean-Baptiste Vilasse, a nail-maker of La Rochelle, accused his wife Marie-Victoire Guyon of 'being unruly and of notorious morals'; in turn she accused him of 'poor treatment' and insisted they had incompatible characters. Jean-Baptiste had forgiven her for making love to another nail-maker, even in front of their children; she had returned to him but insisted 'that she would not abandon the other man, whom she loved'. Now it was Jean-Baptiste's turn to be intransigent, and he filed for divorce. However, in contrast to Rouen, there were only 34 divorces compared with 780 marriages in La Rochelle in the period 1 January 1793–27 June 1795.

An important and heated debate in August 1793 confronted the question of the wife's rights to an equal role in decisions concerning the family's property. Whereas Merlin de Douai argued that 'woman is generally incapable of administration and men, having a natural superiority over her, must protect her'; he was countered by Georges Couthon: 'Woman is born with as many capacities as man. If she has not demonstrated it until now, it is not the fault of Nature but of our former institutions.' Couthon was supported by Camille Desmoulins, who admitted that 'in support of my opinion is the political consideration that it is important to make women love the Revolution'. They carried the day, but the law was never fully applied.[9]

The nature of the marriage ceremony—as of baptism and burial—also changed. Now the mayor entered these rites in a 'civic register', with the priest performing only an optional blessing if indeed a priest was available at all. Religious strictures against marriage in Advent, Lent, on Fridays and Sundays were now ignored. There were also good reasons—the exemption of married men from conscription—for *de facto* couples to marry and for people to marry younger: compared with a pre-revolutionary annual average of 240,000 marriages, there were over 325,000 in both 1793 and 1794.

Despite their contempt for 'superstition', the radical Jacobins of the capital were often self-consciously moralistic, damning what they described as 'loose morals' as smacking of *ancien régime* laxity and corruption. On 2 October 1793 the Commune of Paris decreed that

It is forbidden to all girls and women of bad morals to parade on the streets, promenades, public squares, and to encourage licentiousness there . . .

The general council calls to its aid for the implementation and maintenance of its decree republicans who are austere and lovers of good morals, fathers and mothers of families . . . invites old people, as ministers of morality, to see that these morals are not outraged . . . [10]

Prostitution itself was banned on 21 Nivôse II (10 January 1794), seen by the Commune as an *ancien régime* practice and in any case unnecessary when there was work in war industries. However, it remained a clandestine last resort for up to 20,000 young women in Paris.

Throughout the Revolution, there had been a gulf of class and politics between the individual advocates of women's rights such as Olympe de Gouges and Etta Palm, now dead or discredited because of their political conservatism, and the *sans-jupons'* support for the subsistence and military goals of the popular movement as a whole. In May 1793 Théroigne de Méricourt, who supported the Girondins, was subject to a beating by Jacobin women from which she never recovered. For five months after May, the Revolutionary Republican Citizenesses, led by Claire Lacombe and Pauline Léon, bridged this gap between women's rights and subsistence politics by organizing as an autonomous women's group and campaigning for women's rights to public office and to bear arms, while remaining linked to the radical wing of the *sans-culottes*, the Enragés. 'All the members of the society', read the rules of the Citizenesses, 'are nothing else than a family of sisters.' A visiting delegation from the Droits de l'Homme Section praised the society:

Your Society is part of the social body and not among the least important. Liberty has found a new school here: mothers, wives, children come here to learn, to stimulate each other in the practice of social virtues. You have broken one of the links in the chain of prejudice. The one which confined women to the narrow sphere of their households, making a half of all individuals into passive and isolated beings, no longer exists for you. You want to take your place in the social order; apathy offends and humiliates you . . .[11]

Several sections in the capital had begun admitting women to their meetings, with the Hommes Libres and Panthéon sections acknowledging full voting rights. Others were more cautious: the Popular Society of the Luxembourg Section admitted women over 21 years and their daughters over 14, but limited females to one-fifth of members. However, Robespierre had never been much taken with the abrasive militancy of the Citizenesses, at one point jotting in his diary 'dissolution des f.r.r.' ('close down the Revolutionary Republican Women').

As criticism mounted, Lacombe confronted the Convention on 8 October 1793:

Our sex has produced only one monster [Marie-Antoinette], while for four years we have been betrayed and assassinated, by monsters without number of the masculine sex. Our rights are those of the people and, if we are oppressed, we will know how to provide resistance to oppression.

However, while the Citizenesses attracted 300 women to their meetings, and claimed the active support of 4,000 more, their challenge foundered on the opposition of market stallholders for whom price controls threatened poverty. On 24 October a group of Citizenesses was severely beaten by market women, giving the Jacobins and the Convention the chance to move against them. Robespierre's associate Amar, from the Committee of General Security, called on the Convention to close the society by appealing to the imperatives of nature's order:

Each sex is called to that kind of occupation which is proper to it, its action is circumscribed within a circle which cannot be broken, since nature, which has placed these limitations on mankind, imperiously commands ... If we reflect that the political education of man is still at its dawning, that the principles are not developed, and that we still stutter over the word 'liberty', how much less are women, whose political education is almost nil, enlightened in those principles. Their presence in the popular societies will concede an active role in government to those persons who are exposed to wrong-thinking and to being led astray.

On 30 October all women's clubs—including up to sixty in the provinces—were closed down.[12]

It was inevitable that the desperate demands of the national mobilization for the war would reverse the decentralization of power of the early years of the Revolution. The civil wars of 1793 had also served to underline the dangers of local autonomy, just as the *armées révolutionnaires*, the surge of radical women's demands, and dechristianization highlighted the challenge of local initiatives. The counter-revolution strengthened Jacobin mistrust of minority languages. In January 1794, Barère (though himself from the Occitan-speaking Pyrenees) inveighed against the 'ignorance and fanaticism' which the foreign coalition manipulated in 'people who are badly instructed or who speak a different idiom from that of public education'.[13] Forgetting the extraordinary sacrifices being made on the borders as he spoke, by patriotic Basques, Catalans, Flamands, and Provençaux, Barère assumed that republicanism, civilization, and the French language were synonymous. In fact, responses to the Revolution were very varied in regions of minority languages. However, the contempt which many 'deputies on mission' and members of the *armées révolutionnaires* expressed towards minority languages and cultures was to exacerbate mistrust of Paris.

The smothering of the most militant *sans-culottes* groups revealed the tensions within the popular alliance of the year II, but no less striking were the achievements of this alliance by the end of 1793. By then, republican forces led by a young artillery officer, Napoleon Bonaparte, had recaptured Toulon and foreign armies had suffered major reverses in the northeast and southeast. Though the 'general maximum' had not been fully implemented, the economic slide had been reversed and the purchasing power of the *assignat* stood at 48 per cent. The Vendéan rebellion had been contained and the Federalist revolt crushed, both at a huge cost in lives. The months of December 1793 and January 1794 were the peak of the executions: 6,882 of the 14,080 people sentenced by tribunals in the year of the Terror died in these months.

It was in this context, of military success but also of excesses and continuing constraints on liberty, that a crucial and fateful debate occurred over the continuation and direction of the Terror, when 'moderate' Jacobins such as Danton and Desmoulins urged an end to the controls of the Terror and the implementation of the Constitution of 1793. On 20 December they interrogated the Committee of Public Safety in *Le Vieux Cordelier*:

You want to remove all your enemies by means of the guillotine! Has there ever been such great folly? Could you make a single man perish on the scaffold, without making ten enemies for yourself from his family or his friends? . . . I think quite differently from those who tell you that terror must remain the order of the day.[14]

However, the danger was not over: in the southwest, Spanish troops remained in control of French territory; in St-Domingue, the offer in June 1793 of freedom to slaves who would fight for the Republic (followed by a general emancipation in July–August, extended to all French colonies by the law of 4 February 1794) had not succeeded in defeating the alliance of white planters and the English fleet. In such a situation, the Convention responded by maintaining the committees and their personnel.

Moreover, as we have seen, to Robespierre and his associates in particular, the Terror had a far higher purpose than simply winning the war. Robespierre's vision of a regenerated, virtuous, and self-abnegating society was, for him, the very *raison d'être* of the Revolution. 'It is time to mark clearly the aim of the Revolution', he intoned to the Convention on 5 February 1794:

We wish an order of things . . . where the country secures the welfare of each individual, and each individual proudly enjoys the prosperity and glory of his country. . . . We wish to substitute in our country . . . the empire of reason for the tyranny of custom . . . a people magnanimous, powerful and happy for a people lovable, frivolous and wretched—that is to say, all the virtues and miracles of the Republic for all the vices and puerilities of the monarchy.[15]

In the end, however, the French people Robespierre saw in the mirror were not a reflection of himself.

For the majority of the Convention, in contrast, the goal of the Terror was the attainment of peace, and economic and political controls were but temporary and regrettable impositions to that end: the regular extension of the powers of the Committee was a recognition of its achievements and the continuing war crisis, but not a measure of support for Jacobin ideology. On the other hand, the *sans-culottes* had developed a radically different vision of a society of small farms and workshops created by property redistribution and underpinned by free education, purges of old elites, and direct democracy. Ultimately, the political and social divisions within the republican alliance were to prove irreconcilable and explain the deadly politics of 1794.

In contrast to the mounting calls for a relaxation of the Terror, Hébert and his allies called for another popular rising like the *journée* of 5–6 September 1793—when the *sans-culottes* had last imposed their will on the National Convention—in order to push the Terror still further. In the process they provided the pretext for the Committee of Public Safety to move against both 'extremists' and 'indulgents'. The smothering of the popular movement in Paris and elsewhere was consummated in the execution of the Cordeliers (Hébert, Ronsin, Vincent, Cloots, and their allies) in March and the closing of thirty-nine popular societies. This freed the Convention's hand to encourage selling on the open market by lifting profit margins. Coupled with the imposition of the wages maximum at September 1793 levels, this dealt a severe blow to wage-earners and the *assignat* once again declined, to 36 per cent by July.

Robespierre's followers were treading a narrowing path between their increasingly alienated supporters inside and outside the Convention, and resorted to attempts to mould public opinion in the name of a revolutionary will and morality they claimed to monopolize. In this context, Saint-Just drew on Rousseau's insistence that the 'general will' was not simply an amalgam of opinion but an uncorrupted knowledge of the public interest: in Robespierre's words 'une volonté une' ('a single will'). On 26 Germinal Year II (15 April 1794), Saint-Just expressed his preference for a politics of 'public conscience . . . composed of the penchant of the people for the common good'. Unfortunately, so he believed, this 'penchant' was perverted by the 'evil intent' of former allies: Saint-Just's speech was made only days after the execution of the Cordeliers and the 'indulgents' (Danton, Desmoulins, and their supporters), and the day before the arrest of Pauline Léon and Claire Lacombe as sympathizers of Hébert (the former was released in August 1794, the latter a year later).

Divisions among 'patriots' made Jacobin leaders increasingly desperate. On 20 April Billaud-Varenne reported to the Convention on behalf of the Committee of Public Safety that what was needed was

to recreate the people one wants to return to liberty . . . strong action is needed therefore, a vehement impulse, appropriate for developing civic virtues and repressing the passions of greed, intrigue and ambition.[16]

Shortly afterwards, too, Robespierre delivered a report on the organization of public festivals, seeking both to ensure their civically instructive function and to control them. The Robespierrist festival culminated in the 'Festival of the Supreme Being' (7 May), which he hoped to use to reunite patriots around a common belief in a higher being. This was a brilliant display choreographed by Jacques-Louis David, and with Robespierre, then president of the Convention, leading the procession in his favourite light-blue coat and holding a posy of blue flowers. However, the festival's lack of spontaneity confirmed Saint-Just's fear that 'the Revolution has frozen over'.

Similarly, the policing functions of the Terror increasingly sought to control the content of theatrical performances. From late 1793, 150 plays were censored by rewriting or outright banning; by March, Corneille and Racine had disappeared from the stage and *William Tell* had had to be rewritten before re-emerging in May 1794 as *Les Sans-culottes suisses*. A vigorous debate ensued about whether non-revolutionary plays were necessarily 'unpatriotic'. In defending the production of the pantomime *Adèle de Sacy* against the accusation that it was counter-revolutionary, the director of the Lycée des Arts argued:

The good republican does not dread denunciations, for they are the touchstone of citizenship; but every denunciation must be examined, tested to its depths; this is the duty of surveillance, and it is only then that public esteem brings justice to the accuser.

In May, Robespierre intervened to allow *ancien régime* plays to be performed intact as a way of resolving the tension in trying to use pre-revolutionary material to revolutionary ends; the following month, however, the debate was continuing as to whether all stage representations should be didactic and 'authentic'.[17]

The direct involvement of the creative arts in the politics of the Terror was to have tragic consequences. In 1788 David had painted a luminous portrait of Antoine Lavoisier and his wife Marie-Anne. Lavoisier was the son of a wealthy bourgeois who had bought a noble title, and in 1768 became a private tax-official. He was also the most brilliant scientist of his age, his most important book being his *Traité élémentaire de la chimie*, published in 1789. As opposed to ancient assumptions that air, water, fire, and earth were indivisible elements, Lavoisier had devised quantitative methods for defining chemical elements and devised the system for naming chemical compounds. He discovered, for example, that water is a compound of hydrogen and oxygen, and the chemical processes of combustion. After 1789 Lavoisier, a close friend of Franklin, threw his energies into the Revolution, acting as a senior administrator during the war and on the commission which devised the metric system, while continuing his experiments. However, he had a powerful enemy in Jean-Paul Marat, whose scientific theories he had exposed as bogus when Marat attempted to join the Royal Academy of Science. In 1791 Marat denounced him:

This contemptible little man who enjoys an income of forty thousand livres has no other claim to fame than that of having put Paris in prison with a wall costing the poor thirty millions. . . . Would to heaven he had been strung up from the nearest lamp-post.

Now, in November 1793 charges were laid against all former tax-farmers. Robespierre intervened to save the life of one of them. However, David, who had joined the Committee of General Security in September, and who signed more than 400 arrest-warrants, apparently made no effort to save the man whose portrait he had painted. Lavoisier appeared before the Revolutionary Tribunal on 5 May 1794 and wrote a last letter to his wife before being executed on the 8th:

I have had a fairly long life, above all a very happy one, and I think that I shall be remembered with some regrets and perhaps leave some reputation behind me. What more could I ask? The events in which I am involved will probably save me from the troubles of old age. I shall die in full possession of my faculties.[18]

There were many other apparently needless deaths in this year, although none so wasteful to humanity as that of Antoine Lavoisier. A revolution that had begun in 1789 with a humanitarian, reforming zeal seemed to have developed into a nightmare of outrageous affronts to individual liberties and the safety of the person. This has always been the most important puzzle of the French Revolution. Why was there a 'Terror' in 1793–4? Was it counter-revolution that made the Revolution violent, or was the revolutionary violence of 1793–4 a disproportionate response to the threat of counter-revolution?

Responses to these questions have always depended both on the particular perspective of the historians and on the context in which they were writing. Sympathetic in tone is R. R. Palmer's classic *Twelve who Ruled*, written in the darkest days of the Second World War, in 1941. Palmer describes Robespierre as 'one of the half-dozen major prophets of democracy':

Since 1940 it is no longer so laughable as it once was to say that democracy is founded upon virtue. As we read through the catalogue of changes which Robespierre announced that the Revolutionary Government wished to see in France, we sense a certain similarity to what we might have read in the morning paper.

To Pierre Chaunu, in contrast, the Terror conjured up the images from Cambodia and of Stalinist prisons current at the time he was writing, in 1983:

The Jacobin period can only appear today as the first act, the foundation stone of a long and bloody series stretching from 1792 to our own times, from Franco-French genocide in the Catholic west to the Soviet gulag, to the destruction caused by the Chinese cultural revolution, to the Khmer Rouge genocide in Cambodia.[19]

In 1804, Tom Paine, the British veteran of the American Revolution who in 1792–4 had been both in the National Convention and in prison, blamed 'the provocative influence of foreign powers' for the 'madness'. Similarly, most historians, whether Marxist or liberal, have seen the Revolution as based on sincere liberal beliefs in tolerance and judicial process until it was forced by the circumstances of violent counter-revolution to compromise some of its founding principles. Recently, however, historians such as François Furet, Patrice Gueniffey, and Simon Schama have argued that the *mentalité* of the

Terror was present at the very outset of the Revolution in May 1789 when, as Gueniffey argues, 'patriots' began stigmatizing their opponents as enemies of the new order of things rather than simply adherents of contrary points of view. The widespread belief in 1789 in an 'aristocratic plot', which allegedly aimed to starve Parisians into inactivity, had underpinned the storming of the Bastille and the October Days, and was echoed each time revolutionaries needed to explain opposition to their policies. William Reddy has argued that 'the history of the Revolution cannot be understood without an adequate theory of emotions', that these extremely 'sentimental' people of the time lived out in public their feelings of grief, fear and envy. Such 'over-sentimentality' might, he suggests, explain the particular obsession revolutionaries had with mostly imaginary conspiracies. For conspiracy was, according to Lynn Hunt, 'the central organizing principle of French revolutionary rhetoric. The narrative of Revolution was dominated by plots.'[20]

To Simon Schama, violence was 'the Revolution's source of collective energy . . . the Terror was merely 1789 with a higher body count'.[21] The primary event in his narrative of 1789—on which he lingers— was the collective homicides of Bertier de Sauvigny and his son-in-law Foulon on 22 July. Of course, one obvious difference between these murders and the Terror of 1793–4 is that the latter was institutionalized state repression rather than popular vengeance. However, the alleged response to Foulon's death by Antoine Barnave—'What then, is the blood which has just flowed so pure?'—is used by Schama to imply that revolutionaries of all backgrounds were saturated in bloodlust. Of course, to focus as does Schama on a horrific incident such as this serves to minimize the significance and to demean the intent of the Revolution of 1789: not the rights of man but the slaughter of innocents was its essence.

It is true that there are traces in revolutionary—and counter-revolutionary—rhetoric of verbal imagery which defined opponents as conspirators, traitors, and enemies. This is not surprising in a society where until 1789 politics was the preserve of court factions and their intrigues and where the Church expelled the troublesome as heretics. When Jacques-Alexis Thuriot adduced his revolutionary record as evidence of his innocence, Hébert retorted: 'What is proved by services rendered to the Revolution? Conspirators always adopt this method. In order to deceive the people, one has to have served it; one has to gain its confidence the better to abuse it.'[22] However, to assume that the essence of the Revolution was therefore violence itself is to miss a far more powerful language of liberalism and regeneration, itself an attempt to escape from the intolerance and violence of the *ancien régime*. Moreover, to reduce the course of the Revolution to a stream of emotional intolerance and paranoid obsession with conspiracies which culminated in the Terror of 1794 is to miss both the continued voices of liberalism and tolerance and the way in which the outbreak of war transformed political divisions into matters of life and death. As Timothy Tackett has demonstrated, until the flight of the king in June 1791, and his fellow crowned heads' noisy (if hollow) warnings after his capture, there was little talk of conspiracy in the assemblies. It was the counter-revolution and the mixed emotions of panic, outrage, pride, and fear that it aroused which fostered a willingness to believe that enemies were omnipresent. The Terror cannot be understood simply as an expression of revolutionary paranoia.

While the military threat remained so could the existence of the Terror be justified. In Prairial II (20 May–18 June), 183 of the 608 decrees of the Committee of Public Safety concerned supply and transport matters signed by Lindet; 114 were to do with munitions and were initiated by Prieur de la Côte-d'Or; and 130 were decrees from Carnot about the army and navy. Certainly, however, by the late spring of 1794, the execution of popular revolutionaries to the right and left of the dominant Jacobins, and the escalation of the Terror at a time of military success, alienated even the most patriotic of *sansculottes*. Those imprisoned as suspects ranged from a hero of 1789 and 1792 , the brewer Santerre, the Marquis de Sade, Rouget de l'Isle and France's greatest poet, André Chénier. For Jacques Ménétra, an active member of a pro-Robespierre section, these months similarly conjured up images of cannibalism, murder, barbarism, and unnecessary death—at least in hindsight.[23] In particular, the Law of 22 Prairial Year II (10 June 1794) dramatically expanded definitions of 'counter-revolutionary':

6. The following are deemed enemies of the people: those who . . . have sought to disparage or dissolve the National Convention . . . have sought to inspire discouragement . . . have sought to mislead opinion . . . to impair the energy and the purity of revolutionary and republican principles . . .

7. The penalty provided for all offences under the jurisdiction of the Revolutionary Tribunal is death.

It was above all the battle of Fleurus (26 June)—finally ending the threat of Austrian troops on French soil—which exposed the contradictions in the popular alliance of the year II. The geographic incidence of executions during the Terror had been concentrated in departments where the military threat had been greatest (see Map 6); now, as the military threat receded, the number of executions for political opposition increased. The removal of the immediate military threat starkly exposed the new purpose for which the Terror was being used: from March 1793 to 10 June 1794, 1,251 people were executed in Paris; following the law of 22 Prairial (10 June), 1,376 were guillotined in just six weeks. These weeks were not a time of unremitting repression; in mid-July, seventy-one Girondin deputies who might have joined their fellows at the guillotine in October 1793 but for Robespierre's intervention were reinstated as full members of the Convention. However, they were not in forgiving mood.

Robespierre's speech to the Convention on 26 July (8 Thermidor), with its vague threat to unnamed deputies, provided the motivation for reaction. Among those who plotted his overthrow were Fouché, Collot d'Herbois, Fréron, and Barras, fearful that Robespierre intended to call them to account for their bloody repression of Federalism in Lyons, Toulon, and Marseilles. When he was arrested the following day, he could not look for support to the *sans-culottes'* movement, shattered by the Jacobins' own measures, the death of its leaders, and the alienation of wage-earners. Only seventeen of the forty-eight sections responded to calls to save him, and soon dispersed. Robespierre shot himself in the jaw, apparently in an attempt to commit suicide. He went to the guillotine in agony on the 28th. A police agent reported that, as Robespierre's head fell, a group of brush-makers shouted 'there goes the maximum into the basket' and the next day struck for a one-third increase in wages.

Ultimately, more than eighty 'Robespierrists' were guillotined. The overthrow of Robespierre and his associates in July 1794 was far more than the ousting of a governing coterie which had outlived its purpose. It was also the end of a regime which had had the twin aims of saving the Revolution and creating a new society. It had achieved the former, at great cost, but the vision of the virtuous, self-abnegating civic warrior embodying the new society had palled. The men in the Convention who rejoiced at Robespierre's overthrow were his old enemies the Girondins, joined by those of his erstwhile supporters who found it expedient to absolve their acquiescence in the Terror by emptying their consciences into his grave.

Notes

1. *Moniteur universel*, no. 91, 21 December 1793, vol. 19, 6. On education policy, see Kennedy, *Cultural History*, 353–62; R. R. Palmer, *The Improvement of Humanity: Education and the French Revolution* (Princeton, 1985), chs. 4–5.

2. *Moniteur universel*, no. 214, 2 August 1793, vol. 17, 287.

3. Serge Bianchi, *La Révolution culturelle de l'an II* (Paris, 1982), 119; Ozouf, *Festivals and the French Revolution*, 89–91. General discussions of the effects on the Church are Gibson, *French Catholicism*, ch. 2; McManners, *French Revolution*, ch. 10; Michel Vovelle, *The Revolution against the Church: From Reason to the Supreme Being*, trans. Alan Jose (Cambridge, 1991).

4. *Les Républicaines: chansons populaires des revolutions de 1789, 1792 et 1830*, 3 vols. (Paris, 1848), vol. 1, 34–6. On the 'cultural revolution', see Bianchi, *Révolution culturelle*, esp. ch. 5; Aileen Ribeiro, *Fashion in the French Revolution* (London, 1988); Kennedy, *Cultural History*, ch. 9, Appendix A.

5. Ozouf, *Festivals and the French Revolution*, 117; Michael Sydenham, *Léonard Bourdon: The Career of a Revolutionary, 1754–1807* (Waterloo, Ont., 1999).

6. John Hardman (ed.), *French Revolution Documents* (Oxford, 1973), vol. 2, 132–3. On popular ideology in Paris, see Soboul, *Parisian Sans-Culottes*, chs. 1–3; William Sewell, *Work and Revolution in France: The Language of Labor from the Old Régime to 1848* (Cambridge, 1980), ch. 5.

7. Max Frey, *Les Transformations du vocabulaire français à l'époque de la Révolution (1789–1800)* (Paris, 1925).

8. Detail on La Rochelle is from departmental and municipal archives. On revolutionary place and given names, see the special issue of *Annales historiques de la Révolution française* 322 (2000); Bianchi, *Révolution culturelle*.

9. André Burguière, 'Politique de la famille et Révolution', in Michael Adcock et al. (eds.), *Revolution, Society and the Politics of Memory* (Melbourne, 1997), 72–3. The divorce law is the subject of Roderick Phillips, *Family Breakdown in Late-Eighteenth Century France: Divorces in Rouen, 1792–1803* (Oxford, 1980); and, much more generally, *Putting Asunder: A History of Divorce in Western Society* (Cambridge, 1988).

10. Hardman (ed.), *French Revolution Documents*, vol. 2, 127–8.

11. R. B. Rose, *Tribunes and Amazons: Men and Women of Revolutionary France*

1789–1871 (Sydney, 1998), 246–8. Rose's argument should be compared with Olwen Hufton, 'Women in Revolution', *French Politics and Society*, 7 (1989), 65–81; Madelyn Gutwirth, *The Twilight of the Goddesses: Women and Representation in the French Revolutionary Era* (New Brunswick, NJ, 1992), ch. 7.

12. This most significant episode in the history of women's political participation is discussed by Desan, 'Jacobin Women's Clubs', in B. T. Ragan and E. A. Williams (eds.), *Re-creating Authority in Revolutionary France* (New Brunswick, NJ, 1992); Scott H. Lytle, 'The Second Sex (September, 1793)', *Journal of Modern History*, 26 (1955), 14–26; Landes, *Women and the Public Sphere*, 140–5, 160–8; Marie Cerati, *Le Club des citoyennes républicaines révolutionnaires* (Paris, 1966); R. B. Rose, *The Enragés: Socialists of the French Revolution?* (Melbourne, 1965), chs. 5–6.

13. Cited in Roger Dupuy, *De la Révolution à la chouannerie: paysans en Bretagne* (Paris, 1988), 7–8; see, too, Patrice Higonnet, 'The Politics of Linguistic Terrorism and Grammatical Hegemony during the French Revolution', *Social History*, 5 (1980), 41–69.

14. *Le Vieux Cordelier*, no. 4, 30 Frimaire II (20 December 1793).

15. R. R. Palmer, *Twelve who Ruled* (Princeton, 1941), 275. The drama of the confrontation between Robespierre and Danton—and of the struggle for power in Poland in the early 1980s—is evoked in Andrjez Wadja's 1982 film *Danton*, based on a 1930s play by Stanislawa Przybyszewska.

16. John M. Burney, 'The Fear of the Executive and the Threat of Conspiracy: Billaud-Varenne's Terroristic Rhetoric in the French Revolution 1788–1794', *French History*, 5 (1991), 162.

17. James H. Johnson, 'Revolutionary Audiences and the Impossible Imperatives of Fraternity', in Ragan and Williams (eds.), *Re-creating Authority*.

18. Stephen Jay Gould, *Bully for Brontosaurus* (New York, 1991), 363–4; Arthur Donovan, *Antoine Lavoisier: Science, Administration, and Revolution* (Oxford, 1993).

19. Palmer, *Twelve who Ruled*, 279; Hugh Gough, 'Genocide and the Bicentenary', *Historical Journal*, 30 (1987), 978.

20. These contrasting explanations of the Terror are from A. Y. Ayer, *Thomas Paine* (London, 1988), 177; Patrice Gueniffey, *La Politique de la Terreur: essai sur la violence révolutionnaire* (Paris, 2000); William M. Reddy, 'Sentimentalism and its Erasure: The Role of Emotions in the Era of the French Revolution', *Journal of Modern History*, 72 (2000), 109–52. See, too, Arno J. Mayer, *The Furies: Violence and Terror in the French and Russian Revolutions* (Princeton, 2000).

21. Schama, *Citizens*, 447.

22. Cited in an important article by Colin Lucas, 'The Theory and Practice of Denunciation in the French Revolution', *Journal of Modern History*, 68 (1996), 784.

23. Jacques-Louis Ménétra, *Journal of My Life*, trans. A. Goldhammer (New York, 1986), 219–20. See, too, Nicolas Ruault, *Gazette d'un parisien sous la Révolution, 1783–1796* (Paris, 1976) (some doubts have been raised over the authenticity of these memoirs).

8

Ending the Revolution, 1795–1799

Ten days after the overthrow of Robespierre on 9 Thermidor, Rose de Beauharnais was released from Les Carmes prison. Her husband Alexandre was not so fortunate: he had resigned from the army in August 1793, but was then tried on a charge of conspiracy with the enemy, and executed on 5 Thermidor. Rose, a woman of 31, was the daughter of the owner of a sugar plantation on the Caribbean island of Martinique; however, she had been pro-revolutionary, comfortable with being addressed as *tu* and *citoyenne*. Nevertheless, her name had made her suspect in the murderous spring of 1794.

Among the other 'suspects' released after Thermidor were many *sans-culottes*, including François-Noël Babeuf (see Chapter 4). Babeuf had been imprisoned early in 1793 for falsifying property registers in order to distribute land to the poor. While in prison he had dropped his earlier adopted name Camille for Gracchus, a second-century BC Roman land reformer. Gracchus Babeuf now moved quickly to establish the *Tribun du peuple* to publicize *sans-culottes* demands. Babeuf was one of a number of militants who imagined that the end of the Terror would allow a new freedom for popular initiative and the implementation of the Constitution of 1793.

The fall of Robespierre was universally welcomed as symbolizing the end of large-scale executions. The expression 'the system of the Terror' was first used two days later by Barère. Histories of the Terror—indeed, of the Revolution itself—therefore often end with the fall of Robespierre. For the better-off all over France, the new régime of the Directory represented much of what they wanted: the guarantee of the revolutionary achievements and the smothering of popular politics. In January 1795, for example, the surveillance committee of

Lagrasse (department of the Aude) celebrated the end of the Terror in an address to the Convention:

The Revolution of 9 Thermidor . . . has seen the rebirth of calm and serenity in the hearts of the French, who, released from the errors into which terrorism had led them, and having broken the iron sceptre under which the scoundrel Robespierre held them subject, are enjoying the fruits of your sublime works, marching with joy along the paths of virtue. . . . Formerly the men of blood slaughtered innocent victims selected by envy, and destiny led to the scaffold how many hardworking and suffering citizens, confounded with the guilty . . . France is free, happy and triumphant.[1]

Yet those who sought to blame Robespierre for the Terror's excesses had often been instrumental or complicit in them. Others who welcomed the lifting of the constraints on freedom were so embittered by their experiences that they unleashed a period of vicious reprisals. Certainly, this could be no easy return to the principles and optimism of 1789: the Revolution had lost its innocence, and the men who now ruled France were hardened pragmatists. The post-Thermidorian regimes would have two fundamental objectives. First, they would be republican, but driven above all else by the need to end the Revolution, most obviously by suppressing the sources of instability represented by the Jacobins and *sans-culottes*. The Thermidorians were hard men, many of them former Girondins, who had lived through the Terror in quiet opposition, and were determined that the experience would not be repeated. Secondly, the rationale for war voiced by their former leaders Brissot and Vergniaud—that this was a defensive war against tyrannical aggression which would naturally become a war of liberation joined by Europe's oppressed—would develop instead into a war of territorial expansion in the name of 'la grande nation'.

Within a month of Robespierre's fall, about 200 provincial Jacobin clubs had complained angrily about the unexpected repercussions. For, side by side with the restriction of the scope of the revolutionary tribunal, which was finally abolished in May 1795, along with the execution of Fouquier-Tinville, public prosecutor in the year II, a bitter social reaction was unleashed. This 'white Terror' was a punitive response of political and social elites to the controls and fears they had undergone. Active Jacobins and *sans-culottes* were arrested in

Paris, Jacobins in provincial towns were assassinated, and the Jacobin club itself, which had been the backbone of the patriotic bourgeoisie's political life throughout the Revolution, was closed down in November.

The vengeful tone of this social reaction was expressed, for example, in Souriguières and Gaveaux's song 'Le Réveil du peuple' ('The Re-awakening of the People'), in January 1795:

> French people, brotherly people,
> Can you see without quivering with horror
> Crime holding its banners
> Of carnage and terror?
> You suffer while a hideous horde
> Of assassins and brigands
> Fouls with its ferocious breath
> The land of the living.
>
> What is this primitive slowness?
> Hurry up, sovereign people,
> To return to the monsters of Tenairon
> All these drinkers of human blood!
> War on all the agents of crime!
> Pursue them to the death!
> Share the horror which drives me!
> They won't escape us!

In Bordeaux, the song was popular among resurgent royalists. In mid-1795, for example, young people crowded the Grand Théâtre to hoot and catcall the anti-clerical play *Jean Calas*, demanding that the actors sing 'Le Réveil du peuple'.[2] The song was banned a year later, after the government became concerned that its bloody call for revenge would act as a cover for a royalist revival.

The cultural revolution of the year II was over. The well-to-do self-consciously began to use 'Monsieur' and 'Madame' instead of 'Citizen'. These years also saw the *de facto* end of *tutoiement* as a political form of address, of revolutionary names and even the *décadi* in many areas. Older patterns of communication quickly re-established themselves: in 1795 the number of new novels doubled—largely sentimental tales and mysteries—while the number of new political songs declined from 701 to 137. In parallel ways to the history of the newspaper press and of painting, the history of publishing bears the marks of the political economy of the period. Originally 'emancipated' from the controls of the privileged guild of Parisian publishers, authors had enjoyed years of unprecedented liberty of expression after 1789 until the sharp political curbs of the Terror. With the overthrow of the Terror in July 1794, authors again were to deal with publishers as free contracting agents; now, however, the regime was to offer subsidies to its literary supporters. Grégoire's report of 17 Vendémiaire III (5 October 1794), which Carla Hesse describes as the 'cultural Thermidor', advocated a deliberate policy of inculcating the right cultural and political values.[3]

The sons and daughters of the well-to-do expressed sartorial contempt for Jacobin 'mediocrity' by parading as *muscadins* and *merveilleuses*, and *jeunesse dorée* ('gilded youth') patrolled the streets spoiling for the chance to take physical revenge on *sans-culottes*.[4] Despite a law of 2 Prairial II (21 May 1795), whereby only the tricolour cockade was permitted as a sign of political affiliation, in Bordeaux the royalist *jeunesse dorée* delighted in wearing the white cockade and in beating *sans-culottes* whom they encountered in the streets. Trees of liberty planted during the Terror had little chance of reaching maturity. The release of social and economic restraints on displays of wealth also allowed the re-emergence of ostentatious consumption, notably balls at which the wealthy demonstrated their antipathy to the Terror—and symbolized their recent fears—by appearing with shaved necks and thin red ribbons around their throats. Prostitutes soliciting wealthy customers now reappeared at the Palais-Royal.

The social outlook of the former Girondins and men of the 'Plain' who now dominated the Convention was evident in their education policy, which retreated from Jacobin commitment to universal, free schooling. The Daunou Law of 3 Brumaire IV (25 October 1795) also envisaged that teachers would be paid from pupils' fees, that girls would be taught 'useful skills' in separate schools, and that there need only be a school in each canton rather than in every commune. The Thermidorians were rather more concerned with élite education. In September 1794, the École Centrale des Travaux Publics (which in September 1795 became the École Polytechnique) was established and linked to specialist engineering and military schools. In October

1795, *ancien régime* academies, abolished in August 1793 as corporate and elitist, were re-established as the Institut de France.

Under the Terror the heroic sacrifice of children like Bara and Viala had been commemorated; now there were contrasting acts of virtue to acknowledge. The Paris Salon of 1796 featured a painting by Pierre-Nicolas Legrand entitled 'A Kind Deed is Never Forgotten'. This celebrated Joseph Cange, the messenger of La Force prison during the Terror. Touched by the misery of a prisoner's family to whom he was entrusted to deliver a message, Cange had given them some of his own money on the pretence that it was from the prisoner, and then did likewise to the prisoner. Only after the Terror did the prisoner, reunited with his family, discover the truth; they also found that Cange was raising six children. Legrand's was one of only a number of portraits of Cange and, shortly after Thermidor, at least eight plays told his moving story, one of them by Marin Gamas, author of *Emigrés in the Austral Lands* (see Chapter 6).

However, despite the strength of political reaction against the Terror, this was still a republican regime at war with old Europe. One of Cange's great virtues was that three of the six children he was raising belonged to a brother-in-law killed at the front. A similar mix of social conservatism and republicanism pervaded the official festivals of the Directory, such as the Festivals of Youth, Old Age, Spouses, and Agriculture, which replaced the Jacobin festivals of Reason and Nature. These official festivals lacked popular support, and the Directory resorted to compulsion to impose its particular brand of republicanism. In January 1796, for example, a government decree required the 'Marseillaise' to be sung in all theatres before the curtain went up. Occasionally, more spontaneous festivals turned the tables on the Jacobins: at Beaumont-de-Périgord on 26 Thermidor V (13 August 1797) young people burned 'a straw man, to whom they gave the name Robespierre'; at Blois, the commemoration of 10 August 1792 in the Year VI also involved burning an effigy of Robespierre.[5] In such ways Robespierre served to personify the bloody images of the Terror for moderate republicans as much as for royalists.

While the removal of economic controls permitted vengeful displays of wealth, the end of all fixed prices in December 1794 unleashed rampant inflation. By April 1795, the general level of prices was about 750 per cent above 1790 levels. This coincided with a severe winter: the Seine froze over and the soil hardened to a depth of half a metre. In this context of social and political reaction, and economic deprivation, the *sans-culottes* made a final desperate attempt to regain the initiative. The risings of Germinal and Prairial year III (April and May 1795) effectively sought a return to the promises of the autumn of 1793, the epitome of the *sans-culottes* movement. With 'Bread and the Constitution of 1793' pinned to their caps, insurgents shouted for the suppression of the *jeunesse dorée* and the release of imprisoned Jacobins and *sans-culottes*, but also for the 'abolition of the revolutionary government'. Van Heck, the commander of the Cité Section, warned the Convention: 'The citizens for whom I am speaking want the constitution of 1793; they are tired of spending nights at the bakers' doors ... We ask liberty for several thousands of fathers of patriot families, who have been incarcerated since 9 Thermidor.' Women played a major part in these insurrections. In the aftermath of the Prairial insurrection, the Convention contradictorily decreed that they had both abused the respect men have 'for the weakness of their sex' and that, unless they immediately respected a curfew, they would be repressed by armed force.[6]

The failure of the May 1795 insurrection unleashed more wide-ranging reaction. Over 4,000 Jacobins and *sans-culottes* were arrested, and 1,700 were stripped of all civil rights. Prison camps were established in the Seychelles and Guiana. Apart from the 'Day of the Black Collars' in July 1795, when *sans-culottes* and some soldiers used the sixth anniversary of the storming of the Bastille to take a short-lived revenge on *jeunesse dorée*, the Parisian popular movement was silenced. In the south of the country, 'Companies of Jesus and the Sun' singled out Jacobins.

Such an atmosphere raised royalist hopes, if not for a return of the *ancien régime*, at least for constitutional monarchy. Once the dauphin, now styled Louis XVII, died in prison of scrofula in June 1795, his uncle, the Count de Provence, assumed the title of Louis XVIII. On 25 June, from Verona, he issued a declaration which ensured that there could be no return to the Constitution of 1791 as a way of stabilizing the Revolution. Indeed, he referred to the restoration of the three estates and of the position of the Catholic Church, as if the Revolution of 1789 had never occurred. Given the depths of hatred between republicans and royalists by 1795, it is doubtful whether a return to a variant of the Constitution of 1791 would have been possible without military defeat and further civil war. In any case, Louis's declaration offered hope only to the most intransigent royalists dreaming of a return to the *ancien régime*. Provence's even more recalcitrant younger brother, the Count d'Artois, attempted later in 1795 to lead a British force into Brittany but failed to link up as planned with the Vendéan leader Charette.[7]

The determination with which the Convention resolved to counter both the popular and royalist challenges was above all apparent in its constitutional arrangements, for there could now be no question of returning to the egalitarian democracy of the Constitution of 1793. The political agenda of the Convention was made plain by its president, Boissy d'Anglas, on 5 Messidor III (23 June 1795):

We should be governed by the best among us; the best are the most highly educated, and those with the greatest interest in upholding the laws; save for the rarest exceptions, you will only find such men among those who, by reason of their owning property, are devoted to the land in which it is situated ... If you were to grant unlimited political rights to men without property, and if they were ever to take their place in the legislative assembly, they would provoke disturbances, or cause them to be provoked, without fear of the consequences; they would levy or permit the levying of taxes fatal to trade and agriculture ...[8]

The deputies now dominant in the Convention sought a political settlement which would stabilize the Revolution and end popular upheaval. In the words of Boissy d'Anglas, 'We have lived through six centuries in six years'. He was instrumental in framing the Constitution of the year III (August 1795) which restricted participation in electoral assemblies by wealth, age, and education as well as by sex. Political life was to be restricted to the act of voting: petitions, political clubs, and even unarmed demonstrations were banned. The social rights promised in the Constitution of 1793 were stripped away; the meaning of equality was now to be sharply restricted in a society where property was the basis of the social order:

3. Equality is a circumstance in which the law is the same for all ...
8. The cultivation of land, all production, every means of labour, and the entire social order are dependent on the maintenance of property ...[9]

It was plain to the Thermidorians that only those with an adequate stake in society could be trusted to govern, that is, wealthy, educated, middle-aged, and married males. While the Constitution of 1795 offered voting rights to all male taxpayers, electoral colleges were to be limited to the wealthiest 30,000 among them, about half of the number in 1791. The emphasis was on avoiding the possibility of abrupt political shifts: only one-third of the Council of 500 would be elected at a time, a Council of Elders (of men over 40 years who were married or widowed) would approve legislation, and one of the executive of five Directors, chosen by the Elders from a list submitted from the Five Hundred, would be replaced annually. A subsequent decree required that two-thirds of the incoming legislature were to be chosen from the men of the Convention.

The Constitution was put to the electorate: perhaps 1.3 million men voted in favour and 50,000 against, considerably fewer than for its predecessor in 1793. Only 208,000 bothered to vote in favour of the Two-Thirds decree. Anger was expressed that the price of social order was to limit democracy. A section of voters in Limoges complained that 'We are deeply disturbed to see the wealthy supplanting all other categories of citizen.' Voters in Triel (Seine-et-Oise) insisted that 'The deputies should not be called Representatives of the Nation . . . they are merely mandatories of the section which has elected them and can recall them if necessary.'[10]

In its essentials, this Constitution was a return to the provisions of the Constitution of 1791: France was again to be governed by representative, parliamentary government based on a property qualification and the safeguarding of economic and civil liberties. To be sure, there were differences between the Constitutions of 1791 and 1795. The regime of the Directory was to be republican, not monarchical, and religious divisions were to be resolved by separating Church and state: 'No-one may be forced to contribute to the expenses of a religion. The Republic does not pay for any.'

Gone now was the optimism of 1789–91, the belief that with the liberation of human creativity all could aspire to the 'active' exercise of their capabilities. The men of 1795 now appended a declaration of 'duties' to their constitution, exhorting respect for the law, the family, and property. In this sense, the constitution marks the end of the Revolution. Moreover, emphasizing as it did individual rights and responsibilities, and political and economic liberalism, the constitution could be said to mark the beginning of the nineteenth century. The question remained whether, after six years of conflict, popular participation, and sacrifice, the exclusions and limitations imposed by these pragmatic, chastened republicans could succeed in achieving stability against disaffected urban and rural working people and royalists.

The regime's unpopularity and the cynicism with which it had excluded the great majority of people from an effective political voice resulted in a resistance of a different type, that of a refusal to participate: in the partial elections of October 1795, only about 15 per cent of the 30,000 electors went to the polls (and elected royalists almost exclusively). The wider electorate for local elections often boycotted polls as a sign of their opposition to the bourgeois republic. The electoral consolidation of communes into municipalities at the cantonal level further divorced rural people from the Directory: in the words of Georges Fournier, referring to Languedoc, 'petty notables dominated soulless cantons'. This forced withdrawal of peasants and artisans from formal political life did not represent a hiatus in popular politics. In the south, smouldering animosities were ignited by the policies of the Directory into direct attacks on the persons and property of Jacobins or the local agents of the new regime. Here and in the west, up to 2,000 Jacobins were killed by 'white Terror' gangs: the victims were usually wealthy purchasers of nationalized property, and were often Protestants.[11]

By excluding royalists and the poor from the political process and by restricting that process to electoral participation, the Directory sought to create a republican regime based on 'capacity' and a stake in society. To avoid a strong executive with its Jacobin taints, there were to be frequent partial elections to the Council of Five Hundred and rotation of executive authority. This combination of a narrow social base and internal instability made the regime vacillate between political alliances to the right and left to broaden its appeal and forced it to resort to draconian repression of opposition and to the use of military force. Hence the regime declared advocacy of the 1793 Constitution to be a capital offence and in March 1796 sharply restricted freedom of the press and association, after calling upon Napoleon Bonaparte to forcibly close the Panthéon Club in Paris which had grouped 3,000 Jacobins.

A royalist insurrection on 13 Vendémiaire IV (5 October 1795) hoped to capitalize on popular antipathy towards the Law of the Two-Thirds but was suppressed by the army, under Napoleon Bonaparte, after heavy fighting, leaving several hundred dead. The coup had also failed because Parisian working people, no matter how resentful towards the bourgeois republic, refused to throw in their lot with royalism. However, many working people elsewhere had come to regret the passing of the union of throne and altar, if not the *ancien régime* itself. By 1795 La Rochelle, for example, was so impoverished that the municipality had to suspend coach and mail services because it no longer had the funds to purchase horse-feed. Commerce slowly picked up: in 1796 ninety-nine ships arrived in the port, compared with twenty-five in 1792: these included shipments of maize, tobacco, cotton, and sugar from the United States. However, it is not surprising that, in the context of economic collapse due to continued warfare and the abolition of slavery, there are many examples from La Rochelle of people openly advocating in these years the return of the monarchy. Others regretted the collapse of the routines of pre-revolutionary life. On 7 Brumaire VII (28 October 1798) twenty-five girls aged 16–20 years employed in a spinning-works at the hospice of La Rochelle refused to work because it was a Sunday. The same year forty-four people, mostly women between 15 and 75 years of age, were arrested after an illegal mass said by a sabot-seller, Baptiste Chain, aged 29. Others protested by avoiding conscription or encouraging others to do so. A poster in La Rochelle in 1798 warned:

Conscripts, if you leave you are cowards. Can you accept that your mothers and fathers have their arms snatched away by you enrolling for the field of glory, to fight for whom? For men thirsty for your blood and your bones. These are the men you are off to fight for. Yes, join together, but let that be to exterminate a government which is odious to all European powers, even the most barbarous.[12]

The Directory had inherited a massive religious problem. Not only had most priests refused or retracted an oath of allegiance to the Civil Constitution of the Clergy in 1791, but the subsequent exile, imprisonment or execution of these priests had created a vengeful, embittered clerical army on France's borders. In many areas constitutional clergy had been unable to overcome local resentment at the departure of the 'bons curés' and in any case were simply too few to minister to spiritual needs: in 1796, there were only perhaps 15,000 priests for France's 40,000 parishes. For the men of the Directory, the religious problem was above all one of public order: mistrustful of 'fanaticism' but conscious of a widespread yearning for a reconstitution of the spiritual community, on 11 Prairial III (30 May 1795) the regime allowed the reopening of churches closed during the Terror and allowed *émigré* priests to return under the decree of 7 Fructidor IV (24 August 1796), but only on condition they took a civic oath. Religious observance was to be a purely private matter: bells and outward signs of religiosity were forbidden, and the regime continued the Convention's separation of Church and state. The Church was to be sustained by the offerings of the faithful.

However, these years were remarkable for a construction from below of a new Catholicism. This renaissance testifies to the widespread resilience of religious faith, but is no less significant for what it revealed of regional and gender variations. In 1796, the *curé* of Menucourt, Thomas Duboscq (see Chapter 6), who had abdicated the priesthood in January 1794, moved to nearby Vaux to resume his priesthood and stayed there until his death in 1825, aged 75. However, this great surge in populist religiosity was above all the work of women, and was at its strongest in certain rural areas (such as parts of the west, Normandy and the southwest) where huge proportions of priests had emigrated, and provincial cities (Bayeux, Arles, Mende, Rouen, Toulouse) where the collapse of the institutions of the *ancien régime* had left women particularly vulnerable to unemployment and destitution. For example, in Bayeux in April 1796, a crowd of furious women invaded the cathedral—converted into a 'temple of reason' during the Terror—and dashed a bust of Rousseau to the floor to cries of 'When the good Lord was there we had bread!' There was no necessary correlation between this yearning for familiar religious rituals and antipathy to the Republic: in the departments of the Yonne and Nord, for example, the devout insisted that they were republicans exercising constitutional guarantees of religious freedom. Petitioners from Chablis (Yonne) claimed that 'we wish to be Catholics and republicans, and we can be both one and the other'. A petition from 900 'Catholics and republicans' in the district of Bousbecque in the department of the Nord demanded the opening of their church in March 1795 with a menacing reference to the Constitution of 1793:

We declare to you ... We will celebrate our divine mysteries in our church on the first of germinal if our priest does not flee, and if he does flee, we will find another one. Remember that insurrection is a duty for the people when their rights are violated.[13]

Elsewhere, people found different ways of sustaining religious practice. When Jacobin armies retook St-Laurent-de-Cerdans (see Chapter 6) from the Spanish in May 1794, there was massive emigration of Laurentins who had fought against the Republic, and the town itself narrowly escaped physical destruction. The *curé* Joseph Sicre had already left Saint-Laurent on 24 September 1792 in what he called 'las circumstancias calamitosas de la Iglesia de la frança'; although he probably returned to his parish with the invading Spanish army in 1793–4, his movements from then until 1796 are unknown. But, from 11 September 1796, the date of the benediction of the little chapel of Sant-Cornélis, he once again began to play a vital role in the lives of his parishioners. Built in a field just across the border at the River Muga, which at that point is no more than a stream, the chapel was to become a sacred place for hundreds of Laurentins who walked for an hour and a half along the rough tracks over the Pyrenees to marry or to bring a baby for baptism. Until his return to Saint-Laurent in December 1800, Sicre baptized 331 Laurentins, many of them brought by their fathers on the day of their birth, as was the practice before the Revolution, and performed 158 marriages involving Laurentins. His presence there was widely known: he also performed 124 other marriages and 281 baptisms of people from other villages of the Vallespir and as far away as the lowlands around Perpignan 60 kilometres to the northeast.[14]

By 1796, however, the Catholic Church was irrevocably shorn of its landed wealth, its privileges, its monopoly, and much of its social authority. Whatever the reasons for female religiosity, men in general were far less likely to return so passionately to the Church: boys born after 1785 would not have attended parish schools, hundreds of thousands of young men had served in secular military units, and the republican calendar itself legitimized an attitude to Sunday as a day like any other. In these ways, a gender-based difference in religiosity, already apparent before the Revolution, was widened. Women, often mistrustful of constitutional clergy and tired of waiting for *émigré* priests to overcome their scruples, expressed a populist religiosity which was profound and self-reliant. Local authorities were forced to reopen churches, as were those who had bought them as national property, venerable lay people said 'messes blanches' while midwives baptized the new born, Sundays were observed as the day of rest rather than the *décadi*, and emptied church treasuries were filled with salvaged relics and venerated objects of devotion.

Shaken by the widespread and often violent contestation by devout women of the civic authority of local representatives of the regime, the Directory attempted in 1798 to intimidate 'disloyal' priests into hiding but with negligible impact on a religiosity which was less general but more intense than a decade earlier. Central to the regime's unease at resurgent Catholicism was the continued presence on foreign soil of huge numbers of *émigrés* and unnerving electoral signs that those eligible to vote for deputies were politically open to a return of monarchy. For, while the Jacobin armies had succeeded in expelling counter-revolutionary armies from French soil, the war— and with it the problem of the *émigrés*—continued.

The hard years of the Directory were often characterized by bitter tensions occasioned by religious resurgence and ecclesiastical disorganization, desertion from the army and avoidance of conscription, political abstention and violent revenge for the deadly politics of the Year II. Underpinning these interlocking tensions, which had their origins in religious and political conflicts since 1790 and the exigencies of war since 1792, was the Directory's political economy, unifying and aggravating other antipathies towards the bourgeois republic. The political economy of the regime alienated the great mass of people.

In an economy still on a war-footing, the abandonment of price controls in December 1794 had unleashed a massive spurt of inflation. By October 1795, the *assignat's* purchasing power stood at only 0.75 per cent of its face value; by the following February, when the paper currency was abandoned, it was just 0.25 per cent. The difficulties for wage-earners created by unchecked price rises were worsened by the harvest failure in autumn 1795. Arguably the worst harvest of the century, and followed by a severe winter, the great subsistence crisis of 1795–6 intensified the volatility of popular responses to the Directory. The regime continued the major revolutionary forms of taxation—on land and personal wealth—but added to them a business tax and a tax on doors and windows; the social effects of these new wealth taxes were more than offset by the reintroduction of indirect taxes on essentials, levied at town gates.

These were hard years for urban wage-earners, but not necessarily for all their rural counterparts. The removal of controls on prices and wages was felt in different ways in parts of the countryside. With hundreds of thousands of men still at the front, rural workers could profit from the shortage of labour at harvest-time to insist on higher wages. At Attichy, in the east of the department of the Oise, harvests in August 1795 were disrupted by strikes by itinerant harvesters insisting on higher payments. Known since the fifteenth century as 'bacchanals' (from 'festivals of Bacchus'), these often violent strikes by harvesters testify to the importance of commercial wheat-growing in the Paris basin.[15] Peasants who had borrowed money to acquire an extra plot during the sale of *émigré* land in 1793–4 were also able to take advantage of rampant inflation to pay back the capital. Large tenant-farmers were also able to take advantage of the escalating prices paid for their produce to buy land, clear taxes, and pay off leases.

Forty-five laws and fifty decrees concerning forests had been passed in 1790–5 with little impact on illegal tree-felling. By 1795 the evidence of clearances and woodcutting, especially in the south, had become of national importance. In a series of reports, the Jacobin agronomist and former priest Coupé de l'Oise argued that southern France was now as denuded as other parts of the Mediterranean coast from Spain to the Near East. He reported that the Narbonnais, 'which the Romans called their province and Italy itself, no longer offers anything but arid mountains for the most part':

Even in living memory, people believe that the climate has changed; vines and olives suffer from frosts now, they perish in places where they used to flourish, and people give the reason: the hillsides and peaks were formerly covered with clumps of woods, bushes, greenery . . . the greedy fury of clearances arrived; everything has been cut down without consideration; people have destroyed the physical conditions which conserved the temperature of the region.[16]

The Directory, however, was no more successful than had been the Jacobin Republic in resolving the issues of the common lands and clearances. Resolutely committed to a *laissez-faire* economy, the regime sought to impose agrarian individualism and the rights of private property. No government since 1789 had been willing to confront fully the ancient mesh of communal controls over forest resources, gleaning, commons, use of uncultivated land, and rights of access across private land. Now the Directory acted to legislate for the priority of the rights of the individual owner of private property in forests and on harvested or uncultivated land, and encouraged the sale of commons by auction. On 21 Prairial IV (9 June 1796), an interim measure was rushed through the legislature and Directory to suspend execution of the decree of 10 June 1793 dividing common lands by head.

The Directory also reversed the Convention's policy of nationalized hospitals and state responsibilities for welfare; in the Year V local hospital boards were given responsibility for administration, and welfare again became based on private charity, despite the pleas of hospitals that they needed state aid because they had lost their pre-revolutionary rights to levy dues on local communities. The regime's philosophy of individual responsibility underscored class antipathies more sharply than at any other period of the Revolution. However, in sharp contrast to such *laissez-faire* attitudes, it reintroduced *ancien régime* controls over prostitution, as always a last resort for young women migrants to Paris and other cities. Prostitutes were placed outside the law but were required to register with police and to work in closed and discreet brothels to control the spread of syphilis and to make public thoroughfares more 'respectable'. No controls were placed on their clients.[17]

The dominant cultural values of these years, symbolized by the construction of a new stock exchange in the capital, were mirrored in literary production. After the hiatus of the Terror, the publication of new books reached pre-revolutionary levels of 815 by 1799; among them were 174 new novels, compared with 99 in 1788 and 16 in 1794. These were predominantly pastoral love-stories, sentimental intrigues and mysteries, but there was also a large number of novels with a specifically religious, educational, or moralizing tone. By the end of the 1790s there were three times as many printers and publishers as a decade earlier. Charles Panckoucke, the producer of the official newspaper for announcements and parliamentary reporting, the *Moniteur universel*, had 800 workers. However, the number of new newspapers declined to 42 (from 226 in 1790 and 78 in 1793) and of political songs to 90 in 1799 and 25 in 1800 (from 701 in 1794).[18]

By its religious, military, economic, and social policies, the Directory had alienated large numbers of people already excluded from legal forms of voicing grievances. The popular response to this 'bourgeois republic' varied widely in form and political content, but was everywhere visceral in its tone. By 1797, communities, individuals and clandestine movements were utilizing a rich array of illegal forms of contestation, ranging from the simple refusal to obey to elaborate programmes for radical change. In the small town of Collioure on the Mediterranean border with Spain, on 13 Germinal An V (2 April 1797), a huge crowd of women returning from mass in a nearby village threatened the officer of a grain-store located in a former Dominican chapel, demanding both bread and the reopening of the chapel. According to Jacques Xinxet, the mayor and local notary, 'fanaticism, the primary source of all our problems', was to blame: 'let's cut the evil at the roots if we want to have internal calm'. The town was deeply divided by the religious schism (Collioure's ten priests and monks had all emigrated) and by its occupation for six months by the Spanish army in 1794.[19]

During the same month that the women of Collioure were demanding the reopening of the chapel, a trial was taking place hundreds of kilometres to the north, in Vendôme. Gracchus Babeuf and 48 of his associates were accused of having plotted to overthrow a lawful government by violent means.[20] Babeuf's own intellectual development since 1794 in the Parisian context of economic misery and political repression had led him to advocate a forcible seizure of power to impose the political democracy of the 1793 Constitution and the collectivization of the means of production—indeed, perhaps of work itself. The programme was to be imposed by a supposedly short period of dictatorship by a small group of revolutionaries. Babeuf's ideology and strategies are of great importance in the history of socialism and communism. His 'Conspiracy of the Equals' was remarkable for the attraction of its political and social radicalism to soldiers, working women and Jacobins. However, these followers were united more by opposition to the Directory than by revolutionary communism, a programme which in any event had little appeal to *sans-culottes* committed to the redistribution but not socialization of private property.

Donald Sutherland has concluded that most French people were engaged in some form of rebellion against the Republic in these years. However, it was not the Republic as such that was being spurned, but rather the class politics of its self-perpetuating elite. There were, in any case, no organizational or ideological links—other than a hatred for the regime and its bourgeois supporters—between those in opposition in 1795–9: royalist plotters and 'white' terrorists, Babouvists and Jacobins, women protesting for Christ and bread, and deserters from the army. Some of the most troublesome challenges to the regime had no clear political overtones. For example, in the Beauce south of Paris in 1796–7 travellers were terrified by the 'bande d'Orgères', an organized, violent subculture of perhaps 150 men and women of all ages whose 95 forays resulted in 75 murders.[21] Stories of the band's humiliation and violation of their victims and of their subsequent orgies horrified polite society (as did those of the *'chauffeurs'* of the south, so-called because they roasted their victims' feet to extract information). When finally arrested in 1798, twenty-two of the band were executed.

The sharp edge of economic deprivation was softened somewhat by several bountiful harvests and a return to metallic currency in 1798, but other sources of antipathy remained towards a regime which conscripted young men to fight in distant lands while denying people the means to reconstruct religion and the economy along populist lines. The same men who in 1792 had advocated wars of revolutionary liberation as the solution to foreign animosity and internal division now conducted foreign affairs in an essentially pragmatic and expansionist manner. A smaller army (382,000 in 1797 compared with 732,000 in August 1794), largely composed of conscripts, was now led by officers appointed from above in order to reward technical expertise and to purge both Jacobins and royalist sympathizers.[22]

Despite the turning fortunes of the war, it continued to take an enormous toll; as many as 200,000 soldiers died in 1794–5, mostly from wounds and diseases in rudimentary hospitals. Lack of adequate supplies led to mutinies in Belgium, Holland, and Italy, and caused officers to turn a blind eye to stealing by troops. Whereas the Jacobins of 1793–4 had insisted on the incompatibility of new France and old Europe, the Directory's peace treaties with Prussia (April 1795) and Spain (July 1795), and the commercial and naval treaty signed with the latter in August 1796, were couched in terms which assumed the coexistence of sovereign states. With the creation of 'sister' Republics in the Low Countries in 1795, these treaties signalled the transition from a war of revolutionary survival to one of expansion and negotiation. The welcome extended to 'enlightened' foreigners in 1792 had given way under the Terror to surveillance and suspicion; now a series of laws, such as that of February 1798 empowering officials to expel foreigners from ports, codified the rights of the state over the right of free entry and asylum.[23]

Moreover, conflict with Britain and Austria continued: while a peace with the latter was signed at Campo-Formio on 27 Vendémiaire VI (18 October 1797), hostilities recommenced in Italy in 1798. This, together with the extension of war with Britain into Ireland and Egypt, convinced the Directory that irregular army levies had to be replaced by an annual conscription of single men aged 20–25 years (the Jourdan Law, 19 Fructidor VI/5 September 1798). This law sharply intensified resentment of military service which had been latent or open since 1793 because it increased the numbers of healthy young men removed from the pool of household labour to fight on foreign, often distant, soil and because it introduced a system of 'replacements' whereby wealthy conscripts could buy a substitute from among the poor who had earlier survived the ballot. Again, those regions where the hold of the royal state before 1789 had been weakest (such as parts of Massif Central, Brittany and the west) or which had been incorporated more recently into the state (the Pyrenees, parts of the southeast), particularly resented the deeper intrusion of the state's exactions. Resistance to conscription often became part of a complex of refusal involving religious and ethnic antipathies: in Brittany and the west *chouannerie*, a potent mix of royalism and banditry, proved to be ineradicable.[24] In areas far from Paris, *insoumission* (refusal of conscripts to join the army) became endemic, often with the tacit approval of most of the community: *insoumis* continued to live and work as before, disappearing only when police appeared. Young men also sought to avoid conscription by self-mutilation or by arranged marriages. Occasionally, attempts were made to thwart military bureaucracy by destroying birth records, as on the night of 5 Nivôse VII (Christmas 1799), when the town hall of St-Girons (Ariège) was destroyed by fire, and with it the district's civil registers. Resistance was most effective when it had general community support. In rural areas, where officials and the dwindling number of supporters of the regime were likely to be involved in agriculture, threats, arson, and other destruction of property could be used to intimidate officials into inaction. By 1798, many parts of the west, Massif Central, and Pyrenees were virtually ungovernable.

The Directory had twice to protect the regime against resurgent political forces on either side. The elections of 1797 returned a majority of royalists of various nuances, resulting in the annulling of the elections of 177 deputies by the directors after calling in troops on 17–18 Fructidor V (3–4 September 1797). A new wave of repression followed against refractory clergy, many of whom had returned in hope after the elections. The Peace of Campo Formio brought the war begun in 1792 to a temporary peace, except with England, against whom Napoleon was dispatched to Egypt in May 1798, with disastrous consequences. Then, on 22 Floréal VI (11 May 1798) a coup was organized to prevent a resurgence of Jacobinism: this time 127 deputies were prevented from taking their seats.

Several years of successful foreign policy were to draw the Directory into disastrous wars of territorial annexation. The Directory established 'sister republics' in Switzerland (January 1798) and the Papal States (February). In April the left bank of the Rhine was incorporated into the 'natural boundaries' of what was increasingly referred to as 'la grande nation' (see Map 3). Local populations were not always convinced that the troops' behaviour expressed mutual respect. Hopes of diverting English naval attention also led the Directory into engagement with Irish patriots. Since the founding of the non-sectarian United Irishmen in Belfast in 1791 their hopes had centred on French assistance in securing independence from Britain. An initial French invasion in December 1796 had been thwarted by storms. In 1798 a second attempt to support an Irish insurrection—and to incapacitate the British—failed miserably after initial successes. In a matter of weeks about 30,000 Irish died in punitive killings, the same number as in the year of the Terror in France, a country with six times the population.

In this atmosphere of cynicism and political instability a brilliant couple came to increasing attention. In 1795 the widow Rose de Beauharnais met a young, uncouth, and brilliant army officer. Both had been marginal to the elaborately graded aristocratic society of pre-revolutionary France: the daughter of an impecunious minor noble who had fumbled the management of his slaves on a sugar plantation in Martinique; the studious, smouldering Corsican Napoleone Buonaparte who had felt desperately awkward in his French military academy. 'Napoléon' (as he gallicized his name) was born to minor Corsican nobles in 1769. Sent to military school in France as a 10-year-old, the brooding, irascible, and diminutive boy responded to his peers' taunts at his accent and name with a steely ambition and occasional violent outbursts.

Neither were physically prepossessing: both were diminutive at a time when height bespoke attractiveness, and Rose's bad teeth (a legacy of her childhood love of sugar-cane) were as notorious as Napoleon's sickly pallor. But both could be charming, and they were bonded by passion and a genuine affection, as well as by a startling ambition. Josephine (as he began to call her) gave him the allure of old noble graces; in return he gave her the thrill of power. The French Revolution and the wars it unleashed offered Napoleon and other ambitious young soldiers the chance of rapid promotion: in 1793, his celebrated recapture of the port of Toulon from Britain catapulted him from captain to brigadier-general. At that time Bonaparte, who had received generous compensation from the Convention as a 'Corsican Jacobin Patriot' after the island's revolt, was a supporter of the Jacobins. In July 1793 he had published the 'Souper de Beaucaire' in which he exclaimed: 'Marat and Robespierre! These are my saints!'[25] By the time of the Directory, however, he had sloughed off such revolutionary rhetoric, and concentrated on military power. His standing was bolstered when, late in 1796, he retook Corsica for the Republic after twenty-eight months as the Anglo-Corsican Kingdom.

The rise of Napoleon in popular repute is clear from the songs of the period. Le Caveau was a small gastronomic society founded in Paris in 1726 whose members contributed gently satiric 'vaudeville' songs as well as the cost of their meals. In 1796 Le Caveau recreated itself as the

Dîners du Vaudeville and adopted a constitution which excluded politics from its members' contributions. Nevertheless, many of the songs were marked by nationalist themes, and in 1797 one of them eulogized the young Napoleon:

Hail to our soldiers' leader,
Who, courageous as well as wise,
Leads the French into combat
Or restrains their bravery.
Of Europe, the victor,
And the pacifier.
Glory to the able warrior,
Who, not yet thirty years old,
Joins the valour of Achilles,
And the virtues of Nestor.[26]

Despite a good harvest in 1798, the French economy was in tatters: the Bas-Rhin had only 146 master-weavers operating compared with 1,800 in 1790, the Basses-Pyrénées had only 1,200 people employed in the woollens industry compared with 6,000 at the start of the decade. Economic resentments and massive popular non-compliance with the demands of the state climaxed in the summer of 1799 in large-scale but uncoordinated royalist risings in the southwest around Toulouse and a resurgence of *chouannerie* in the west in October. By that time, too, the requisitioning, anticlericalism and repression of putatively liberating French armies was provoking discontent and insurrection in all of the 'sister republics'. This and the initial successes of the second coalition formed between Russia, Austria, and England provided a military pretext for a fourth challenge to the Directory, this time led successfully by Napoleon, the army officer who had dispersed the royalist insurgents in 1795 and who now abandoned his shattered forces in Egypt. In this he was supported by his brother, then president of the Five Hundred, Sieyès and Talleyrand, two of the architects of revolutionary change in 1789–91, and Fouché, a former priest from the Vendée turned dechristianizer in 1793. On 18–19 Brumaire VIII (9–10 November 1799), the furious members of the Five Hundred were driven out by troops and a decade of parliamentary rule was over.

On 24 Frimaire (15 December), the Consuls (Bonaparte, Sieyès, and Ducos, who had sat on the 'Plain' during the Terror) announced that a new constitution would terminate uncertainty while being based on 'the sacred rights of property, equality, and liberty':

The powers which it institutes will be strong and stable, as they must be in order to guarantee the rights of citizens and the interests of the State.

Citizens, the Revolution is established upon the principles which began it: it is ended.[27]

The pronouncement was made more in hope than in confidence: many provincial Jacobins shared the deputies' outrage that a republican legislature had been dispersed by the army. In the plebiscite on the Constitution of the Year VIII Napoleon's younger brother Lucien nearly doubled the 'yes' votes from 1.6 million to more than 3 million; only 1,562 had supposedly voted 'no'.

However, within a few years Napoleon had moved to meet major sources of instability. A decree of 29 Vendémiaire IX (20 October 1800) permitted *émigrés* who had not taken up arms to return; then, on 6 Floréal X (26 April 1802), the path was opened to all other exiles. With them came the bulk of the non-juring priests, convinced of the foolishness of the First Estate's rallying to secular reform in 1789 and of the burning need, after ten years of divine retribution, for a purified Catholicism to rechristianize France. On 15 July 1801 a Concordat was signed with the papacy, formally celebrated at Easter mass at Notre Dame de Paris in 1802. The treaty of Lunéville was signed with Austria on 21 Pluviôse IX (9 February 1801) and that of Amiens with Britain on 5 Germinal X (25 March 1802). The end (albeit temporary) of war offered the chance for deserters to be amnestied, and for returning *émigrés* and priests to be reintegrated into their communities in a climate of reconciliation. The sunny calm of the summer of 1802 created the perfect conditions for the plebiscite on the new Constitution of the year X, by which Napoleon became Consul for life. The Revolution was indeed over.

Notes

1. McPhee, *Revolution and Environment*, 120.

2. Alan Forrest, *The Revolution in Provincial France: Aquitaine, 1789–1799* (Oxford, 1996), 334; Mason, *Singing the French Revolution*, ch. 5. The reference to

Tenairon is to a cape on the Peloponnese, testimony to the classical education of middle-class Parisians.

3. Carla Hesse, *Publishing and Cultural Politics in Revolutionary Paris, 1789–1810* (Berkeley and Los Angeles, 1991).

4. François Gendron, *The Gilded Youth of Thermidor*, trans. James Cookson (Montreal, 1993). The best overview of the Thermidorian period remains Georges Lefebvre, *The Thermidorians*, trans. R. Baldick (London, 1965). See, too, Bronislaw Baczko, *Ending the Terror: The French Revolution after Robespierre* (Cambridge, 1994).

5. Ozouf, *Festivals and the French Revolution*, 96.

6. Philip Dawson (ed.), *The French Revolution* (Englewood Cliffs, NJ, 1967), 152–3. On these *journées*, see Rudé, *Crowd in the French Revolution*, ch. 10; Bertaud, *Army of the French Revolution*, ch. 12.

7. On the links between internal and external counter-revolution, see Maurice Hutt, *Chouannerie and Counter-Revolution: Puisaye, the Princes and the British Government in the 1790s*, 2 vols. (Cambridge, 1983); William Fryer, *Republic or Restoration in France? 1794–1797: The Politics of French Royalism* (Manchester, 1965); Harvey Mitchell, *The Underground War against Revolutionary France: The Missions of William Wickham, 1794–1800* (Oxford, 1965).

8. *Moniteur universel*, no. 281, 11 Messisor III [29 June 1795], vol. 25, 81, 92; Soboul, *French Revolution*, 453–5.

9. John Hall Stewart (ed.), *A Documentary Survey of the French Revolution* (New York, 1951), 572–612.

10. Crook, *Elections in the French Revolution*, 124–8.

11. McPhee, *Revolution and Environment*, 136. Popular politics in the countryside are studied by Lewis, *Second Vendée*, ch. 3; Colin Lucas, 'Themes in Southern Violence after 9 Thermidor', in Lewis and Lucas (eds.), *Beyond the Terror*, 152–94; Richard Cobb, *Reactions to the French Revolution* (Oxford, 1972), 19–62; Jones, *Peasantry*, 240–7.

12. Archives Départementales de la Charente-Maritime; Jean-Marie Augustin, *La Révolution française en Haut-Poitou et pays Charentais* (Toulouse, 1989).

13. Suzanne Desan, *Reclaiming the Sacred: Lay Religion and Popular Politics in Revolutionary France* (Ithaca, NY, 1990), 146, 162. Useful general surveys of the Church under the Directory are McManners, *French Revolution*, chs. 13–14; Olwen Hufton, 'The Reconstruction of a Church 1796–1801', in Lewis and Lucas (eds.), *Beyond the Terror*, 21–52, and Olwen Hufton, 'Women in Revolution', *French Politics and Society*, 7 (1989), 65–81.

14. These figures come from a register Sicre brought back with him to St-Laurent and which is today in the archives of the parish church: Peter McPhee, 'Counter-Revolution in the Pyrenees', *French History*, 7 (1993).

15. Jacques Bernet, 'Les Grèves de moissonneurs ou "bacchanals" dans les campagnes d'Île-de-France et de Picardie au XVIIIe siècle', *Histoire et sociétés rurales*, 11 (1999), 153–86.

16. McPhee, *Revolution and Environment*, 132.

17. Richard Cobb, *The Police and the People: French Popular Protest 1789–1820* (Oxford, 1970), 234–39; Colin Jones, 'Picking up the Pieces: The Politics and the Personnel of Social Welfare from the Convention to the Consulate', in Lewis and Lucas (eds.), *Beyond the Terror*, 53–91.

18. Research on 'cultural production' is conveniently tabulated in Colin Jones, *The Longman Companion to the French Revolution* (London, 1989), 260–2. On changes to festivals, see Ozouf, *Festivals and the French Revolution*, ch. 5.

19. Peter McPhee, *Collioure 1780–1815: The French Revolution in a Mediterranean Community* (Melbourne, 1989), 72–3.

20. R. B. Rose, *Gracchus Babeuf 1760–1797* (Stanford, Calif., 1978); J. A. Scott (ed. and trans.), *The Defense of Gracchus Babeuf before the High Court of Vendôme* (Amherst, Mass., 1967).

21. This violence is examined by Sutherland, *France 1789–1815*, ch. 8; Cobb, *Reactions*, ch. 5; Michel Vovelle, 'From Beggary to Brigandage: The Wanderers in the Beauce during the French Revolution', in Jeffry Kaplow (ed.), *New Perspectives on the French Revolution* (New York, 1965), 287–304.

22. On the army under the Directory, see Bertaud, *Army of the French Revolution*, chs. 10–11. The question of how 'liberating' French armies were divides historians: see Robert R. Palmer, *The Age of the Democratic Revolution: A Political History of Europe and America, 1760–1800*, vol. 2 (Princeton, 1964); T. C. W. Blanning, *French Revolution in Germany: Occupation and Resistance in the Rhineland, 1792–1802* (Oxford, 1983).

23. Michael Rapport, *Nationality and Citizenship in Revolutionary France: The Treatment of Foreigners, 1789–1799* (Oxford, 2000).

24. Alan Forrest, 'Conscription and Crime in Rural France during the Directory and Consulate', in Lewis and Lucas (eds.), *Beyond the Terror*, 92–120.

25. Evangeline Bruce, *Napoleon and Josephine: An Improbable Marriage* (London, 1995), 97. Two most accessible accounts of Napoleon's rise are Malcolm Crook, *Napoleon Comes to Power: Democracy and Dictatorship in Revolutionary France, 1795–1804* (Cardiff, 1998); and Robert Asprey, *The Rise of Napoleon Bonaparte* (New York, 2000).

26. From Mason, *Singing the French Revolution*, 199; Brigitte Level, *A travers deux siècles. Le Caveau: société bachique et chantante 1726–1939* (Paris, 1996).

27. Stewart (ed.), *Documentary Survey*, 780.

9

The Significance of
the Revolution

A Revolution which had begun in 1789 with boundless hopes for a golden era of political liberty and social change had ended in 1799 with a military seizure of power. It had not proved possible to stabilize the Revolution after the initial overthrow of the *ancien régime* and the proclamation of the Declaration of the Rights of Man and the Citizen in August 1789. Instead, French people had had to endure a decade of political instability, civil war, and armed conflict with the rest of Europe.

In 1889, on the centenary of the French Revolution, Samuel Langhorne Clemens—the author, as Mark Twain, of *Huckleberry Finn* and *The Adventures of Tom Sawyer*—published *A Connecticut Yankee in King Arthur's Court*. The sprightly novel imagines the visit by a nineteenth-century American to sixth-century Britain as a way of evaluating human progress and includes a ringing justification of the French Revolution and the Terror:

There were two 'Reigns of Terror', if we would but remember it and consider it; the one wrought murder in hot passion, the other in heartless cold blood; the one lasted mere months, the other had lasted a thousand years; the one inflicted death upon ten thousand persons, the other upon a hundred millions; but our shudders are all for the horrors of the minor Terror.[1]

Of course, any judgement about whether the French Revolution was, on balance, beneficial to humanity must be more nuanced than Twain's. There is no doubt that the 300,000 nobles and clergy would have judged these years to have been disastrous in every way. So, too, would have those who had been dependent on the privileged for employment or for charity, and the families of scores of thousands of young men whose lives had ended prematurely on battlefields or in hospitals. Had they died in vain? Too many discussions of the consequences of the Revolution have in fact been reduced to personal judgements about whether or not it was 'a good thing'. This is not the same as evaluating its consequences for the world in which French people lived. How 'revolutionary' had been the experience of twenty-five years of Revolution and Empire?

Responses to these questions go to the heart of important and often trenchant divisions among historians. Ever since the Revolution itself, most historians have argued that, for better or for worse, the Revolution profoundly altered most aspects of life in France. However, in recent decades, some historians have argued that its consequences were minimal in terms of real social change. François Furet, for example, argues that well into the nineteenth century French society remained much as it had under the *ancien régime*.[2] Until France went through its own industrial revolution from the 1830s, so his argument goes, the patterns of work and daily life would be much the same as before the Revolution.

Certainly, such 'minimalist' historians agree with their opponents that French political life had been fundamentally transformed. For the first time, a large and populous country had been reformed along democratic, republican lines. Even the restoration of monarchy in 1814 could not reverse the revolutionary change from royal absolutism to constitutional, representative government. Moreover, the experience of years of political debate, election campaigns and new political rights meant that the idea of citizenship was now deeply ingrained. Such new ideas had been spread by word of mouth, the printed word, and imagery, part of what may be described as a revolution in 'political culture'. The years of liberty after 1788 unleashed an unprecedented outpouring of the printed word: hundreds of newspapers, perhaps one thousand plays, and many thousands of brochures and handbills. But this revolution of ideas went far beyond this, for such printed material was accompanied by a flowering of popular revolutionary art in the form of woodcuts, prints and paintings. Millions of people had become accustomed to the assumption that any form of government could only be legitimate if it was based on some form of popular sovereignty. Malcolm Crook has estimated that about three million men had been involved in voting across the revolutionary decade; indeed, there were so many elections (several per year), and such lengthy voting procedures, that a certain lassitude developed. The Constitution of 1793 made provision for direct elections, but this was never implemented.

Historians also agree about the ideological importance of the Revolution. Twenty-five years of political upheaval and division left a legacy of memories, both bitter and sweet, and of conflicting ideologies which has lasted until our own times. The Revolution was a rich seedbed of ideologies ranging from communism to authoritarian royalism via liberal constitutionalism and social democracy. French people were to remain divided about which political system was best able to reconcile authority, liberty, and equality. Should the head of government be a king, an emperor or an elected executive? Should 'liberty' mean political and civic freedoms or economic freedom (a free enterprise economy) as well? And how was 'equality' to be understood: as equality before the law, of political rights, of social status, of economic well-being, of the races, of the sexes? Such questions were at the heart of political and social divisions during the Revolution; they remain unresolved today.

None of the ideologies which developed during the Revolution could claim to represent the views of a majority of French people. While Bonapartism and Jacobinism claimed to be based on popular sovereignty, both were ambiguous about the forms that democratic government should take. The memory of Napoleon would cast a long shadow of the strong man who had restored order and stability but at the cost of military rule and almost continuous war. The period of Jacobin rule remained attractive in hindsight for its emphasis on democracy and social equality and its heroic defence of the Revolution in 1793–4, but also conjured up negative images of the Terror and controls on civil liberties. In areas of the south with significant Protestant populations the deadly political divisions of 1793–5 had often followed denominational lines, leaving a legacy of hatred which henceforth ensured that Protestants would support left-wing, secular political parties. A century later, a Protestant rural labourer, Jean Fontane from Anduze (department of the Gard), recalled that, 'if a majority of us were republicans, it was in memory of our beautiful Revolution of 1793, of which our fathers had inculcated the principles which still survive in our hearts. Above all, we were children of the Revolution.'[3]

In contrast, there would always be large numbers of people for whom the memory of the Revolution evoked negative images of suffering and horror. The many liberal nobles and the great mass of parish priests who had thrown in their lot with the Third Estate in 1789 had experienced a protracted nightmare as the Revolution abolished noble privileges and titles and made sweeping changes to the Church. Most of the clerical deputies had arrived at the Estates-General of 1789 critical of both the monarchy and their own bishops and eager to participate in a project of regenerating the country. Their hopes had been dashed by more radical reform agendas for the Church, culminating in the Civil Constitution of the Clergy. The involvement—whether active or complicit—of non-juring clergy in the counter-revolution and the subsequent proscription and dechristianization during the Terror was to reunite Church and monarchy in a royalist ideology of the Right, one of the major political movements in France for the next 150 years.

Memories of the Terror and of mass conscription and war were etched deep into the memories of every individual and community. In the west, where the civil war in the Vendée had cost perhaps 400,000 lives, there was general rejection of republicanism for a century or more. In the village of Chanzeaux, for example, the church built on the ruins of the old in the nineteenth century features stained glass windows listing the names of the dead of 1793 and visual images which have taught generations of villagers until this day that the rising was one of devout peasants defending beloved priests. Similarly, the discovery of masses of bones in Lucs-Vendée by the parish priest in 1860 was to result in another myth, still potent today, of the 'Bethlehem of the Vendée', according to which 564 women, 107 children and many men were massacred on a single day, on 28 February 1794. In 1804, La Roche-sur-Yon, destroyed by Jacobin armies in 1794 was rebuilt as Napoléonville. The town was ordered around three major open spaces: for the market, in front of the Prefecture, and for troop reviews.[4] There is perhaps no better statement of the values underpinning the Napoleonic vision of social order in post-revolutionary France; his conquest of space could not, however, obliterate memories of its earlier role at the heart of the Vendéan rebellion. Two hundred years later, the insurrection remains the central element in the collective identity of the people of the west of France.

Whatever the importance of these changes to government, political ideas and memories, however, 'minimalists' have argued that the essentials of daily life continued largely unchanged: especially patterns of work, the position of the poor, social inequalities, and the inferior status of women.

First, the great mass of working people in town and country continued to work and survive in the same ways as they had before 1789. Most French people remained, like their parents, owners or renters of small plots of land. The abolition of seigneurial dues, finally achieved by reforms in 1792–3, and the purchase of the smaller pieces of church and *émigré* property made it possible for millions of peasant landowners to stay on the land. France remained essentially a rural society dominated by small farm units on which households used ancient methods and techniques to produce mainly for their own survival. In urban areas, too, most work continued to be done in small workplaces, where master craftsmen worked side by side with three or four skilled workers and apprentices. Many decades would pass before a substantial minority of wage-earners were employed in large, mechanized workshops of the type starting to become common in the new industrial cities in the north of England.

Secondly, whatever the grand schemes of the Jacobins in 1793–4, the destitute continued to constitute a major urban and rural underclass swollen in times of crisis by unemployed rural labourers and urban workers. The position of the poor had always been appalling, dependent as they were on haphazard and often inadequate relief from the Church. But worse was to come. In 1791, the National Assembly had removed the Church's capacity to dispense charity when it abolished the tithe and sold off church property. The subsequent realization that local government could simply not cope with poor relief led governments to set up a series of work schemes and temporary relief measures which were always piecemeal and never adequately financed by governments preoccupied with war. After 1794 the situation of the poor became truly desperate, as conservative governments abolished controls on prices and the Jacobins' social welfare measures. This coincided with several poor harvests and harsh winters. In the winter of 1795–6 the river Seine froze solid and ravenous wolves were reported roaming the streets of Paris among the bodies of the destitute who had died of hunger. Even when the Catholic Church was restored to its position as religion of state by Napoleon, it never again had the material resources to minister to the needs of the poor even in the limited way it had before 1789.

Among the initial supporters of the Revolution, perhaps urban working people had sacrificed most and gained least. The *sans-culottes* of Paris, Marseilles and other cities had been the backbone of the Revolution, but they won few tangible benefits. Their demands in 1793 for property redistribution failed to achieve results; in contrast, a major grievance in 1789, indirect taxation, had been reintroduced and customs houses ringing cities and towns had been re-erected. To be sure, moments of popular power and hope left potent traces in the collective memories of the descendants of *sans-culottes* and sections of the peasantry. Even so, it could be argued that, for working people, fond memories of 1792–4 were to be cold comfort for dashed expectations of real social change. The descendants of the radicals of the 1790s had to wait many decades for the realization of such hopes: until 1848 for the durable implementation of manhood suffrage (for women not until 1944), until 1864 for the right to strike and twenty years more for the right to form trade unions, until the 1880s for free, secular, and compulsory education, and until well into the twentieth century for an income tax and social welfare provisions for the sick, the elderly, and the unemployed.

Thirdly, France remained a sharply inegalitarian, hierarchical society, even if the new hierarchy was to be one in which wealth rather than the family name was seen as the best gauge of personal merit. Many of the battles of the revolutionary period were fought over the question of what 'equality' should mean in practice, but the campaigns of the *sans-culottes* and poorer peasants for concrete measures to reduce economic inequalities were ultimately unsuccessful. The constitution of 1793 had been the first to codify public responsibilities for social welfare and education, but it had never been put into effect.

In the colonies, too, the pre-revolutionary hierarchies of race were reimposed, with one exception. In January 1802, 12,000 French troops landed in St-Domingue to reimpose colonial control; after two years of bloody fighting the first post-colonial black nation—Haiti—was born. Elsewhere, however, Napoleon reversed the Jacobin abolition of slavery in 1794 and in 1802 reintroduced the 'Code noir' of 1685, which denied slaves legal recourse and assumed their children to be the slave-owner's property. The slave trade would not be abolished until 1815–18; slavery itself not until 1848.

Moreover, in the new hierarchy of wealth which was to rule the country after 1799, most *ancien régime* nobles continued to be pre-eminent. According to Donald Greer, 13,925 male nobles over 12 years of age had emigrated; in all, 1,158 noble men and women were executed during the Terror. Historians now argue that there were perhaps only 125,000 nobles in the 1780s, many fewer than previously estimated. Consequently, virtually every noble family was directly affected by emigration, imprisonment or death. Even so, it is clear that the Revolution was not a holocaust of nobles. Those nobles who steered clear of political trouble and kept their lands intact during the Revolution could continue to play a leading economic and political role into the nineteenth century. Of the 281 men Napoleon appointed as his 'prefects' to administer the provinces, 41 per cent were drawn from old noble families. In 1830, two-thirds of the 387 richest men in France were nobles; and, as late as 1846, 25 per cent of parliamentary deputies were nobles from *ancien régime* families.

On 28 Pluviôse An VIII (16 February 1800), just three months after seizing power, Napoleon issued a new administrative decree which effectively reduced local government to a rubber stamp. Henceforth councils were to restrict themselves to the management of communal finances and resources within rigid formulae of administration. The mayors and deputy-mayors of towns with more than 5,000 people were to be directly appointed by the first Consul, while others were to be named by the prefect of the department. In this way prefects had the powers of the pre-revolutionary *intendants*, and local councils, elected for twenty years on a property qualification, were decidedly less democratic and unfettered than ever before. Judges, too, were once again to be appointed rather than elected.

Finally, 'minimalists' argue that the inferior status of women emerged little changed, or even more entrenched. Women had always been the linchpin of the fragile family economy and, as such, had injected an extraordinary strength and hope into the early years of the Revolution. But, as women, they seem to have gained little: only the right to inherit equally with their brothers and to sign legal contracts, if they were unmarried, survived the Empire. The liberal 1792 divorce laws, used by perhaps 30,000 women, were sharply curtailed in 1804 by Napoleon and finally abolished altogether in 1816. Despite the energetic campaigns of individual feminists in the early years of the Revolution, the repeated intervention of working women in collective action in Paris and their presence in clubs and societies, the great majority of politicians of whatever type were firmly opposed to women's political rights. During the Terror, the government newspaper, *La Feuille du salut public*, asked:

Women, do you wish to be republicans? Love, follow and teach the laws which recall your husbands and your children to the exercise of their rights . . . never follow the popular assemblies with the desire of speaking there.

Indeed, the strength of the political challenge women represented may be gauged by the often violent attacks upon them. Politicians ranging from royalists to Napoleon would have agreed with the Jacobin Amar, of the Committee of General Security, who justified the banning of the militant women's organization, the Revolutionary Republican Citizenesses, to the Convention on 30 October 1793 by describing men as

strong, robust, born with great energy, audacity and courage . . . destined for agriculture, commerce, navigation, travel, war . . . he alone seems suited for serious, deep thought . . . Women are unsuited for advanced thinking and serious reflection . . . more exposed to error and an exultation which would be disastrous in public life.[5]

The ambiguities in men's attitudes to women—drawing on ingrained assumptions about 'women's nature'—are also evident in revolutionary iconography: the protective Virgin Mary of *ancien régime* imagery gave way to the Marianne of the Republic, now in classical garb and liberty cap, but still a feminine allegory watching protectively but passively over active men. Lynn Hunt has argued that despite, or because of, the political challenge of radical women, the transition from absolutism—under which all were subjects of the king—to a republican fraternity of male citizens had in fact reinforced the subordinate political position of women.

The implication of this 'minimalist' view of the significance of the Revolution is that those few changes it made to French politics and society were simply not worth the cost. The fatal legacy of the Revolution according to Simon Schama was the violent and naive certainty that 'connected social distress with political change'; the great mistake of Louis XVI had been to ask the masses for their *cahiers de doléances* at a time of famine and political uncertainty. From that point, the Revolution was 'doomed to self-destruct from over-inflated expectations'. For Schama, the only significant social change was the death of the innocent at the hands of unscrupulous demagogues and brutish mobs.[6]

Other historians, such as Albert Soboul and Gwynne Lewis, have argued that the Revolution was profoundly transforming. While they recognize that there were important continuities in French society, they insist that the 'minimalists' have ignored other important consequences. To Soboul, the 'minimalist' perspective was born of a political antipathy to the possibilities of revolutionary transformation: 'the vain attempts to deny the French Revolution—that dangerous precedent—its historical reality'. For Soboul, the Revolution was profoundly revolutionary in its short and long-term outcomes: 'A classic bourgeois revolution, its uncompromising abolition of the feudal system and the seigneurial regime make it the starting-point for capitalist society and the liberal representative system in the history of France.'[7]

These 'maximalist' historians argue that the Revolution was a triumph for the bourgeoisie and for the landowning peasantry. Moreover, the Revolution transformed the institutional structures of France—indeed, the very meaning of 'France' itself. It also led to lasting changes to the nature of the Church and of the family.

The Revolution represented an abrupt change in cultural and institutional structures of identity. France in 1789 had been a society in which people's main allegiance had been to their particular region: France had a unity only because of the monarchy's claim that this was its territory and the people its subjects. Most people did not use the French language in daily life and looked to elites in provincial capitals such as Toulouse, Rennes and Grenoble to defend them against the increasing claims of the royal state for taxes and conscripts. The strength of local loyalties was reinforced by economic practices which sought to meet the needs of the household and exchanged produce mainly within local markets. Since the twelfth century, the cost to the monarchy of establishing territorial control over France had been to accept a patchwork of regional and local privileges, exemptions and rights. On the eve of the Revolution, every aspect of the institutions of public life—in administration, customs and measures, the law, taxation, and the Church—was still marked by regional exceptions and privileges. Not only were the clergy, nobility, and certain corporate bodies such as guilds privileged in law and taxation, but the provinces also had their own law codes, degrees of self-government, levels of taxation, and systems of currency, weights, and measures.

In 1789–91 revolutionaries reshaped every aspect of institutional and public life according to principles of rationality, uniformity, and efficiency. Underpinning this sweeping reform was an administrative system of departments, districts, cantons, and communes. These 83 departments (today 96) were henceforth to be administered in precisely the same way; they were to have an identical structure of responsibilities, personnel, and powers. Diocesan boundaries coincided with departmental limits, and cathedrals were usually located in departmental capitals. The uniformity of administrative structures was reflected, too, in the imposition of a national system of weights, measures, and currency based on new, decimal measures. For example, the department of the Lot-et-Garonne in the southwest covered an area where before 1789 there had been sixty-five different ways of measuring length and twenty-six measures of the weight of grain: now there was just one national way of measuring. These evident benefits to business and commerce were accentuated by the abolition of tolls paid to towns and nobles and of internal customs. Before 1789, for example, a merchant taking a load of wood from Lorraine to Sète on the Mediterranean had had to pass through thirty-four separate toll-gates in twenty-one different places. Henceforth governments legislated on the basis of free trade within a national market.

From 1789, all French citizens, whatever their social background and residence, were to be judged according to a single uniform legal code, and taxed by the same obligatory proportional taxes on wealth, especially landed property. This is a key meaning of 'fraternity' and 'national unity'. The years of Revolution and Empire intensified the administrative unity of France, sustained by a new political culture of citizenship and the celebration of national heroes drawn from antiquity or the revolutionary struggle itself. Not only was the Revolution a turning-point in the uniformity of state institutions, but, for the first time, the state was also understood as representing a more emotional entity, 'the nation', based on citizenship. It is for this reason that the French Revolution is so often seen by historians as the seedbed of modern nationalism, a classic example of Benedict Anderson's concept of 'imagined community' as the basis of national identity.[8]

National unity was not only achieved at the expense of privileged social orders, occupations, and localities, but also assumed that all individuals were now first and foremost French citizens, members of the new nation. Before 1789, the major form of redistribution of wealth or surplus extraction had been the payment of 'tribute' or 'surplus' of various types to the state, the Church, and seigneurs, in the form of taxes, dues, and tithes. By 1800 the claims of the privileged orders were irredeemably lost; now wealth was appropriated from its producers by the state and through economic structures (through rent, markets and labour). Now, to follow Eric Wolf's argument, the state alone could levy tribute of taxes, men, and obedience, indicating its growing power and pre-eminence as an agent of social control.[9]

The emotional power of the nation-state often led revolutionaries in Paris to claim that French alone was the 'language of liberty' and that minority languages were part of the archaic *ancien régime* which had been overthrown. In fact, popular attitudes to the Revolution among the ethnic minorities who together made up a majority of the population varied from enthusiasm to outright hostility across time and place. But the Revolution and Empire everywhere had a profound impact on collective identity, on the *francisation* ('Frenchification') of the citizens of a new society, both because of participation in elections and referenda within a national context and because, in the years of revolutionary wars, millions of young men were conscripted to fight for the *patrie*, the safety of the Revolution and the Republic. In the Year III, General Kléber asked that his Alsacien compatriot Ney accompany him in the Army of the Rhine 'so that . . . I can at least speak immediately with someone who knows my language'. Napoleon, who himself was not fully at ease in French, perhaps had them in mind when he supposedly quipped: 'let these courageous men have their Alsacien dialect; they always fight in French'.[10]

In his memoirs, the eminent Catalan noble Jaubert de Passa recalled nostalgically the years before 1789 when 'I was completely ignorant of the French language and ... even felt a lively enough revulsion towards it'. Two of Jaubert's close relatives had been guillotined for collaborating with the Spanish armies in 1793–4. Now, in 1830, he wrote his memoirs in perfect French.[11] Whether or not speakers of minority languages were enthusiastic or hostile towards revolutionary change, the years after 1789 represented an acceleration of the process of *francisation*, whereby they came to perceive themselves as citizens of the French nation as well as Bretons, Catalans, or Basques. However, this change in self-identity should not be exaggerated. This 'double identity' was limited to an acceptance of national institutions and the vocabulary of a new, French politics. There is little evidence that popular cultures and minority languages were thereby eroded. French remained the daily language of a minority of people and France a land of great cultural and linguistic diversity.

Central to the 'minimalist' perspective on the significance of the Revolution is the argument that, as a victory of the landowning peasantry and because of the lost decades of overseas trade due to protracted warfare, these years actually retarded the development of a capitalist or market economy. Similarly, it could be argued that many of those bourgeois whom Soboul sees as the victors of the Revolution in fact suffered during it.

There were certainly many bourgeois for whom the Revolution and Empire were economically difficult periods. This was particularly the case in the great coastal towns where the uncertainties caused by wars and blockades and the temporary abolition of slavery (1794–1802) hit overseas trade hard: by 1815, French external trade was only half the 1789 volume and did not regain pre-revolutionary levels until 1830. Between 1790 and 1806, the downturn in trade caused the population of Marseilles to fall from 120,000 to 99,000, that of Nantes from perhaps 90,000 to 77,000 and that of Bordeaux from 110,000 to 92,000. In Languedoc, the textile towns of Lodève, Carcassonne, and Sommières had already been in crisis by the 1780s, largely because of English industrial competition, and the decades of war provided only temporary respite through army supplies before they went into permanent decline.

However, despite the economic difficulties felt by entrepreneurs and merchants in such towns, there were others where the cotton, iron, and coal industries were stimulated during the Napoleonic period by France's role in the continental system and by protection from British imports. One of them was the small Norman textile town of Elbeuf. Here the manufacturing bourgeoisie had been quite specific about their grievances in their *cahier* of 1789, fulminating against:

the inefficient administration of finances ... these constraints, these impediments to commerce: barriers reaching to the very heart of the kingdom; endless obstacles to the circulation of commodities ... representatives of manufacturing industries and Chambers of Commerce totally ignored and despised; an indifference on the part of the government towards manufacturers ...

The 'indifference' which so rankled with these men referred to the 1786 free trade treaty with Britain which had exposed them to cheap competition. After 1789, these budding industrialists achieved their goals, including the new recognition of their own importance: in the Year V, they were asked for the first time their opinion on a number of commercial treaties, and in the Year IX the advisory role of Chambers of Commerce was formally institutionalized. While Elbeuf felt the full brunt of trade blockades and food shortages, the decades after 1789 mark an important phase in the mechanization and concentration of the textile industry in the town rather than in rural piecework. By 1815 the population had increased some 50 per cent, and the number of enterprises had doubled. Political power was now fully concentrated in the hands of these local manufacturers.[12]

The essence of capitalism is market-oriented production by large and small entrepreneurs in town and countryside in order to make a profit. Even though many entrepreneurs, particularly in the seaports, actually suffered during the Revolution, in a more general sense, fundamental changes to the nature of the French economy were accelerated by the Revolution, changes which were to facilitate capitalist practices. From 1789 there was a series of institutional, legal, and social changes creating the environment within which capitalist industry and agriculture would thrive. The free enterprise and free trade (*laissez-faire*, *laissez-passer*) legislation of the Revolution guaranteed that manufacturers, farmers, and merchants could commit themselves to the market economy secure in the knowledge that they could trade without the impediments of internal customs and tolls, differing systems of measurement, and a multitude of law codes. The position of employers was strengthened by the Le Chapelier law of June 1791, outlawing associations of workers, and by the reintroduction by Napoleon of the *livret*, an *ancien régime* practice requiring workers to carry a booklet detailing their employment record and conduct.

Economic change in the countryside may also have been accelerated by land sales. Research on the extent and social incidence of such sales during the Revolution remains piecemeal, but there is no question that it was significant in most areas. An estimate would be that about 20 per cent of land changed hands as a result of the expropriation of the Church and *émigrés*. For example, in 1786 the Thomassin family of Puiseux-Pontoise (just to the north of Menucourt) owned 3.86 hectares and rented 180 more from the seigneur, the Marquis de Girardin. They then bought up large amounts of nationalized property seized during the Revolution from the abbey of St-Martin-de-Pontoise, the Sisters of Charity and eight other ecclesiastical land-owners: by 1822 they owned 150.64 hectares, 27.5 per cent of the land in the commune, including much of the marquis's estate. This land was used for commercial grain-growing and, finally, for sugar-beet and a sugar distillery.[13]

Church land in particular was usually of prime quality, sold in large lots by auction and purchased by urban and rural bourgeois—and many nobles—with the capital to thus expand pre-existing holdings. In and around Angers, for example, the extensive ecclesiastical property was auctioned on the first possible day, and the eager local bourgeoisie paid 40 per cent above its estimated value. Moreover, while most nobles kept their lands intact (Robert Forster estimates that about one-fifth of noble holdings were seized and sold), their method of exploiting the soil of necessity changed fundamentally. The final abolition of feudal dues in 1793 implied that nobles' income from property would henceforth be based on rents charged to tenants and sharecroppers or on direct exploitation of noble holdings by farm managers employing labour. Efficient use of landed resources rather than control over persons was now the basis of rural wealth.

Peasants who owned their own land were among the direct and most substantial beneficiaries of the Revolution. After the abolition of feudal dues and the church tithe, both of which had normally been paid in grain, farmers were in a better position to concentrate on using the land for its most productive purposes. For example, in the countryside around Bayeux, the heavy, damp soils were quickly converted to cattle-raising once the Church ceased exacting a fixed tithe in grain. In Gabian, peasants started extending their vineyards into fields formerly used for growing grain. As a result of land sales, peasant holdings increased from perhaps one-third to two-fifths of the total land of France (for example, from 31 to 42 per cent in the department of the Nord studied by Georges Lefebvre), and were no longer subject to tithe or seigneurial dues. The weight of such exactions had varied enormously, but a total weight of 20–25 per cent of the produce of peasant proprietors (not to mention the *corvée*, seigneurial monopolies, and irregular payments) was common outside the west of France. Producers now retained an extra portion of their output which was often directly consumed by a better-fed population: in 1792, only one in seven of the army recruits from the impoverished mountain village of Pont-de-Montvert (Lozère) had been 1.6 metres or taller; by 1830, that was the average height of conscripts.[14]

The reforms and wars of the revolutionary period had disparate effects on rural economies. At the northern extremity of the country, in Montigny and its region of Cambrésis, the period saw the collapse of the distinctive rural textile economy. The free trade treaty with England in 1786 had been a body blow to the textile industry; now the revolutionary and imperial wars of 1792–1815, which swept back and forth across the region, would destroy the market for linen. When the vast church lands were sold as national property after 1790, the merchant-weavers rushed to buy them as a refuge from a collapsing industry. Consequently, by 1815 the countryside was again as rural as it had been a century earlier, and a reconstructed textile industry was centred in towns. In the southern department of the Aude, in contrast, the ending of seigneurial and church exactions, coupled with the collapse of the textile industry, encouraged peasants to turn to wine as a cash crop. Across the thirty years after 1789, the estimates provided by mayors for the area under vines in the department showed an increase of 75 per cent, from 29,300 to 51,100 hectares. The volume of wine produced may well have trebled to 900,000 hectolitres across these years.

This first viticultural revolution 'from below' is important evidence for an ongoing debate about the extent and nature of economic change wrought by the Revolution. Echoing Georges Lefebvre's famous statement that the peasantry 'destroyed the feudal regime, but consolidated the agrarian structure of France', Peter Jones has concluded that 'the desperately poor, that is to say the landless or virtually landless peasantry, nearly always demanded the complete restoration of collective rights . . .' and that 'the revolution boosted the "dead weight" or subsistence sector of the rural economy'.[15] The awkwardness of such an argument for a Marxist analysis of the Revolution as the decisive moment in the transformation from feudalism to capitalism has long been evident.

Certainly there is plentiful evidence of the poorest sections of rural communities clinging to collective rights as a buffer against destitution. However, the Russian historian Anatolï Ado has argued that the constraints on a more rapid transition to agrarian capitalism in post-revolutionary France came not so much from the entrenching of small peasant ownership but from the survival of large holdings rented out on restrictive short-term leases or by sharecropping. Certainly, in some areas close to cities or good transport the retention of a greater share of produce increased the safety margin for middling and larger peasant landholders and facilitated the contemplation of the risks of market specialization. In this way, too, the Revolution may have speeded up the expansion of capitalism in the countryside.[16]

Not all sectors of the rural population benefited equally. Napoleon could draw on extensive support from those who valued both the imposition of social order and the guaranteeing of revolutionary gains. For example, the Chartier family of Gonesse, just north of Paris, had been tenant-farmers but took advantage of the sale of church lands in 1791 to buy up a large holding. A Chartier became mayor in 1802, beginning a line that would last until 1940. Apart from those able to take advantage of the rampant inflation of 1795–7 to buy their way out of leases or to purchase land, tenants and sharecroppers experienced limited material improvements from the Revolution. However, like every other group in the rural community, they had been affected by seigneurial *banalités* (monopolies of mills, bake-houses, wine and oil presses) and *corvées* (unpaid labour) and, with rural labourers, had been those most vulnerable to the often arbitrary justice of the seigneur's court. John Markoff's exhaustive study of the origins and course of the peasant revolution has led him to conclude that the Anglophone 'revisionists', notably Alfred Cobban, William Doyle, and George Taylor, are fundamentally incorrect in their minimizing or misreading of the extent of peasant political initiative and of the significance of the abolition of feudalism.

The direct benefits that rural people, particularly peasant landowners, drew from the Revolution were not just at the expense of the Church and nobility. In many ways the provincial towns which were centres of *ancien régime* institutions had been parasitic on the countryside. In provincial towns such as Bayeux, Dijon, and Angers, the revenue from feudal dues and tithes was expended by cathedral chapters, religious orders, and resident nobles on the employment of domestic servants, purchases from skilled trades, especially of luxury goods, and in provision of charity. As a direct result of the Revolution, the countryside largely freed itself from such control by towns, leaving marketing and administration as the remaining links. It was this which made the lot of the destitute so desperate in such towns and which caused the impoverishment of those directly or indirectly dependent on clerical and noble elites. For example, before the Revolution, the bishop of Mende in the southern Massif Central had given 10,000 livres worth of bread to the destitute each year, paid for from the tithe collected in the countryside; after 1789, the peasantry consumed that part of their produce and the town's destitute were in an even more precarious situation.

The gains for the peasantry went beyond tangible economic benefits. The abolition of seigneurialism underpinned a revolutionary change in rural social relations, voiced in political behaviour after 1789. The social authority many nobles retained in the rural community was now based on personal esteem and direct economic power over the dependent rather than on claims to deference due to a superior order of society. Nor was Napoleon's reinforcement of notables' power at the local level meekly accepted: as the prefect of the Aisne in the northeast wrote to him in 1811, 'the principles subversive of all public order which were popular during the Revolution cannot be easily erased'. In 1822, during a protracted battle with the mayor, who had inherited the noble properties at Rennes-les-Bains (department of the Aude), locals petitioned the Prefect that they do not regard M. de Fleury as other than their mayor, who cannot have any special power, being simply responsible for the expenses of the commune according to the budget allocations, and not their former seigneur armed with feudal power, the arbitrary dispenser of the product of their sweat.[17]

These 'subversive principles' were commonly adduced by administrators to explain their inability to control 'the misguided greed of peasants' in seizing and clearing the vast areas of *vacants* or 'wastelands' which became common lands during the Revolution. From this point began the *légende noire* of the peasant revolution, that the revolutionary period was an unmitigated disaster for the natural environment until the re-emergence of effective authority under Napoleon and the Restoration. There is no doubt that there was massive land clearance during the revolutionary period: in the southern department of the Aude, for example, as much as 20 per cent of the land surface may have been cleared. However, this only accelerated the environmental pressures unleashed in 1760 by Louis XV's decrees encouraging clearances. In the decades after 1750, it was estimated that some 600,000 *arpents* (about 250,000 hectares) of France was cleared, some 3 per cent of the total land area. Nor were the peasantry those who alone destroyed more forests than they planted: the loss of half the French fleet at the battle of Trafalgar was to destroy about 80,000 oak trees more than 150 years old.

Certainly, however, the Napoleonic regime permitted the forest administration to have a series of laws promulgated reorganizing its personnel and re-establishing a centralized forests policy along similar lines to that of Colbert in 1669. These laws represented a reversal of the liberalism of the early years of the Revolution, when owners of private forests had been explicitly authorized to use their resources as they wished. Forests belonging to communes were now placed under the same controls as state forests. However, in creating a centralized and enforced system of controls over forest resources, the state was to attract decades of resentment over its attempts to end the collective use of forests.

There is evidence, therefore, that the Revolution had created the institutional foundations on which capitalism could thrive. However, to what extent did it also represent the coming to power of a new class? At first glance, the continued economic prominence of the old nobility is remarkable: a major element of the 'minimalist' view of the

Revolution seems undeniable. Despite the loss of seigneurial rights and, for *émigrés*, land, nobles remained at the pinnacle of landholding, and landholding remained the major source of wealth in France. According to a survey compiled in 1802, across half of the country a majority of the wealthiest landowners were nobles, and they dominated some of the richest agricultural regions, such as the Paris basin, the valley of the Rhône, Burgundy, Picardy, Normandy, and parts of Brittany.

Nevertheless, the wealthy survivors of the landholding élite of the *ancien régime* were now only part of a far broader elite which included all of the wealthy, whatever their social background, and embraced bourgeois in agriculture, business, and administration. The rapid expansion of the bureaucracy after 1789 broke down barriers in recruitment and opened opportunities to able young bourgeois. More than in the 1780s or 1790s, the ruling class in the early nineteenth century brought together those at the pinnacle of economic, social, and political power. David Garrioch describes the Parisian bourgeoisie which emerged from the Revolution as far more powerful and self-conscious. It was an amalgam of the old parish 'notables' of the *ancien régime* and new men who had seized the opportunities which came with the selling of church lands, the availability of army contracts, and the new freedoms offered by the abolition of guilds.

Those who had taken the initiative in creating the new France after 1789 had been the bourgeoisie, whether professional, administrative, commercial, landowning, or manufacturing. For them, the Revolution represented the changes to political structures and dominant social values necessary to recognize their importance in the life of the nation. The Revolution was their triumph. The cultural values of post-revolutionary France were to be characterized by an amalgam of bourgeois and aristocratic values in a culture of 'notables'. This was reflected in a myriad of ways. For example, Paris's first restaurants or 'houses of health' pre-dated the Revolution: from the 1760s they were advertised as places to 'restore' the appetite with small portions and as providing small private spaces for intimacy. It was during the Revolution, however, that they began supplying full meals in dining-rooms for the middle classes, a function they were never to lose. The sharper articulation of a world of 'separate spheres' for men and women among the middle classes was revealed by a clearer contrast between men's and women's clothing. The sober colours and plain design of bourgeois male attire signified the world of endeavour and seriousness; his wife's costume was to be ultra-feminine, signifying by its material the wealth of his spouse.[18]

Most nobles had been pragmatic enough to withdraw from public life and accept, however begrudgingly, the institutional changes of the Revolution. However, despite the continued importance of the wealthiest nobility, their losses had still been considerable. Robert Forster's judgement, though based on scattered and contrasting case-studies, is that, in real terms, an average provincial noble family's income fell from 8,000 to 5,200 francs. Seigneurial dues had represented as little as 5 per cent of noble income near Bordeaux, while immediately to the north, in Aunis and Saintonge, they amounted to 63 per cent. While many noble families survived with their lands intact, some 12,500—up to one-half of all families—lost some land, and a few lost virtually everything. Overall, perhaps one-fifth of noble land changed hands. To an extent, the losses of lands and dues were compensated for by charging higher rents to tenants and share-croppers, but no longer could nobles avoid paying the same taxes as everyone else. Whereas 5 per cent at most of noble wealth was taken by state taxes before 1789, thereafter the uniform land tax was levied at approximately 16 per cent of the estimated annual product of the land.

Moreover, nothing could compensate the nobles for the loss of judicial rights and power—ranging from seigneurial courts to the *parlements*—or the incalculable loss of prestige and deference caused by the practice of legal equality. The *émigré* noble returned to a transformed world, of litigation by creditors and peasants, the erosion of the mystique of nobility, and the need to run an estate as a business. Lucy de La Tour du Pin, who had fled to the United States in the 1790s, looked back in 1820 on the abolition of feudalism during the Revolution. She claimed that:

This decree ruined my father-in-law and our family fortunes never recovered . . . It was a veritable orgy of iniquities . . . Since then, we have been forced to contrive a living, sometimes by sale of some of the few possessions remaining to us, sometimes by taking salaried posts . . . And so it is that, inch by inch, over a long period of years, we have gradually slid to the bottom of an abyss from which we shall not emerge in our generation.

The loss of feudal dues, rents and tolls (one of which brought in 12,000 francs per year) was enormous: the marquise estimated that her family had lost 58,000 of its original annual income of 80,000 francs.[19]

Even when nobles survived the Revolution with landholdings intact, their social relations with others underwent a major change. In the Provençal village of Lourmarin, Jean-Baptiste Jérôme de Bruny, a former member of the *parlement* at Aix, retained his extensive property but became the largest taxpayer, assessed for 14 per cent of all taxes payable by the community. His seigneurial dues (the *tasque* of one-eighth of harvested grain and olive oil), monopolies, and other levies were gone. The estimated annual value of his *seigneurie* had been about 16,000 livres, but by 1791 the taxable revenue from his lands was estimated at only 4,696 livres, a fall of 71 per cent. Relations between him and the village quickly became those between rich and poor citizens rather than between peasants and their lord, suggested by the speed with which locals began litigation with 'citizen Bruny' after 1789. In the decades after 1800, they fought a protracted, successful battle with Bruny over his attempts to ignore ancient collective rights in his woods: in the words of Thomas Sheppard, 'dealing not with their seigneur but simply with another French citizen'.[20]

One reason for the enthusiasm with which Lourmarinois supported the Revolution—though they were temporarily divided during the 'Federalist' revolt of 1793—was that some 80 per cent of them were Protestants. Oral memories of earlier religious atrocities against them had been kept alive within the community. The construction of a Protestant church in 1805 was to be a tangible reminder of the significance of the Revolution for religious minorities. For revolutionaries, too, religious freedom exemplified their achievements: in a 1790 version of 'snakes and ladders', the emancipation of Jews was represented to children as one of the ladders leading to the new France. For Protestants and Jews, the legislation of 1789–91 represented legal emancipation, civil equality and the freedom to worship. Only later would some of them regret that the price of emancipation had been pressure to assimilate by subordinating their religious identity into a wider Frenchness.

The Revolution marks the end of the near-universal practice of church-going among Catholics in France. As many priests refused to accept the 1790 reforms to the Church, thousands of villages found themselves without a priest and church education. Once war was declared in 1792, the support given by the pope to the counter-revolutionary armies made the Church an object of suspicion, even hatred, for revolutionaries. The Catholic Church was devastated during the height of the war and the Terror of 1793–4. The frequent abdications further decimated the ranks of the constitutional clergy, leaving a land almost devoid of priests; indeed, many thousands of parishes had no priest for up to a decade after 1791. Among 3,000 violent clerical deaths in these years were at least 920 clergy who were publicly executed as counter-revolutionaries, and probably 30,000–40,000 (up to 25 per cent) of all clergy had emigrated. The former First Estate was thereby affected more directly than the nobility: the number of noble *émigrés* (16,431) was about 15 per cent of the Second Estate. The adoption of revolutionary names for people and their communities may have been only temporary, but it expressed an antipathy towards the status of ecclesiastical authority which was corrosive.

In 1789, the mass of parish priests had supported the claims of the Third Estate while calling vigorously for a Catholic monopoly of worship and morality. Instead, the Catholic Church emerged from Revolution without its extensive property, internally divided between those who had accepted the Revolution and those who fled to years of exile, and with several thousand of its clergy prematurely dead. The Revolution had created a secular state; although the Restoration was to pronounce Catholicism the state religion, an important legacy of the Revolution was the creation of an ethos among public functionaries that their primary allegiance was to the ideal of a secular state which transcended particular interests. Never again could the Catholic Church claim pre-revolutionary levels of obedience or acceptance among the people. Consequently, most priests—and many of the devout—were to become implacably opposed to republicanism and secularism. Nor was it ever to regain its old monopoly of morality; for example, Napoleon continued the revolutionary abolition of laws against homosexuality, even though police continued to harass homosexuals using other charges, such as 'outraging moral decency'.

Despite this, the laity—especially women—had proved their religious commitment in large areas of the countryside; from women, too, would come a widening stream of recruits to religious orders in the nineteenth century. The devastating impact of the French Revolution on the institutional structures of the Catholic Church and the initiative women in particular had taken in rebuilding the Church 'from below' after 1794 had developed the basis for a less authoritarian relationship of clergy and laity in the nineteenth century. In the words of a citizen from Sens to the Abbé Grégoire in January 1795:

I think it will be difficult to restrain the countryside back within the narrow boundaries of society except by giving them back their churches and the freedom to practice the religion in which they have been brought up and nourished.[21]

A reconciled Catholic Church was to be one support for the new Napoleonic regime; reinforced familial authority was to be another. The new regime's sympathy for the rights of fathers and of private property as the basis of the social order was revealed in attempts to modify revolutionary changes to the transmission of property by testament. The right of primogeniture in noble families had been abolished on 15 March 1790 as a way of undermining the economic and social power of great families. Then, in a law on inheritance passed by the National Convention on 7 March 1793, this principle was extended to all wills, requiring all children to inherit equally, extended later in the year to children born outside wedlock. The Napoleonic regime sought to modify what it saw as a threat to the authority of fathers, as well as to economically viable landed holdings. On 4 Germinal VIII (25 March 1800), a law was passed introducing a 'disposable portion' which a parent might leave to a favoured child in order to increase the inheritance. This provision was later enshrined in Napoleon's Civil Code of March 1804, which also ended the claims of children born outside marriage: henceforth they were entered in birth registers as 'born of an unknown father' and without rights to initiate claims of paternity.

However, no government—not even the Restoration—tampered with the principle of equal inheritance. If one son was now to inherit the family holding, other children had to renounce their share or be compensated in other ways. Since parents were able to transfer their property at any time, they retained an important measure of control over their offspring. But they could no longer threaten to disinherit them, for example, over the choice of a marriage partner. Whatever the case, the social consequence of this legislation was to focus attention on children's rights as well as on the family estate, especially in Normandy and the south, where pre-revolutionary law had allowed complete testamentary freedom to parents. In countless households after 1790, the rights of daughters became a family issue—just as the divorce law empowered wives—and in this may lie the most significant shift in the status of women in these years. A study of 83 court-cases in Caen over wills contested between siblings between 1790 and 1796 shows that 45 were won by sisters. The citizeness Montfreulle stated to the court in 1795: 'I was married in 1773 "for a bouquet of roses", to use the Norman expression. That was how girls were married then. Greed was in the air and one often sacrificed the daughters for the happiness of one son.'[22] Women may have emerged from the revolution with no political rights and limited legal rights, but the effects of the new inheritance law and the abolition of seigneurialism may well have meant that women were both better nourished and in a stronger position within the family. Another consequence of the legislation may have been a sudden drop in the national birth rate, from 38.8 per thousand in 1789 to 32.9 in 1804, as parents sought to limit family size and therefore the likelihood of subdivision of the family's farm.

While there is no doubt that the Revolution had entrenched political power in men's hands, this was primarily due to the unease, then anger, that scores of women's political clubs in Paris and the provinces had aroused in men. This, too, Napoleon sought to stabilize in the Civil Code of 1804. The Code was to be the cornerstone of the regime's administration of civil society and sought both to guarantee the essentials of revolutionary principles and to consolidate a social order based on wealth and patriarchy. Napoleon's authoritarian imposition of public order was, however, balanced by the rule of law and religious tolerance within a fluid social hierarchy of 'talent'. In Napoleon's words, it was 'the great glory of my reign'.

The Code was remarkable for its juxtaposition of the essentials of revolutionary principles with the consolidation of hierarchy and patriarchy. On the one hand, the code was predicated on the revolutionary assumption of a secular society of citizens equal before the law: 'talent' was seen to be the rationale of social hierarchy, and success in the use of one's individual private property was the proof of that talent. On the other, the exercise of talent was to be the preserve of men: married women no longer had the right to independently make legal contracts. They were bound as before 1789 to the authority of fathers, then to their husbands. Henceforth wives would only sue for divorce if their husband's mistress was brought into the marital home. In contrast, a simple act of adultery by a wife sufficed for a husband to sue, and the adulterous woman was liable to imprisonment for up to two years. This ideology of patriarchal authority extended to children, for fathers were authorized to request detention for disobedient offspring for one month, if under 16 years, and six months, if aged 16 to 21.

However, despite the conservatism of the Code, no French adult alive in 1804 was in any doubt that they had lived through a revolutionary upheaval. Despite the claims of 'minimalist' historians that they were mistaken, a consideration of the social, political, and economic outcomes of the Revolution suggests that this was no illusion. Life could never be the same again. As a revolution for liberty, equality, and fraternity, it would inspire others as diverse as the leader of Latin American struggles for national independence, Simon Bolivar (who attended Napoleon's coronation in 1804), one of the early Indian nationalists of the 1830s, Ram Mohan Roy, and even the Chinese students on Tiananmen Square in 1989.

The best gauge of the Revolution's outcome is to compare the *cahiers de doléances* of 1789 with the nature of French politics and society in 1795 or 1804. Ultimately, the social changes wrought by the Revolution endured because they corresponded to some of the deepest grievances of the bourgeoisie and peasantry in their *cahiers*: popular sovereignty (even if stopping short of full democracy), civil equality, careers open to 'talent', and the abolition of the seigneurial system. Whatever the popular resentments expressed towards warfare, conscription and church reform in many regions, particularly in 1795–9, there was never a serious possibility of mass support for a return to the *ancien régime*. At the same time, the thwarted aspirations of working people by 1795, and the potency of the revolutionary tradition they had created, meant that the new regime would not be uncontested, as evidenced by the revolutions of 1830, 1848, and 1870–1.

This book began in the little village of Menucourt north of Paris, and should end there. Although today Menucourt has almost been engulfed by the suburban sprawl of Cergy-Pontoise, it was then far enough from Paris to avoid direct involvement in the upheavals in the capital. While the rest of their family emigrated, Chassepot de Beaumont and his wife stayed on in the chateau at Menucourt, accepting the loss of their seigneurial dues and prerogatives, but keeping their land intact. They were imprisoned as 'suspects' in Pontoise in late 1793, but the municipality's willingness to vouch for their good conduct was instrumental in their release shortly thereafter. Chassepot died in 1803, aged 90. Nevertheless, the Revolution had changed a great deal about life in Menucourt. Seigneurial dues were no longer paid; the expenses of the Church were funded from general taxation; no longer did the people of Menucourt pay a tithe to a priory at Évecquemont. However, while this had been a revolution for civil equality it had not fundamentally altered the vulnerable position of the wage-earning majority of the population. As before 1789, most of Menucourt's households survived from work as farm-labourers, and by quarrying, woodcutting, and tilling small plots. In the words of three of their descendents, who wrote the village history for the bicentenary of the Revolution in 1989, 'The labourers would have to wait nearly two centuries and live through other revolutions—political, industrial and, above all, cultural—for inequalities to be significantly reduced and for liberty to become meaningful.'[23]

Notes

1. Mark Twain, *A Connecticut Yankee in King Arthur's Court* (London, 1971), 127.

2. François Furet, *The French Revolution 1774–1884* (Oxford, 1992).

3. Peter McPhee, *The Politics of Rural Life: Political Mobilization in the French Countryside 1846–1852* (Oxford, 1992), 161.

4. Between 300 and 500 of Luc's 2,320 people were killed in all the fighting during the Vendéen insurrection: Jean-Clément Martin and Xavier Lardière, *Le Massacre des Lucs-Vendée 1794* (Vouillé, 1992). On Chanzeaux, see Lawrence Wylie, *Chanzeaux: A Village in Anjou* (Cambridge, Mass., 1966). On La Roche-sur-Yon, see John M. Merriman, *The Margins of City Life: Explorations on the French Urban Frontier, 1815–1851* (Oxford, 1991), 101–12.

5. *La Feuille du salut public*, November 1793. On women's participation in the Revolution, see Rose, *Tribunes and Amazons*; Landes, *Women and the Public Sphere*, ch. 6, Conclusion; Hufton, *The Prospect before Her*, ch. 12.

6. Schama, *Citizens*, 906, Epilogue. Contrasting conclusions about the significance of the Revolution are Doyle, *Oxford History of the French Revolution*, ch. 17; and Martyn Lyons, *Napoleon Bonaparte and the Legacy of the French Revolution* (London, 1994), ch. 5.

7. Soboul, *French Revolution 1787–1799*, 19.

8. Benedict Anderson, *Imagined Communities: Reflections on the Origin and Spread of Nationalism* (London, 1983).

9. Eric Wolf, *Europe and the People without History* (Berkeley, Calif., 1982), ch. 3.

10. Martyn Lyons, 'Politics and Patois: The Linguistic Policy of the French Revolution', *Australian Journal of French Studies*, 18 (1981), 264–81.

11. Peter McPhee, 'A Case-Study of Internal Colonization: The *Francisation* of Northern Catalonia', *Review: A Journal of the Fernand Braudel Center*, 3 (1980), 399–428.

12. Jeffry Kaplow, *Elbeuf during the Revolutionary Period: History and Social Structure* (Baltimore, 1964), 193–209, and chs. 3, 5.

13. Albert Soboul, 'Concentration agraire en pays de grande culture: Puiseux-Pontoise (Seine-et-Oise) et la propriété Thomassin', in Soboul, *Problèmes paysans de la Révolution, 1789–1848* (Paris, 1976), ch. 11.

14. Patrice Higonnet, *Pont-de-Montvert: Social Structure and Politics in a French Village, 1700–1914* (Cambridge, Mass., 1971), 97.

15. Jones, *Peasantry*, 255–9; Georges Lefebvre, 'La Révolution française et les paysans', *Études sur la Révolution française* (Paris, 1954), 257.

16. Anatolï Ado, *Paysans en Révolution* (Paris, 1996), 6, Conclusion; McPhee, *Revolution and Environment*, ch. 7.

17. McPhee, *Revolution and Environment*, 168.

18. Rebecca Spang, *The Invention of the Restaurant* (Cambridge, Mass., 2000); Amy Trubeck, *Haute Cuisine: How the French invented the Culinary Profession* (Philadelphia, 2000); Ribeiro, *Fashion in the French Revolution*, 141.

19. Felice Harcourt (ed.), *Escape from the Terror: The Journal of Madame la Tour du Pin* (London, 1979), 93–4, 243–4. This noblewoman is the heroine of Schama's conclusion: *Citizens*, 861–6.

20. Sheppard, *Lourmarin*, 211 and ch. 8. Sheppard himself prefers to emphasize the continuities of daily life in Lourmarin.

21. Suzanne Desan, *Reclaiming the Sacred* (Ithaca, NY, 1990), 225.

22. Suzanne Desan, '"War between Brothers and Sisters": Inheritance Law and Gender Politics in Revolutionary France', *French Historical Studies*, 20 (1997), 628.

23. Denise, Maurice, and Robert Bréant, *Menucourt* (Menucourt, 1989).

Maps

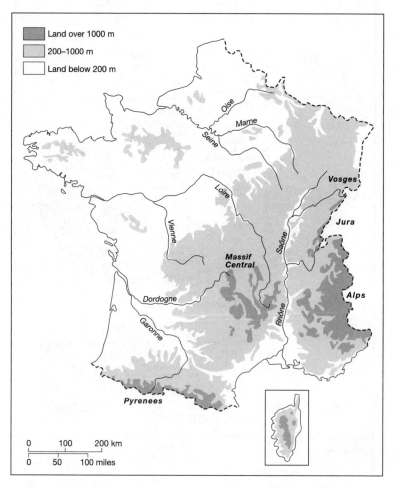

Map 1. France—physical.

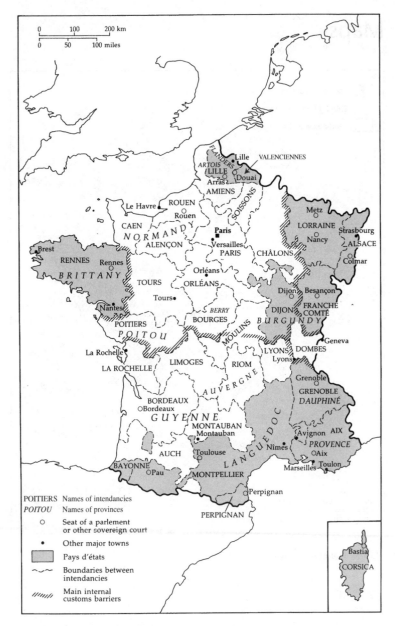

Map 2. Pre-revolutionary France, showing principal administrative, judicial and fiscal boundaries. Large italicized names are of major provinces.

Map 3. The departments of revolutionary France, 1790, and some major cities and towns, plus departments created after annexations 1791–8.

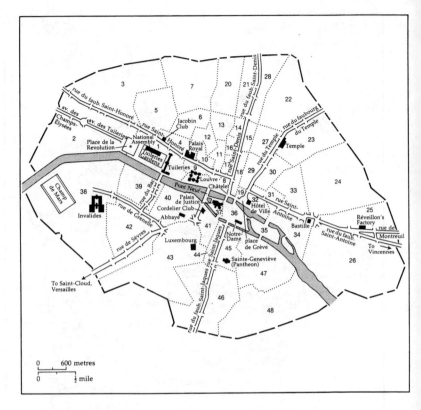

Map 4. Revolutionary Paris, showing major places named in the text and the 48 sections of local government.

Paris Sections:

1 Tuileries	17 Marché des Innocents	33 Place Royale
2 Champs-Élysées	18 Lombards	34 Arsenal
3 Roule	19 Arcis	35 Île Saint-Louis
4 Palais Royal	20 Faub. Montmartre	36 Notre-Dame
5 Place Vendôme	21 Poissonnière	37 Henri IV
6 Bibliothèque	22 Bondy	38 Invalides
7 Grange Batelière	23 Temple	39 Fontaine de Grenelle
8 Louvre	24 Popincourt	40 Quatre Nations
9 Oratoire	25 Montreuil	41 Théâtre-Français
10 Halle au Blé	26 Quinze Vingts	42 Croix Rouge
11 Postes	27 Gravilliers	43 Luxembourg
12 Place Louis XIV	28 Faub. Saint-Denis	44 Thermes de Julien
13 Fontaine Montmorency	29 Beaubourg	45 Saint-Geneviève
14 Bonne Nouvelle	30 Enfants Rouges	46 Observatoire
15 Ponceau	31 Roi de Sicile	47 Jardine des Plantes
16 Mauconseil	32 Hôtel de Ville	48 Gobelins

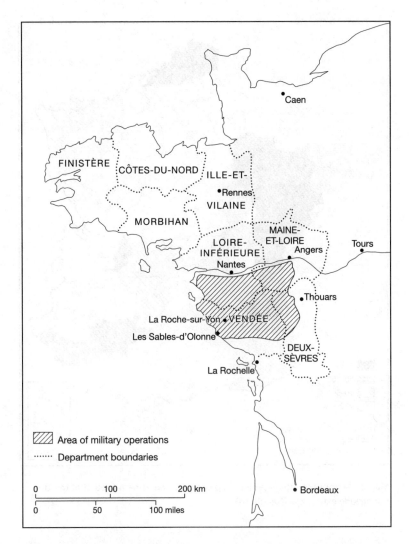

Map 5. The 'Vendée militaire' (note that this is not congruent with the boundaries of the department of the Vendée).

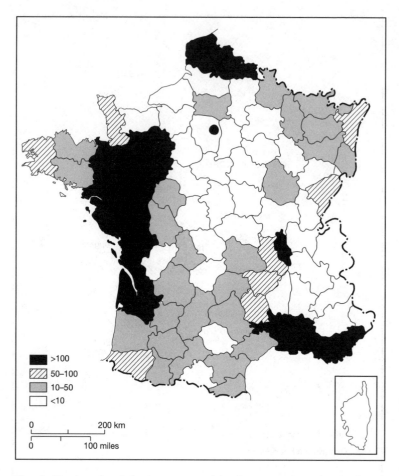

Map 6. Number of capital sentences passed, by department (note that this does not include extra-legal executions).

Chronology

22 February 1787	Meeting of the Assembly of Notables.
June–August 1787	Refusal of *parlement* of Paris to register royal reforms; exile of *parlementaires*.
8 May 1788	Lamoignon's reforms to reduce power of *parlements*.
7 June 1788	'Journée des Tuiles' at Grenoble.
8 August 1788	Estates-General convened for 1 May 1789.
27 December 1788	Royal Council decrees doubling of the number of Third Estate's representatives.
January 1789	Sieyès publishes *Qu'est-ce que le Tiers État?*
March–April 1789	Elections to the Estates-General.

The Estates-General (5 May 1789–27 June 1789)

5 May 1789	Opening of the Estates-General at Versailles.
17 June 1789	Declaration of the National Assembly.
20 June 1789	Tennis Court Oath.
23 June 1789	King's Declaration concerning the Estates-General.

The National Constituent Assembly
(28 June 1789–30 September 1791)

11 July 1789	Dismissal of Necker.
14 July 1789	Taking of the Bastille.
Late July–early August 1789	Municipal revolutions, peasant revolts, Great Fear.
4–11 August 1789	The August Decrees on feudalism.
10 August 1789	Decree Establishing National Guards.
27 August 1789	Declaration of the Rights of Man and Citizen.
11 September 1789	National Assembly grants suspensive, rather than absolute, veto to king.

5–6 October 1789	March of the Parisian women on Versailles; royal family brought back to Paris.
21 October 1789	Decree on Martial Law.
2 November 1789	Church property placed at the disposal of the nation.
14 December 1789	Decree establishing municipalities.
19 December 1789	First issue of *assignats* (revolutionary currency).
24 December 1789	Grant of religious liberty to Protestants.
28 January 1790	Sephardim Jews granted equal rights.
13 February 1790	Decree prohibiting monastic vows in France.
26 February 1790	Decree dividing France into departments.
22 May 1790	National Assembly renounces wars of conquest.
10 June 1790	Request from Avignon for annexation into France.
19 June 1790	Decree abolishing hereditary nobility and titles.
12 July 1790	The Civil Constitution of the Clergy.
14 July 1790	Fête de la Fédération.
18 August 1790	First counter-revolutionary assembly at Jalès.
29 October 1790	Revolt of slaves and free blacks in St-Domingue.
27 November 1790	Decree requiring the clerical oath.
2 March 1791	Suppression of the guilds.
13 April 1791	The Papal Bull *Charitas*.
15 May 1791	Children of free blacks in colonies granted equal rights.
14 June 1791	The Le Chapelier Law.
20 June 1791	The king's declaration and flight to Varennes.
5 July 1791	The Padua Circular.
17 July 1791	Petition and 'massacre' of the Champ de Mars.
27 August 1791	The Declaration of Pillnitz.
3 September 1791	The Constitution of 1791.
14 September 1791	Louis XVI accepts the new constitution.
14 September 1791	Annexation of Avignon and the Comtat-Venaissin.
28 September 1791	Ashkenazim Jews granted equal rights; Rural Code.

The Legislative Assembly (1 October 1791–20 September 1792)

9 November 1791	Decree against *émigrés* (vetoed by king 12 November).
29 November 1791	Priests refusing to take oath to constitution suspended from functions.
9 February 1792	Decree nationalizing *émigré* property.
20 April 1792	Declaration of war on Austria.
27 May 1792	Decree on deportation of non-juring priests (vetoed 19 June).
12 June 1792	Dismissal of Girondin ministers.
20 June 1792	Invasion of the Tuileries by the Paris crowd.
11 July 1792	Declaration of the 'patrie en danger'.
25 July 1792	Publication of the Brunswick Manifesto.
10 August 1792	Storming of the Tuileries and suspension of the king.
19 August 1792	Defection of Lafayette to Austrians.
25 August 1792	Decree on feudalism.
2 September 1792	Fall of Verdun to Prussians
2–6 September 1792	'September massacres' in the prisons of Paris.

The First Phase of the National Convention
(20 September 1792–2 June 1793)

20 September 1792	First session of the National Convention.
20 September 1792	Victory at Valmy.
6 November 1792	Victory at Jemappes.
27 November 1792	French annexation of Savoy.
11 December 1792	First appearance of Louis XVI before the Convention.
14–17 January 1793	King's trial.
21 January 1793	Execution of Louis XVI.
1 February 1793	French declaration of war on England and Holland.
24 February 1793	Decree for a Levy of 300,000 men.
7 March 1793	Declaration of war on Spain.
10 March 1793	Creation of special revolutionary tribunal.

10 March 1793	Creation of surveillance committees.
10–11 March 1793	Massacres at Machecoul and start of Vendéan insurrection.
19 March 1793	Decree on Public Relief.
28 March 1793	Decree against *émigrés*.
4 April 1793	Defection of Dumouriez to the Austrians.
6 April 1793	Decree on the Formation of a Committee of Public Safety.
9 April 1793	Decree establishing 'deputies on mission'.
4 May 1793	The first law of the Maximum.
31 May–2 June 1793	Invasion of Convention by Paris sections; fall of Girondins.
7 June 1793	Federalist revolts in Bordeaux and the Calvados.

The Second Phase of the Convention: The Terror
(3 June 1793–28 July 1794)

10 June 1793	Decree authorizing communes to divide common lands by head.
24 June 1793	The Constitution of 1793.
13 July 1793	Assassination of Marat.
17 July 1793	Definitive abolition of feudalism.
27 July 1793	Robespierre appointed to Committee of Public Safety.
1 August 1793	Decree establishing a uniform system of weights and measures.
23 August 1793	Decree establishing the *levée en masse*.
27 August 1793	Toulon surrenders to the British navy.
5–6 September 1793	Popular 'journée' pressures the Convention into radical measures.
17 September 1793	The Law of Suspects.
29 September 1793	The Law of the General Maximum.
5 October 1793	Decree Establishing the French Era (14 Vendémiaire II).
9 October 1793	Suppression of 'Federalist' insurrection in Lyons.

10 October 1793	Declaration of Revolutionary Government (19 Vendémiaire II).
16 October 1793	Execution of Marie-Antoinette.
31 October 1793	Execution of the Girondin leaders.
4 December 1793	The Constitution of the Terror (Law of 14 Frimaire Year II).
8 December 1793	Decree concerning Religious Liberty (18 Frimaire II).
19 December 1793	Decree concerning Public Education (29 Frimaire II).
4 February 1794	Abolition of slavery in French colonies.
3 March 1794	The Ventôse Decrees (13 Ventôse II).
13–24 March 1794	Arrest and execution of Hébertistes.
30 March–6 April 1794	Arrest and execution of Dantonists.
8 June 1794	Festival of Supreme Being in Paris.
10 June 1794	The Law of 22 Prairial (22 Prairial II).
26 June 1794	Victory at Fleurus.
23 July 1794	Introduction of wage regulation in Paris.
27 July 1794	The 9th Thermidor: overthrow of Robespierre.
28 July 1794	Execution of Robespierre, Saint-Just and associates.

The Third Phase of the Convention: The Thermidorian Reaction (29 July 1794–26 October 1795)

12 November 1794	Closure of Jacobin club.
17 November 1794	Decree on Primary Schools (27 Brumaire III).
24 December 1794	Abolition of General Maximum.
28 December 1794	Decree Reorganizing the Revolutionary Tribunal (8 Nivôse III).
1 April 1795	Germinal: popular *journée* in Paris.
5 April 1795	The Treaty of Basle with Prussia (16 Germinal III).
7 April 1795	Decree on weights and measures (18 Germinal III).
April–May 1975	'White Terror' in southern France.
16 May 1795	The Treaty of The Hague (27 Floréal III).
20 May 1795	Prairial: invasion of Convention by Parisian crowd.

8 June 1795	Death of Louis XVII; Count de Provence becomes pretender to French throne (Louis XVIII).
22 July 1795	Peace signed with Spain.
22 August 1795	The Constitution of the Year III (5 Fructidor III).
30 August 1795	Decree of the Two-Thirds (13 Fructidor III).
29 September 1795	Decree on the Exercise of Worship (7 Vendémiaire IV).
5 October 1795	Vendémiaire: royalist rising in Paris.
25 October 1795	Decree concerning the organization of Public Education (3 Brumaire IV).
26 October 1795	Dissolution of the Convention.

The Directory

3 November 1795	Installation of the Directory.
19 February 1796	Withdrawal of the *assignats*.
2 March 1796	Bonaparte appointed General-in-Chief of the Army in Italy.
10 May 1796	Conspiracy of the Equals; Babeuf arrested.
December 1796	Failure of Hoche's Irish expedition.
March–April 1797	Royalist successes in legislative elections.
27 May 1797	Execution of Babeuf.
4 September 1797	18 Fructidor: *coup d'état* against royalist deputies.
17 October 1797	Treaty of Campo Formio (27 Vendémiaire VI).
11 May 1798	22 Floréal: removal from office of extreme republican deputies.
19 May 1798	Bonaparte leaves on Egyptian Campaign.
1 August 1798	Battle of the Nile: French fleet defeated.
5 September 1798	The First General Conscription Law (19 Fructidor VI).
March 1799	War of the Second Coalition.
April 1799	Legislative elections favour neo-Jacobins.
23 August 1799	Bonaparte embarks for France.
9 October 1799	Bonaparte's return to France.
18 October 1799	Decree on Francs and Livres (26 Vendémiaire VIII).

10 November 1799	The Brumaire Decree (19 Brumaire VIII).
13 December 1799	The Constitution of the Year VIII (22 Frimaire VIII).
28 December 1799	Churches reopened for worship on Sundays.

Appendix
The Revolutionary Calendar

The calendar was introduced to mark the first anniversary of the proclamation of the Republic on 22 September 1792. 14 Vendémiaire II (5 October 1793) was the day of the calendar's introduction by a 'Decree establishing the French Era'. The calendar represented a repudiation of the Gregorian calendar and its saints' names; instead, there would be 'rational' months of 30 days, each with three *décades* (unfortunately for the decimally minded, there had to be twelve rather than ten months), and each day would have a name drawn from nature: in Frimaire, for example, cauliflower, bees-wax and truffle. The *décadi* or tenth days were named after farm implements. The calendar lasted until New Year's Day 1806.

Autumn:	Vendémiaire	(month of vintage)	22 Sept.–21 Oct.
	Brumaire	(month of fog)	22 Oct.–20 Nov.
	Frimaire	(month of frost)	21 Nov.–20 Dec.
Winter:	Nivôse	(month of snow)	21 Dec.–19 Jan.
	Pluviôse	(month of rain)	20 Jan.–18 Feb.
	Ventôse	(month of wind)	19 Feb.–20 Mar.
Spring:	Germinal	(month of budding)	21 Mar.–19 Apr.
	Floréal	(month of flowers)	20 Apr.–19 May
	Prairial	(month of meadows)	20 May–18 June
Summer:	Messidor	(month of harvest)	19 June–18 July
	Thermidor	(month of heat)	19 July–17 Aug.
	Fructidor	(month of fruit)	18 Aug.–16 Sept.

Sans-culottides: 17–21 Sept. inclusive plus extra day in leap years.

A Guide to Further Reading in English

The best introduction to eighteenth-century France is Daniel Roche, *France in the Enlightenment*, trans. Arthur Goldhammer (Cambridge, Mass., 1998). An enormous amount may be learned about French society as a whole from John McManners, *Church and Society in Eighteenth-Century France*, 2 vols. (Oxford, 1998). Local studies permit a closer approach to French society; among them are Robert Forster, *The Nobility of Toulouse in the Eighteenth Century* (Baltimore, 1971), and *The House of Saulx-Tavanes: Versailles and Burgundy 1700–1830* (Baltimore, 1977); Daniel Roche, *The People of Paris: An Essay in Popular Culture in the 18th Century*, trans. Marie Evans (Berkeley, Calif., 1987); Thomas Sheppard, *Lourmarin in the Eighteenth Century: A Study of a French Village* (Baltimore, 1971); Olwen Hufton, *Bayeux in the Late Eighteenth Century: A Social Study* (Oxford, 1967); John McManners, *French Ecclesiastical Society under the Ancien Régime* (Manchester, 1960); Patrice Higonnet, *Pont-de-Montvert: Social Structure and Politics in a French Village, 1700–1914* (Cambridge, Mass., 1971), and Liana Vardi, *The Land and the Loom: Peasants and Profit in Northern France 1680–1800* (Durham, NC, 1993). The crucial roles of women in household work strategies are discussed in Olwen Hufton's important *The Prospect before Her: A History of Women in Western Europe, 1500–1800* (New York, 1996).

Debates on the origins of the Revolution are summarized from a non-Marxist or 'revisionist' perspective in William Doyle, *Origins of the French Revolution*, 2nd edn. (Oxford, 1980), while Colin Jones synthesizes a mass of recent research into an effective riposte in Colin Lucas (ed.), *Rewriting the French Revolution* (Oxford, 1991). The continuity of attempts at reform is stressed by Peter Jones, *Reform and Revolution in France: The Politics of Transition, 1774–1791* (Cambridge, 1995). Increasing attention has been paid to the cultural origins of the Revolution, well summarized in Roger Chartier, *The Cultural Origins of the French Revolution* (Durham, NC, 1991); Emmet Kennedy, *A Cultural History of the French Revolution* (New Haven, 1989); and the deservedly influential work of Robert Darnton, *The Great Cat Massacre and Other Episodes in French Cultural History* (New York, 1984), and *The Literary Underground of the Old Regime* (Cambridge, Mass., 1982).

Forty years after its publication in French, the classic Marxist narrative by Albert Soboul, *The French Revolution 1787–1799: From the Storming of the*

Bastille to Napoleon, trans. Alan Forrest and Colin Jones (London, 1989) remains a powerful, cohesive analysis. Very different in tone is the detailed political history by William Doyle, *The Oxford History of the French Revolution* (Oxford, 1989); here international affairs and counter-revolution are properly emphasized. Michel Vovelle, *The Fall of the French Monarchy 1787–1792*, trans. S. Burke (Cambridge, 1984) is a fluent narrative of the origins and early years of the Revolution. A lucid recent overview is David Andress, *French Society in Revolution, 1789–1799* (Manchester, 1999); this includes a superb collection of documents translated from *French Revolution Documents*, vol. 1, ed. J. M. Roberts and Richard Cobb (Oxford, 1966), vol. 2, ed. J. M. Roberts and John Hardman (Oxford, 1973). Richard Cobb and Colin Jones (eds.), *Voices of the French Revolution* (Topsfield, Mass., 1988) is an expertly chosen and illustrated collection of documents. Donald Sutherland's *France 1789–1815: Revolution and Counterrevolution* (London, 1985) is a detailed, provocative overview which succeeds in viewing the Revolution from a national rather than Parisian perspective.

Apart from Andress, none of these books pays more than passing attention to women's participation or issues of gender, on which see Donimique Godineau, *The Women of Paris and their French Revolution*, trans. Katherine Streip (Berkeley, Calif., 1998); Joan Landes, *Women and the Public Sphere in the Age of the French Revolution* (Ithaca, NY, 1988); R. B. Rose, *Tribunes and Amazons: Men and Women of Revolutionary France 1789–1871* (Sydney, 1998), and Margaret Darrow's innovative *Revolution in the House: Family, Class and Inheritance in Southern France, 1775–1825* (Princeton, 1989).

Three succinct and sprightly overviews which address recent debates are by Tim Blanning, *The French Revolution: Aristocrat versus Bourgeois?* (London, 1989); Alan Forrest, *The French Revolution* (Oxford, 1995), and Gwynne Lewis, *The French Revolution: Rethinking the Debate* (London, 1993). A collection of recent articles, mostly from a cultural history perspective, is Ronald Schechter (ed.), *The French Revolution: Blackwell Essential Readings* (Oxford, 2001). More inclusive and helpful is the collection edited by Peter Jones, *The French Revolution in Social and Political Perspective* (London, 1996). Colin Jones, *The Longman Companion to the French Revolution* (London, 1988) is a treasure-trove of helpful detail.

Successive revolutionary assemblies are studied by Timothy Tackett, *Becoming a Revolutionary: The Deputies of the French National Assembly and the Emergence of a Revolutionary Culture (1789–1790)* (Princeton, 1996); C. J. Mitchell, *The French Legislative Assembly of 1791* (Leiden, 1989); and Alison Patrick, *The Men of the First French Republic* (Baltimore, 1972).

Peter Jones, *The Peasantry in the French Revolution* (Cambridge, 1988); and John Markoff, *The Abolition of Feudalism: Peasants, Lords, and Legislators in the French Revolution* (Philadelphia, 1996) extend the 1932 classic by Georges Lefebvre, *The Great Fear of 1789: Rural Panic in Revolutionary France* (New York, 1973). On rural resistance to the Revolution, see Charles Tilly's pathbreaking *The Vendée* (Cambridge, Mass., 1964); Donald Sutherland, *The Chouans: The Social Origins of Popular Counter-Revolution in Upper Brittany, 1770–1796* (Oxford, 1982); and Gwynne Lewis, *The Second Vendée: The Continuity of Counter-Revolution in the Department of the Gard, 1789–1815* (Oxford, 1978). A study of a pro-revolutionary region is Peter McPhee, *Revolution and Environment in Southern France: Peasants, Lords, and Murder in the Corbières, 1780–1830* (Oxford, 1999).

Apart from the local studies cited earlier, the urban, provincial face of the Revolution is expertly traced in Gail Bossenga, *The Politics of Privilege: Old Regime and Revolution in Lille* (Cambridge, 1991); Alan Forrest, *Society and Politics in Revolutionary Bordeaux* (Oxford, 1975); Bill Edmonds, *Jacobinism and the Revolt of Lyon, 1789–1793* (Oxford, 1990); David Garrioch, *The Formation of the Parisian Bourgeoisie 1690–1830* (Cambridge, Mass., 1996); William Scott, *Terror and Repression in Revolutionary Marseilles* (London, 1973); Paul Hanson, *Provincial Politics in the French Revolution: Caen and Limoges, 1789–1794* (Baton Rouge, La., 1989); Ted W. Margadant, *Urban Rivalries in the French Revolution* (Princeton, 1992); and Richard Andrews's engrossing essay on revolutionary Paris in Gene Brucker (ed.), *People and Communities in the Western World*, vol. 2 (Homewood, Ill., 1979).

John McManners's *The French Revolution and the Church* (London, 1969) remains a readable, perceptive introduction to the religious conflicts of the revolutionary period, as is Ralph Gibson, *A Social History of French Catholicism, 1789–1914* (London, 1989). More detailed recent analyses include Timothy Tackett's illuminating *Religion, Revolution, and Regional Culture in Eighteenth-Century France* (Princeton, 1986). Social policy during the Revolution is studied by Colin Jones, *The Charitable Imperative: Hospitals and Nursing in Ancien Régime and Revolutionary France* (1989); Alan Forrest, *The French Revolution and the Poor* (Oxford, 1981); Antoinette Wills, *Crime and Punishment in Revolutionary Paris* (New York, 1981); and Isser Woloch, *The French Veteran from the Revolution to the Restoration* (Chapel Hill, NC, 1979). An important study of the impact of the 1792 divorce law is Roderick Phillips, *Family Breakdown in Late-Eighteenth Century France: Divorces in Rouen 1792–1803* (Oxford, 1980).

The fundamental works on the Parisian popular movement remain George Rudé, *The Crowd in the French Revolution* (Oxford, 1959), and Albert Soboul, *The Parisian Sans-Culottes and the French Revolution, 1793–4* (Oxford, 1964). They have been supplemented by William Sewell, *Work and Revolution in France: The Language of Labor from the Old Régime to 1848* (Cambridge,

1980). 'The Revolution armed' has been studied by Jean-Paul Bertaud, *The Army of the French Revolution: From Citizen-Soldiers to Instrument of Power*, trans. R. R. Palmer (Princeton, 1988), Alan Forrest, *Soldiers of the French Revolution* (Durham, NC, 1989), and, in different guise, by Richard Cobb, *The People's Armies*, trans. Marianne Elliott (New Haven, 1987). Popular political life is the focus of R. B. Rose, *The Making of the 'sans-culottes': Democratic Ideas and Institutions in Paris, 1789–1792* (1983), and, nationally, of Michael Kennedy, *The Jacobin Clubs in the French Revolution*, 2 vols. (1982, 1988).

The period 1795–9 remains relatively neglected. Useful surveys are by Denis Woronoff, *The Thermidorian Regime and the Directory* (1984); and Martyn Lyons, *France under the Directory* (1975). The Directory and Consulate are expertly linked by Malcolm Crook, *Napoleon Comes to Power: Democracy and Dictatorship in Revolutionary France, 1795–1804* (Cardiff, 1998). There are relevant chapters in Richard Cobb, *The Police and the People: French Popular Protest 1789–1820* (Oxford, 1970), and *Reactions to the French Revolution* (Oxford, 1972). On the social history of these years, see Gwynne Lewis and Colin Lucas (eds.), *Beyond the Terror: Essays in French Regional and Social History, 1794–1815* (Cambridge, 1983).

The social impact of the Revolution remains contentious. Among the 'minimalist' overviews are Olwen Hufton, 'Women in Revolution 1789–1796', *Past & Present* (1971); Robert Forster, in Jaroslaw Pelenski (ed.), *The American and European Revolutions, 1776–1848* (1980) and the conclusions to Doyle, *French Revolution* and Simon Schama, *Citizens: A Chronicle of the French Revolution* (London, 1989). These may be contrasted with the concluding chapters of Soboul, *French Revolution*; Jones, *Peasantry*; and Bill Edmonds, 'Successes and Excesses of Revisionist Writing about the French Revolution', *European Historical Quarterly*, 17 (1987), 195–217.

The impact of the Revolution on 'political culture' is stressed by Lynn Hunt, *Politics, Culture, and Class in the French Revolution* (London, 1984); Carla Hesse, *Publishing and Cultural Politics in Revolutionary Paris 1789–1810* (Berkeley, Calif., 1991); the contributors to the three volumes of *The French Revolution and the Creation of Modern Political Culture* (Oxford, 1987–9); Isser Woloch, *The New Regime: Transformations of the French Civic Order, 1789–1820s* (New York, 1994); and Kennedy, *Cultural History*. These are largely concerned with literate, urban culture: more wide-ranging is Mona Ozouf, *Festivals and the French Revolution*, trans. Alan Sheridan (Cambridge, Mass., 1988). The Revolution's musical expression is studied by Laura Mason, *Singing the French Revolution: Popular Culture and Politics, 1787–1799* (Ithaca, NY, 1996); Malcolm Boyd (ed.), *Music and the French Revolution* (Cambridge, 1990); Jean Mongrédien, *French Music from the Enlightenment to Romanticism*

1789–1830 (Portland, Ore., 1989). Aileen Ribeiro, *Fashion in the French Revolution* (London, 1988) is an interesting survey of the politics of fashion. Particularly useful is Malcolm Crook, *Elections in the French Revolution: An Apprenticeship in Democracy, 1789–1799* (Cambridge, 1996). Most readable is Maurice Agulhon, *Marianne into Battle: Republican Imagery and Symbolism in France, 1789–1880*, trans. Janet Lloyd (Cambridge, 1981). The Revolution's impact on state structures and national identity is discussed in Howard G. Brown, *War, Revolution and the Bureaucratic State: Politics and Army Administration in France, 1791–1799* (Oxford, 1995); Clive Church, *Revolution and Red Tape: The French Ministerial Bureaucracy, 1770–1850* (Oxford, 1981); and John Bosher, *The French Revolution* (London, 1989). The impact on the colonies and racial attitudes has received belated attention, from Carolyn Fick and Pierre Boulle in Frederick Krantz (ed.), *History from Below: Studies in Popular Protest and Popular Ideology in Honour of George Rudé* (Montreal, 1985).

Index